DISCIPLINE
DEVOTION
and DISSENT

DISCIPLINE DEVOTION *and* DISSENT

Jewish, Catholic, *and* Islamic Schooling in Canada

Graham P. McDonough, Nadeem A. Memon,
and Avi I. Mintz, *editors*

WILFRID LAURIER
UNIVERSITY PRESS

Wilfrid Laurier University Press acknowledges the financial support of the Government of Canada through the Canada Book Fund for its publishing activities.

Library and Archives Canada Cataloguing in Publication

Discipline, devotion, and dissent : Jewish, Catholic, and Islamic schooling in Canada / Graham P. McDonough, Nadeem A. Memon, and Avi I. Mintz, editors.

Includes bibliographical references and index.
Issued also in electronic formats.
ISBN 978-1-55458-841-1

1. Jewish day schools—Canada. 2. Catholic schools—Canada. 3. Islamic education—Canada. 4. Religious education—Canada. I. McDonough, Graham Patrick, 1975– II. Memon, Nadeem A. (Nadeem Ahmed), 1980– III. Mintz, Avi I., 1977–

LC114.D58 2013   371.070971   C2012-904288-9

———

Electronic monograph.
Issued also in print format.
ISBN 978-1-55458-868-8 (PDF).—ISBN 978-1-55458-869-5 (EPUB)

1. Jewish day schools—Canada. 2. Catholic schools—Canada. 3. Islamic education—Canada. 4. Religious education—Canada. I. McDonough, Graham Patrick, 1975– II. Memon, Nadeem A. (Nadeem Ahmed), 1980– III. Mintz, Avi I., 1977–

LC114.D58 2013   371.070971   C2012-904289-7

Cover design by Martyn Schmoll. Text design by Sandra Friesen.

© 2013 Wilfrid Laurier University Press
Waterloo, Ontario, Canada
www.wlupress.wlu.ca

This book is printed on FSC recycled paper and is certified Ecologo. It is made from 100% post-consumer fibre, processed chlorine free, and manufactured using biogas energy.

Printed in Canada

Every reasonable effort has been made to acquire permission for copyright material used in this text, and to acknowledge all such indebtedness accurately. Any errors and omissions called to the publisher's attention will be corrected in future printings.

No part of this publication may be reproduced, stored in a retrieval system, or transmitted, in any form or by any means, without the prior written consent of the publisher or a licence from the Canadian Copyright Licensing Agency (Access Copyright). For an Access Copyright licence, visit http://www.accesscopyright.ca or call toll free to 1-800-893-5777.

CONTENTS

ACKNOWLEDGEMENTS   vii

INTRODUCTION   1
Graham P. McDonough, Nadeem A. Memon, and Avi I. Mintz

Part A: Aims and Practices

1 The Jewish Day Schools of Canada   25
  Seymour Epstein
2 The Distinctiveness of Catholic Education   45
  Mario O. D'Souza, csb
3 Between Immigrating and Integrating: The Challenge of
  Defining an Islamic Pedagogy in Canadian Islamic Schools   73
  Nadeem A. Memon

Part B: Faith and Citizenship

4 Jewish Education, Democracy, and Pluralistic Engagement   101
  Greg Beiles
5 Canadian Catholic Schools: Sacred and Secular Tensions in
  a Free and Democratic Society   121
  J. Kent Donlevy
6 London Islamic School: Millstone or Milestone?   145
  Asma Ahmed

CONTENTS

Part C: Dissent and Critical Thinking

7 The Changed Context for Jewish Day-School Education   171
Alex Pomson and Randal F. Schnoor

8 Teaching Subject Matter That Is Controversial among Catholics: Implications for Intellectual Growth in the Church   189
Graham P. McDonough

9 A Canadian Islamic School in Perspective: A Critique of the "Moderate" and "Strong" Categories in Faith-Based Schooling   213
Qaiser Ahmad

Conclusion

10 Diversity and Deliberation in Faith-Based Schools: Implications for Educating Canadian Citizens   237
Avi I. Mintz

GLOSSARY   251

THE CONTRIBUTORS   259

INDEX   265

ACKNOWLEDGEMENTS

The editors gratefully acknowledge financial support for this book from the Dean's Office at the University of Victoria's Faculty of Education, the University of Tulsa's Office of Research and Sponsored Programs, and RAZI Group. In addition, Avi Mintz's work on this project was made possible through a Summer Fellowship granted from the University of Tulsa. We also thank two graduate assistants, Diane McCrackin and Irina Malova, for their diligent assistance at various stages of the manuscript's preparation, and Rabbi Marc Boone Fitzerman for his suggested revisions of glossary items. Lastly, we thank our editor at Wilfrid Laurier University Press, Lisa Quinn, both for her support of the book and for her sage advice.

We are also grateful for the encouragement and patience of our spouses throughout this project.

Previously Published Material

Portions of the Introduction and Chapter 8 were published previously in G.P. McDonough, *Beyond Obedience and Abandonment: Toward a Theory of Dissent in Catholic Education* (Montreal: McGill-Queen's University Press, 2012), and appear here with the kind permission of that Press.

INTRODUCTION

Graham P. McDonough, Nadeem A. Memon, and Avi I. Mintz

The 2007 Ontario provincial election brought educational questions of faith-based schools and social cohesion into high relief. The Progressive Conservative Party, under the leadership of John Tory, campaigned with, among other things, a promise to extend full funding to all faith-based schools (pre-kindergarten through high school) in Ontario. A heated debate ensued and featured a variety of concerns, including a question of whether public funding for these schools would divert tax dollars from the current public school systems. The main focus of the debate, however, became a concern that faith-based schools are a threat to social cohesion. For instance, Dalton McGuinty, the Liberal premier, said that when he travels around the world, people ask him, "Why have I not seen on your television screens what I have seen on the streets of London, Germany, Paris, the Netherlands? Why is there not more strife, struggle, and controversy?" He reported his reply to these questions: "It's because we bring our kids together in the same classrooms."[1] But to many observers, McGuinty's comment seemed to reveal an element of Islamophobia that is unfortunately common in the post-9/11 discourse on faith-based schooling. As Andrew Coyne wrote: "all of the examples cited—London, Germany, Paris, the Netherlands—are places with significant Muslim populations, and significant Muslim unrest—not to say terrorism. The only thing standing between them and us, McGuinty suggests, is our public school system."[2] Coyne called McGuinty's stance on the issue of faith-based schools "fearmonger-

INTRODUCTION

ing" and "demagoguery," and others in the media were quick to pass similar judgments.[3]

Tory's proposal resurrected more than simply the debate about Ontario's current public funding model for faith-based schools. It also raised fundamental questions about the place of faith-based schools in Canada: What really are the aims of these schools? How do they nurture religious belief and culture? How do they understand good Canadian citizenship? In the 2007 debate, there was a lack of meaningful engagement with questions of the nature and practice of secular and faith-based schooling. This did not serve the public well, regardless of one's final opinion on Tory's proposal.

What was clear in the debate in Ontario and elsewhere in Canada is that faith-based schools are often discussed in only superficial ways and are sometimes viewed with suspicion, if not hostility. While it is often the case that public discourse lacks the nuance and depth of academic scholarship, in the case of faith-based schooling in Canada, anyone who turns to academic scholarship would not find much help. The majority of such work in Canada has focused on its historical significance to Canada's early development, the issue of public funding, important legal challenges, and the way in which religious pluralism is accommodated within *secular* public schools.[4] The current scholarship has generally neglected to consider what Canadian faith-based schools actually aim to accomplish, how citizenship is broached in them, and how controversies are addressed in classrooms. *Discipline, Devotion, and Dissent* provides a starting point for understanding how some Canadian faith-based schools develop educational visions that seek to cultivate both members of a faith community and members of the broader Canadian society. Before we continue to describe the purpose and scope of this book, it is worthwhile to reflect on the political negotiation in Canada that has made faith-based schools so controversial.

The Controversial Place of Faith-Based Schools in Canada: A Historical Overview

The role of religion in schooling has been a flashpoint for debate and conflict from the earliest moments of Canadian history. The institutions of formal education that existed in seventeenth-century New France were established and controlled by Catholic religious orders such as the Ursulines, Jesuits, and Congrégation de Notre-Dame. These schools sought to "convert and acculturate the Aboriginal people" into white, Christian society, and they also provided religious and social instruction to the children of French settlers.[5] State initiatives into public education did not occur until

2

INTRODUCTION

the first half of the nineteenth century, and even during that period, in what had by then become the British-controlled provinces of Upper and Lower Canada (antecedents of today's Ontario and Quebec), the kind of state-controlled institutions of common education that are found today did not exist; schooling remained in the control of Catholic and, by that time, Protestant churches. For instance, while the Legislature of Upper Canada passed *An Act to establish Public Schools in each and every District of this Province* in 1807, the funding for these institutions was "scandalously insufficient," thus leaving public education in the de facto control of Catholic and Protestant religious institutions.[6]

The desirability of denominational, Church-run schools versus a public system beyond direct Church control is thus a subject that has long been a focus of Canada's educational policy. The particular experiences of Upper Canada are most instructive in this respect, as they established the basis on which Canada's Constitution currently recognizes separate faith-based education for Catholics and Protestants. Nineteenth-century Upper Canada saw at least two competing trends: one that pressed for common schools, and another that opposed the removal of religious, denominational influence from institutions of public education. One of the major objections to common schools—and a source of great conflict—within the mainly Protestant and minority Catholic province was the question of whether education in a "common Christianity" could somehow transcend disagreements about denominational control over schools. All denominations of Protestants generally agreed that their religious education could be conducted in common schools, but Catholics did not agree.[7] The Catholic bishops opposed what they viewed as a Protestant approach to teaching the Bible that was the foundation of "common Christianity" and fought for Catholics to operate their own, separate schools.[8] In addition to tensions about whether Catholics should accept schools teaching "common Christianity," Catholics were alarmed at—and resisted—the state's attempts to interfere with the content of, and approach to, religious and moral education within Catholic schools.[9]

Because of the disagreement between the Protestant majority and the Catholics over the place of religion in schooling, the 1843 *Act for the Establishment of Common Schools in Upper Canada* was passed and maintained funding for Protestant and Catholic separate schools. This public funding of separate faith-based schools "set the pattern for education in Upper Canada."[10] In Lower Canada, the minority objections to a majority institution were similar, although the denominational roles were reversed.[11]

INTRODUCTION

There, it was the Protestant minority's objections to the prevailing Catholicism that was the foundation of their separate faith-based schools. By the time of Canada's Confederation in 1867, separate education for Catholics or Protestants who found themselves the minority in an Ontario or Quebec school district had been established and was protected in section 93 of the *British North America Act*.

The establishment of education as a provincial responsibility in the *British North America Act* has played an important part in the evolving role of faith-based schooling in Canada as waves of immigrants have made the country much more religiously diverse. Canada's accommodation of religious diversity in some provinces allowed deep religious tensions to simmer, instead of boil. By allowing Protestant and Catholic families to school their children in separate schools in the nineteenth century, difficult decisions about how a genuinely inclusive school might accommodate all Christians were avoided. The *British North America Act* also presents one of the earliest foundational frameworks through which difference and minority rights have been recognized and accommodated as part of the fabric of Canada's national identity.

Although the efforts to establish schools based on a "common Christianity" in Ontario failed as a province-wide attempt to offer a sufficiently broad religious teaching that would be inoffensive to all Christians, it was nonetheless assumed in the nineteenth century that the moral aims of schooling must be met through religious instruction of some sort. As religion has become less central to the identities of many Canadians, however, this assumption is no longer widely shared. Indeed, secular public schools have been embraced by many Canadians as the most promising and/or politically desirable schooling institution.

Perhaps the increasing movement toward secular schools in many provinces is evidence that support for faith-based schools in Canada is eroding. Newfoundland joined Canada in 1949 with terms stipulating full support for all of its denominational schools. This model was maintained until a referendum was held in 1997 on a proposal to create a single school system that had no denominational affiliation. The public voted overwhelmingly (73%) in support of this single-system model. Now Newfoundland and Labrador provide secular public schooling and no public support at all for its faith-based schools. A major impetus for the 1997 establishment of secular schools in Newfoundland and Labrador was the inefficiency and costliness of many small denominational schools and multiple school boards. However, the debate also revealed a deep concern that faith-based schools

INTRODUCTION

are a threat to social unity. The president of the Newfoundland and Labrador Teachers' Association, Brendan Doyle, framed his support for a single secular system as follows: "Our children must learn to live together, grow together and learn together. They must be freed from the bonds of denominational isolationism and discrimination."[12] Notably, Doyle's point does not speak to the efficiency of a single system but instead emphasizes that separation of schooling by faith is socially divisive. Faith-based schools in Quebec have gone through a similar change. The Catholic and Protestant school boards that once were the dominant public bodies controlling public schooling in Quebec gave way in 1998 to non-denominational school boards and non-denominational public schools.

The variation in public funding for faith-based schools across Canada's provinces has an impact on the affordability, and consequently the availability, of the schools for faith communities. While no funding is provided for faith-based schools in Newfoundland and Labrador, New Brunswick, Nova Scotia, or Prince Edward Island, most other provinces offer at least partial funding for faith-based schools that follow the provincial curriculum. Saskatchewan fully funds historic Catholic and Protestant separate faith-based schools and provides partial funding for some other schools. Alberta, like Saskatchewan and Ontario, fully funds Catholic and Protestant separate schools, but Alberta also goes further than other provinces by fully funding some faith-based schools that operate through charters or as part of a public school board. For example, there is a Jewish school and an Islamic school operated within the administration of Edmonton's public school district. British Columbia entered Confederation without any provision for public support of separate religious education, but the province currently provides up to 50-per-cent funding for some independent faith-based schools. Manitoba publicly supported separate religious education until 1890, when it was ended with the passage of the *Manitoba Schools Act* and the subsequent resolution of the Manitoba Schools Question, whereby, over the following two decades, electoral and legal challenges to the Act were defeated in favour of maintaining the status quo.[13] Manitoba, like British Columbia, currently provides up to 50-per-cent funding for some independent faith-based schools. Yukon and the Northwest Territories have constitutionally established separate Catholic schools like those in Alberta, Ontario, and Saskatchewan; and while Nunavut has the same constitutional provision, currently it has no separate schools in existence.

It is often during debates about public funding or regulation of faith-based schools that faith-based schools become the subject of controversy.

INTRODUCTION

Ontario's policies on faith-based schools are perhaps the most contentious in Canada today because the province has continued to maintain the original terms of Confederation by funding its Catholic schools, while refusing to provide funding for other faith-based schools.[14] The funding situation in Ontario has resulted in several legal disputes and led to a UN Human Rights Committee hearing, at which Ontario's funding model was found to be discriminatory. As Ontario's provincial elections in 2007 revealed, the legacy of Canada's accommodation and support of faith-based schools remains an important legal, political, and social issue. Further, it remains a matter of public concern even in provinces in which the subject has not been contested as recently and forcefully as it has been in Ontario.

Shaping *Discipline, Devotion, and Dissent*

Discipline, Devotion and Dissent offers a starting point for investigation into the place of faith-based schools in Canada by offering perspectives on some of their aims and practices. The contributors as a whole do not seek to defend faith-based schools, though some of them explicitly or implicitly offer defences. Indeed, a significant body of literature defending faith-based schools already exists.[15] Rather, the contributors to this book seek primarily to illuminate the lived experience of Canada's faith-based schools by exploring three questions:

1. What aims and practices inform and characterize Canada's faith-based schools?
2. How do faith-based schools negotiate the tension between the demands of the faith and the expectation that they educate Canadian citizens?
3. How do faith-based schools respond to internal dissent?

A summary of the three parts, and each of the book's chapters, follows below. But we believe that it will be helpful if we first explain the scope of the responses we have provided to these three questions.

Writing on a topic as broad as Canada's faith-based schools raises some difficulties. It would be virtually impossible to survey the theory and practice of all Canadian faith-based schools in order to respond to our three questions with comprehensive breadth. Canada has sizable populations of many religious communities, including Christians, Jews, Muslims, Sikhs, Buddhists, and Hindus. Within these faith communities there are multiple denominations. A survey of the faith-based schools of each denomination would have resulted in an enormous volume and would not have allowed

INTRODUCTION

multiple contributors to explore each type of faith-based school from different perspectives. Furthermore, there was also a practical concern about identifying a critical mass of scholars who have spent time within faith-based schools and who were willing and able to contribute a chapter to this book. It would have been fascinating, for example, to include chapters on the increasing number of fundamentalist, Evangelical Protestant schools in Canada (which are described in more detail below). However, administrators and faculty in these schools have been reluctant to allow scholars to enter them, study them, and criticize them. As a result, there is not nearly enough scholarship available on these schools. In contrast, however, there are many scholars who have been studying and writing about Canada's Catholic schools. There is much need and room for research on different Canadian faith-based schools, and we look forward to seeing scholars continue to contribute to the existing scholarship. Yet, for the purposes of this collection, we asked scholars who were already engaged in research in faith-based schools to contribute original works of scholarship. We maintain that we have identified a group of scholars whose work offers important insights into faith-based schooling in Canada.

In essence, we were faced with a choice between, on the one hand, seeking breadth in representing Canada's many types of religious schools in the collection and abandoning the idea of exploring a particular type of faith-school from multiple perspectives and, on the other hand, seeking depth by answering the three questions we identified as particularly illuminating from within the perspective of a single type of faith-based school. In the end, we sought to seek some depth, while allowing for some breadth as well. We decided to seek multiple answers to the questions that struck us as essential to better understanding the place of faith-based schools in Canada. At the same time, we aimed for breadth in the responses to these questions from different faith perspectives so as to provide some means of comparison. Hence, we made the following decision. We located three qualitatively unique institutional "clusters" of points on the map of Canadian religious schooling that are of ongoing theoretical interest in terms of the questions we have raised above. These clusters of interest are Jewish, Catholic, and Islamic schools. We name these groups clusters because as religious traditions they appear as incommensurable as comparing one apple with two oranges: Catholicism is a denomination of the larger Christian tradition, which in a survey of religions would stand parallel to one of the denominations of Islam or Judaism. This volume does not primarily contribute to *comparative* religious studies, however; rather, it aims to

INTRODUCTION

illuminate some aspects of faith-based schools in Canada. We believe that Jewish, Catholic, and Islamic schools in this respect offer unique and qualitatively rich material to do so.

Jewish schools in Canada have been present in one form or another since the late nineteenth century. This long history of non-Christian religious education in Canada makes Jewish schools interesting because they have evolved and become established in Canada through implicit negotiation with the larger Canadian society. On the other hand, the rise of Islamic schooling in Canada is a relatively recent phenomenon—dating only from the late 1970s. Yet Islamic schools currently serve as the most identifiable object of public concern about faith-based schooling in Canada in the post-9/11 era, as Premier McGuinty's comments (cited above) demonstrate. How Islamic schools educate their students is therefore of great concern to many. Thus, by offering perspectives on Jewish and Islamic schools, a revealing juxtaposition emerges about the educational theories and practices of both a long-established and a more recent religious minority in Canada.

In contrast, Catholic schools represent the largest and most recognizable form of established faith-based education in Canada. Furthermore, Catholic schools in Canada are uniquely united by their normative reference to Catholic educational philosophy, the Catholic faith and theology, the administrative-juridical aspect of the Catholic Church, and the broader community of Catholic persons. As a result of these phenomena, Catholic schools in localized places across the country have much in common in their pedagogical philosophy and practices. Given the historical and widespread prominence of Catholic schools in Canada, in this context they lend themselves to scholarly scrutiny as an entity.

In addition, by limiting our focus to Catholic schools rather than all Christian schools, we have been able to balance the book's chapters in a significant way. One of the characteristics of Canada's diverse array of faith-based schools is that some are interdenominational and others represent a single denomination of a religion. In the second and third parts of the book, the contributors writing on Jewish schools each offer a case study of an interdenominational school. The Islamic schools described in the second and third parts of the book are both broadly **Sunni** and therefore denominational, but they are populated by students representing a broader spectrum of theological perspectives (e.g., **Salafi**, **Sufi**, **Deobandi**) and therefore fall somewhere between the Catholic schools and the interdenominational Jewish schools explored. Interdenominational faith-based schools face different challenges and present different opportunities than single-denomi-

INTRODUCTION

national schools. For example, an interdenominational school must labour to create stability for the institution in its educational and religious policies while simultaneously respecting the differences in doctrines, practices, and beliefs of each part of its school community. On the positive side, an interdenominational school is well positioned to create space for discussion across deeply felt differences, an experience that is often believed to be an important element of citizenship education. Thus, by focusing on Catholic schools rather than all Christian schools, the book as a whole manages to address both denominational and interdenominational schools.

In addition to the fact that this volume restricts its examination of schooling to Judaism, Islam, and a single Christian denomination, it narrows its focus in another sense as well. Faith-based schools differ in that some schools embrace a mission of cultivating civic virtues while others emphasize isolation from the broader Canadian community, and some even include teachings that run counter to civic education. There are schools in Canada that, from the Canadian perspective, are difficult to justify if one is at all concerned with children receiving some semblance of a multicultural education. Accelerated Christian Education (ACE) schools, for instance, are fundamentalist, Evangelical Protestant schools that typically feature classrooms without a teacher. In the teacher's place there is an invigilating adult who enforces strict discipline, sometimes through corporal punishment. Children sit quietly and ply through workbooks designed by a group in Texas, where the ACE program was founded.[16] There is little discussion or other interaction among students and limited discussions with the supervising adult present; the students spend their days learning by rote. This is a type of school that discourages critical thinking and not only fails to instill understanding and respect for people of other faiths or no faith, but treats them as inferior.[17]

Although only one contributor, Seymour Epstein, describes some faith-based schools that are relatively more isolationist than others, in general this book offers no detailed examination of what many scholars of faith-based schooling and the general public would identify as the most worrisome aims and practices of these schools. Furthermore, the Jewish schools that are discussed in chapters four and seven are each progressive in that they actively seek to provide a kind of education appropriate for multicultural citizenship. Chapters six and nine each focus on a particular Islamic school and, although aspects of these schools are noted that might fall short of the demands that some scholars and many within the general public might demand of civic education, the authors of these chapters find much to

INTRODUCTION

extol in these schools' approaches to multicultural education. Chapter eight, on the other hand, is highly critical of Catholic schools' failure to articulate a meaningful way to validate and encourage students' faithful dissent. In short, no chapters in this volume offer a strong critique of faith-based schooling in general or of any particular faith-based schools. As editors, we asked our contributors neither to defend nor to critique the schools they discuss. Rather, we asked them to present their research and experiences of the schools they have studied as an honest response to the questions that govern this book. All in all, the most important quality of these chapters, in our view, is that they collectively illuminate the aims and practices of a selection of Canada's faith-based schools. We describe next in detail the various perspectives on faith-based schooling offered in this book.

Overview of *Discipline, Devotion, and Dissent*

In this section, we provide an overview of each of the book's three sections, describing how each section responds to the book's governing questions. We also offer brief summaries of each of the book's chapters.

Part A: Aims and Practices

Part A explores how Canadian Jewish, Catholic, and Muslim communities have conceived of the aims of their schools and how these aims are manifested in their curricula and teaching methods. Central to each chapter in this part is an emphasis on defining the vision that informs faith-based schooling. As a whole, the first three chapters of the book offer a foundational understanding of the trajectory, diversities, challenges, and distinctions that define the aims of education in each cluster.

In chapter one, Seymour Epstein offers a comprehensive overview of Canada's 74 Jewish schools. His overview contains three parts. First, he proposes that Canada's Jewish schools can be understood to fall into one of seven categories. Some of these categories are those of a particular Jewish denomination, such as **Reform**, **Conservative**, Modern **Orthodox** and Charedi (fervently Orthodox). Additionally, there are Jewish community schools that are pluralistic and interdenominational and might pursue a specific curricular theme such as arts-based education. Lastly, there is a history of secular Jewish schools in Canada that focus on Yiddish and Jewish culture rather than Jewish religion. The second part of Epstein's chapter identifies various components of the curriculum in Canada's Jewish schools. He describes the role of prayer, the Hebrew language, the Bible, the Talmud, laws and customs, the calendar cycle, history, literature, and values

10

INTRODUCTION

in the curriculum and highlights some of the differences in approaches to these elements of the curriculum among the schools in the seven categories. In the third part of the chapter, Epstein discusses how the various Jewish schools differ or are united in aspects of their teaching methods. Overall, Epstein's chapter reveals the tremendous diversity among Canada's Jewish schools in their pedagogical missions, curricula, and teaching methods.

According to Mario D'Souza in chapter two, it is imperative that discussion of the aims of Catholic education be articulated in terms that outline a clear relationship between philosophy and theology. For his discussion on what constitutes these aims, he points toward an enabling of human freedom and enhancement of the common good as Catholic education's fundamental cornerstones. D'Souza observes that Catholicism's aim to achieve human freedom is based upon a positive ontology and anthropology; hence, in Catholic education all knowledge and activities are aimed toward the development of a person's metaphysical, existential, ethical, and religious freedom. Where subject matter may tend to become compartmentalized and even fragmented, it is the teacher who serves as the first example and touchstone upon which a synthesis of faith, knowledge, and culture may obtain. This unity is not dispassionate, nor is its expressed interest in human freedom trivial. To the contrary, D'Souza firmly articulates the aim of Catholic education in opposition to trends of "human miniaturization" in contemporary secular society that threaten the freedom and dignity of persons. The final section of D'Souza's chapter explores the meaning of Catholic education for the common good in terms of its relationship with democracy in a pluralistic society. Anticipating the issues raised by J. Kent Donlevy's chapter in Part B, D'Souza notes that all religions encounter strains when living within plurality. The Catholic response to this tension, D'Souza argues, is to emphasize that religion need not be hidden from public view, and that it should instead be "de-privatized" so as to acknowledge its contribution to the freedom of persons and hence the common good.

In chapter three, Nadeem Memon traces the historical growth of Islamic schooling in Canada. The chapter explores the purpose of Islamic schooling, the challenges of establishing schools, and the way in which both its articulated purpose and the response to its initial growing pains combined to shape the curriculum. Although it has a relatively short (thirty-year) history when compared to Jewish and Catholic education in Canada, Memon maintains that Islamic schooling nonetheless has a complex history here. With his observation that Toronto houses the largest concentration of Islamic schools in North America, Memon insists that the diversity of

INTRODUCTION

voices and historical influences in the field of Islamic education is arguably most evident in Canada. He connects the ways in which national networks and organizations such as the Muslim Students' Association and the Islamic Society of North America, both initiated in the United States, helped establish Canada's first Islamic school. Aside from cross-border influences, he also maps the divergent aspirations and conceptions that varying segments of the Canadian Muslim diaspora understand as the role of Islamic schools. The chapter closes by exploring the recent interest in redefining the purpose of Islamic schools in light of a changing conception of what it means to be a Canadian Muslim in the post-9/11 era.

Part B: Faith and Citizenship

As discussed above, one of the main concerns raised about faith-based schools in liberal democracies is that they pose a threat to social cohesion. At the heart of this concern is the idea that faith-based schools are unable to, or do not adequately, address the education of citizens. The chapters in Part B all address the question of how faith-based schools respond to the challenge of educating Canadian citizens. Whereas the chapters in Part A focus on how faith-based schools might broadly conceive of their aims, curricula, and methods, in Part B the chapters focus specifically on the extent to which faith-based schools manage to address the values deemed important for citizenship in multicultural Canada. The three chapters in this part of the book demonstrate that the schools described here, at least, do indeed take citizenship education seriously. Each chapter reflects a different approach. The chapters on Jewish and Islamic faith-based schooling are each a case study of a single school's efforts to address citizenship. In contrast, the chapter on Catholic schools examines a number of legal disputes that reveal that certain key values relating to citizenship education have been interpreted differently by the Church and by secular Canada. The result is that the civic values taught in Catholic schools are indeed sometimes in tension with the broader Canadian society, despite the fact that Catholic schools understand civic education to be part and parcel of religious teaching.

In chapter four, Greg Beiles explores how the subject of citizenship is broached in The Toronto Heschel School, an interdenominational Jewish community school. Beiles draws on interviews, student work samples, and his own experiences as a teacher at the school to present a case study of how one particular school manages to offer a robust education for multicultural citizenship within a Jewish framework. Beiles describes how the Heschel

INTRODUCTION

curriculum identifies and emphasizes correlations between secular democratic institutions, processes, and values and those that are part of the Jewish tradition. Perhaps most importantly, Beiles provides intriguing examples of the attempt at Heschel to incorporate divergent ideas and voices in the Jewish tradition into the curriculum. The pluralism that animates Heschel's curriculum is designed to provide opportunities for students both to learn to reflect critically on their own circumstances and to appreciate the value of coming to understand and respect differences. The curriculum at Heschel goes beyond the recognition and appreciation of difference by fostering students' abilities to work through difference as well: it requires students to confront tensions in identity formation, both their own and others'. Beiles's overall assessment is that the Heschel School has managed to enact an educational culture that honours and nurtures Jewish faith while cultivating the values necessary for meaningful engagement with the broader Canadian society.

In chapter five, J. Kent Donlevy explores tensions between competing Catholic and secular conceptions of the values of respect for the Other, fairness, the common good, and democracy. Through an exposition of several prominent cases recently argued before Canadian courts and human rights tribunals, Donlevy points to examples of the "sacred–secular divide" along these four values, and then relates how the issues and judgments in those cases affect the ways in which Catholic education is theorized and practised. While there are arguably many points of congruence between Catholic and secular values, the cases Donlevy presents show that there are also some places where important differences exist. He explores these differences through their philosophical, anthropological, political, and legal foundations. These differences, Donlevy argues, create difficulties in Catholic schools' ability to defend some of their policies in the public square. He concludes that the intersection of these competing foundations within Catholic institutions creates the optimal conditions for an apparent sense of paradox for instructional and political leaders in Catholic education. In the end, this paradox presents a "teachable moment" for those on both sides of the value divide. For Catholics, it provides a meaningful context within which one must become aware of one's Church, its value commitments, and the question of how they are to be coordinated with non-Catholic values in secular society. For secular Canadian society, Catholic schools stand as a challenge to its commitment in rhetoric to embrace all cultures. Donlevy asks, how can a religious Other be seen to be acting with rational sincerity,

INTRODUCTION

honour, and faith in the interests of the common good, if those interests do not completely match with the prevailing secular norms?

In chapter six, Asma Ahmed explores how Canadian Islamic schools can educate young Muslim students in a way that fosters social integration. Ahmed describes her research on the London (Ontario) Islamic school, where she encountered young Muslim students struggling with balancing their religious, national, and cultural identities. Ahmed frames the chapter around Muslim youth who struggle between a strong religious identity and Canadian values of citizenship and social responsibility. To ground her analysis, Ahmed builds on the works of Tariq Ramadan to question whether Islamic schools hinder the social growth and integration of Muslim youth, or whether they are able to nurture effectively the multiple identities of students.

Ahmed argues that Islamic schools are enmeshed in a complex crisis of identities, so they need not only to nurture a sense of integration that entails a psychological sense of belonging but to move toward a stage of "post-integration," where attitudes of civic participation are fostered among youth. Ahmed provides a balanced analysis that both highlights the ways in which the London Islamic School fosters integration and at the same time requires institutional development through a structured curriculum that would cultivate socially and spiritually grounded young people.

Part C: Dissent and Critical Thinking

Whereas Part A opens the volume with perspectives on how some Canadian faith-based schools conceive of their aims and pedagogy, and Part B carries that discussion of aims into how they (or similar institutions) view their relationships with the rest of Canadian society along a "sacred–secular" divide, Part C examines the ways in which faith-based schools might view and respond to dissent.[18] The focus of this part is how faith-based schools handle dissenting views within classrooms. The chapters in Part C therefore explore the social questions that elicit internal differences within a religious school and point to larger foundational questions at the core of the school's mission. All three chapters raise this question: what is the most appropriate approach that teachers and administrators should take to deal with the dissent in their schools?

In chapter seven, Alex Pomson and Randal Schnoor explore the various discussions of values, commitments, and expectations that have occurred at the Downtown Jewish Day School (DJDS), a pluralistic community day

INTRODUCTION

school in Toronto. The school's explicitly pluralistic framework seeks to enable students' appreciation of the importance of, and respect for, diversity and difference. As a group, DJDS's parents are characterized by a great deal of sociological diversity, including varied levels of Jewish observance and differing religious commitments. Pomson and Schnoor discovered that the significant sociological diversity of the parents of DJDS's students leads to a number of "collisions" among administrators, teachers, and parents. They observe that during the school's formative years there was constant debate about the school's policies and practices, debates that were reopened even some time after they apparently had been settled. Based on their findings at DJDS, Pomson and Schnoor demonstrate that the sociological diversity of parents at DJDS makes it difficult to build a stable community. Yet, on the other hand, the members of the school community do share a strong commitment to Jewish pluralism and to religious heterodoxy. Therefore, Pomson and Schnoor argue, DJDS can be viewed as a "postmodern community of difference" that, at its best, becomes a community that overcomes and benefits from the instability resulting from the tensions, disagreements, and disputes caused by the community's religious pluralism.

In chapter eight, Graham McDonough shows that Catholic students and their families experience doctrine in multifaceted ways. As an example of a controversial internal issue that Catholic schools struggle to present in terms that are true to the interests of (a) the Church's authorities, (b) those in the community who do agree with official Church teaching, and (c) those voices that remain faithful but nonetheless find strong reasons within the Church's own history and theology with which to dissent, he focuses on the widespread disagreement with Pope Paul VI's 1968 **encyclical** letter *Humanae Vitae*, which proscribes artificial contraception. In his discussion of how the school might respond to the disagreement over this encyclical, McDonough finds that the pedagogical question of how to treat intra-Church controversies is itself a controversial subject within the school and Church. Should students who disagree with *Humanae Vitae* (like many of their parents do) be taught how to do so with the best intellectual resources available in the interests of renewing the Church? Should the role of the school be to defend the prevailing view and even persuade dissenting students that the encyclical has merit? Or is some middle path the best option? McDonough offers a twofold conclusion. First, in cases like this, explicit statements are required as to the aims of engaging with students in discussions of internally controversial issues. Second, teaching students rigorous

INTRODUCTION

and scholarly ways to disagree is preferable to leaving them without the resources to make a fair defence of their conscientious view.

In chapter 9, Qaiser Ahmad challenges the dichotomy which maintains that faith-based schools can be characterized as either "strong" or "moderate." He notes that in the prevailing theoretical discourse, "moderate" faith-based schools are portrayed as being more committed to (a) fostering individual autonomy and critical thinking, and (b) preparing students to live cohesively with other citizens; on the other hand, "strong" schools are portrayed as inculcating a comprehensive religious identity that is determined and not open to challenge. He observes that for this reason, strong schools are often charged with providing an insular, undemocratic, and uncritical education that is antithetical to the values of integration, tolerance, and student autonomy. Reflecting on his experience teaching at an Islamic school in Toronto for over six years, Ahmad contends that cultivating a critical disposition often associated only with moderate schools was central at his school, but that it also featured many elements that characterize strong schools. By relating specific classroom examples and reflections on his own teaching, Ahmad shows how an encouragement of and respect for critical thinking, differences of opinion, and nurturing of liberal values can be taught in schools where the educational aims include a strong religious identity.

In the tenth and final chapter, Avi Mintz provides some concluding remarks that highlight an important theme of citizenship education that emerges throughout the book. He discusses how many of the faith-based schools described in the book create spaces within the school and within classrooms for meaningful deliberation across differences. In these spaces, heated conversation may occur about issues that are of fundamental importance to the faith community and to the school's students. Mintz contends that the diversity of priorities, interests, beliefs, and expectations among administrators, teachers, parents, students, and community members found in many of Canada's faith-based schools can serve as a dynamic and valuable wellspring of citizenship education, should school leaders recognize and embrace it. The diversity within a faith-based school's community requires students and community members to respect opinions different from their own, articulate clearly their own positions, and then consider what would be required to address the differences present. Such conversations may go some length toward cultivating the kind of citizens who are able to interact productively with Canadians outside of their faith, and

INTRODUCTION

Mintz argues that such deliberative spaces provide positive support for the faith-based schools that embrace them. Indeed, it may be that faith-based schools that encourage deliberation and meaningful engagement with dissent form a bridge to the creation of robust multicultural Canadian citizens.

The Promise and Problems of Faith-Based Schooling in Canada

At the dawn of Canada, great efforts were made to think through how the religiously diverse population could be educated. Today, with a Canadian population that is much more diverse than it was in the nineteenth century, the question of how the country should accommodate faith-based schools remains as salient as it is controversial. The contributors to this book approach the question of faith-based schooling from perspectives located within faith-based schools themselves, thereby illuminating the aims and practices of these institutions. The schools discussed in this book face many challenges: some struggle to promote religious faith while maintaining a distinct identity within a secular national culture; some struggle with defending themselves from external criticism that their mission is incompatible with Canadian values and that segregating students exacerbates social tensions; and some struggle to articulate and practise foundationally rigorous responses to internal differences and dissent.

At the same time there is much promise across faith-based schools, and their potential emerges throughout the book's chapters. The Canadian faith-based schools described in this book generally take seriously their responsibility to provide students with high-quality academic preparation, meaningful religious instruction, *and* an education appropriate for citizenship in a multicultural democracy. These schools represent many ways in which Canadian citizens have been educated and are currently being educated. Moreover, they are incarnations of the hopes that religious groups have for their futures. Whatever their failures, many of Canada's faith-based schools are struggling with their place in Canada just as much as Canada in general has struggled with the question of how to accommodate them.

Notes

1 Cited in Andrew Coyne, "Strife," 12 Oct. 2007, http://andrewcoyne.com
2 Coyne, "Strife."
3 To provide only a few more examples, the charge of Islamophobia appears in Christina Blizzard, "A One-Issue Campaign: Faith-Based School Funding Overshadows All," *Toronto Sun*, 3 Oct. 2007: 5, and Lorrie Goldstein, "Hijabs,

INTRODUCTION

Turbans Aren't a Threat," *Toronto Sun*, 21 Oct. 2007: C5. Robin Sears argued that McGuinty's appeal to Islamophobia eroded Tory's support by 10 points in three weeks. Sears claimed that this was "a clear appeal to Islamophobia" and that "at Toronto dinner parties one heard 'progressive' downtown Liberals muttering quietly that Tory's policy would fund 'some crazy imam's Mississauga madrassa.'" Sears, "How Ontario Got a One-Issue Campaign," *Policy Options* 28, no. 10 (Nov. 2007): 17–24.

4 For literature on Public Funding and Legal Challenges, see, for example, Greg M. Dickinson and W. Rod Dolmage, "Education, Religion, and the Courts in Ontario," *Canadian Journal of Education* 21, no. 4 (1996): 363–83; Paul Clarke, "Religion, Public Education and the Charter: Where Do We Go Now?" *McGill Journal of Education* 40, no. 3 (2005): 351–81; and Anwar N. Khan, "Religious Education in Canadian Public Schools," *Journal of Law and Education* 28, no. 3 (1999): 431–42. For literature on religious accommodations in public schools, see David Seljak, "Education, Multiculturalism, and Religion," in *Religion and Ethnicity in Canada*, ed. P. Bramadat and D. Seljak (Toronto: University of Toronto Press, 2009), 178–200; R.D. Gidney, *From Hope to Harris: The Reshaping of Ontario's Schools* (Toronto: University of Toronto Press, 1999); Stephen Lawton, "Public, Private and Separate Schools in Ontario: Developing a New Social Contract for Education?" In *Private Schools and Public Policy*, ed. William Lowe Boyd and James G. Cibulka (American Educational Research Association, 1989), 171–92.

5 Micheline Dumont, "Education in New France," *The Oxford Companion to Canadian History*, ed. Gerald Hallowell (Oxford: Oxford University Press, 2004), Oxford Reference Online, http://www.oxfordreference.com/views/ENTRY.html?subview=Main&entry=t148.e509

6 Franklin A. Walker, *Catholic Education and Politics in Upper Canada* (Toronto: J.M. Dent, 1976), 36.

7 Walker, *Catholic Education and Politics*, 43.

8 Walker, *Catholic Education and Politics*, 55.

9 For examples of such Catholic resistance, see Mark G. McGowan, *The Waning of the Green: Catholics, the Irish, and Identity in Toronto 1887–1922* (Montreal and Kingston: McGill-Queen's University Press, 1999), especially 134.

10 Charles B. Sissons, *Church and State in Canadian Education* (Toronto: Ryerson Press, 1959), 18.

11 See Sissons, *Church and State*, 135ff. for a description of Lower Canada's School Act of 1846.

12 Cited in Alan Wright, Véronique Brunet and Marie-Jeanne Monette, "Policy Narrative for Newfoundland and Labrador," in *The Evolution of Professional-*

INTRODUCTION

ism: Educational Policy in the Provinces and Territories of Canada, ed. Adrienne Chan, Donald Fisher, and Kjell Rubenson (Vancouver: University of British Columbia Press, 2007), 173.

13 Roberto Perin, "Manitoba Schools Question," *The Oxford Companion to Canadian History*, ed. Gerald Hallowell (Oxford: Oxford University Press, 2004), Oxford Reference Online, http://www.oxfordreference.com/views/ENTRY.html?subview=Main&entry=+148.e977

14 There are several Roman Catholic separate school districts in Ontario, but only one fully funded Protestant separate school district remains, located in Penetanguishene.

15 Of the many works in this "defence" genre, a fine example, and one that draws on the Canadian context, is Thiessen, *In Defence of Religious Schools and Colleges*. See also Geoffrey Short, "Faith–Based Schools: A Threat to Social Cohesion?" *Journal of Philosophy of Education* 36, no. 4 (2002): 559–72; Anthony S. Bryk, Valerie E. Lee, and Peter Blakeley Holland, *Catholic Schools and the Common Good* (Cambridge, MA: Harvard University Press, 1993); Walter Feinberg, *For Goodness Sake: Religious Schools and Education for Democratic Society* (New York: Routledge, 2006); and Jasmin Zine, *Canadian Islamic Schools: Unraveling the Politics of Faith, Gender, Knowledge, and Identity* (Toronto: University of Toronto Press, 2008).

16 For a discussion of ACE schools in Canada, see Lois Sweet, *God in the Classroom: The Controversial Issue of Religion in the Classroom* (Toronto: McClelland & Stewart, 1997), 88–92.

17 For a discussion of the texts of ACE schools, see James Dwyer, *Religious Schools v. Children's Rights* (Ithaca, NY: Cornell University Press1988), 14–15.

18 See Graham P. McDonough, "Why Dissent Is a Vital Concept in Moral Education," *Journal of Moral Education* 39, no. 4 (2010): 421–36, for the conceptual analysis of dissent as the act of internal criticism. Also see Margaret O'Gara, *The Ecumenical Gift Exchange* (Collegeville, MN: Liturgical Press, 1998); Steven H. Shiffrin, *Dissent, Injustice, and the Meanings of America* (Princeton, NJ: Princeton University Press, 1999); and Cass R. Sunstein, *Why Societies Need Dissent* (Cambridge, MA: Harvard University Press, 2003).

Bibliography

Blizzard, Christina. "A One-Issue Campaign: Faith-Based School Funding Overshadows All." *Toronto Sun*, 3 Oct. 2007: 5.

Bryk, Anthony S., Valerie E. Lee, and Peter Blakeley Holland. *Catholic Schools and the Common Good*. Cambridge, MA: Harvard University Press, 1993.

Clarke, Paul. "Religion, Public Education and the Charter: Where Do We Go Now?" *McGill Journal of Education* 40, no. 3 (2005): 351–81.

Coyne, Andrew. "Strife." 12 Oct. 2007. http://andrewcoyne.com

Dickinson, Greg M., and W. Rod Dolmage. "Education, Religion, and the Courts in Ontario." *Canadian Journal of Education* 21, no. 4 (1996): 363–83.

Dumont, Micheline. "Education in New France." *The Oxford Companion to Canadian History*. Edited by Gerald Hallowell. Oxford: Oxford University Press, 2004. Oxford Reference Online, http://www.oxfordreference.com/views/ENTRY.html?subview=Main&entry=t148.e509

Dwyer, James. *Religious Schools v. Children's Rights*. Ithaca, NY: Cornell University Press, 1998.

Feinberg, Walter. *For Goodness Sake: Religious Schools and Education for Democratic Society*. New York: Routledge, 2006.

Gidney, R. D. *From Hope to Harris: The Reshaping of Ontario's Schools*. Toronto: University of Toronto Press, 1999.

Goldstein, Lorrie. "Hijabs, Turbans Aren't a Threat." *Toronto Sun*, 21 Oct. 2007: C5.

Khan, Anwar N. "Religious Education in Canadian Public Schools." *Journal of Law and Education* 28, no. 3 (1999): 431–42.

Lawton, Stephen. "Public, Private and Separate Schools in Ontario: Developing a New Social Contract for Education?" In *Private Schools and Public Policy*, edited by William Lowe Boyd and James G. Cibulka, 171–92. New York: Falmer Press, 1989.

McDonough, Graham P. "Why Dissent Is a Vital Concept in Moral Education." *Journal of Moral Education* 39, no. 4 (2010): 421–36.

McGowan, Mark G. *The Waning of the Green: Catholics, the Irish, and Identity in Toronto 1887–1922*. Montreal and Kingston: McGill-Queen's University Press, 1999.

O'Gara, Margaret. *The Ecumenical Gift Exchange*. Collegeville, MN: Liturgical Press, 1998.

Perin, Roberto. "Manitoba Schools Question." *The Oxford Companion to Canadian History*. Edited by Gerald Hallowell. Oxford: Oxford University Press, 2004. Oxford Reference Online, http://www.oxfordreference.com/views/ENTRY.html?subview=Main&entry=+148.e977

Sears, Robin. "How Ontario Got a One-Issue Campaign." *Policy Options* 28, no. 10 (Nov. 2007): 17–24.

Seljak, David, "Education, Multiculturalism, and Religion." In *Religion and Ethnicity in Canada*, edited by P. Bramadat and D. Seljak, 178–200. Toronto: University of Toronto Press, 2009).

Shiffrin, Steven H. *Dissent, Injustice, and the Meanings of America*. Princeton, NJ: Princeton University Press, 1999.

Short, Geoffrey. "Faith–Based Schools: A Threat to Social Cohesion?" *Journal of Philosophy of Education* 36, no. 4 (2002): 559–72.

Sissons, Charles B. *Church and State in Canadian Education*. Toronto: Ryerson Press, 1959.

Sunstein, Cass R. *Why Societies Need Dissent*. Cambridge, MA: Harvard University Press, 2003.

Sweet, Lois. *God in the Classroom: The Controversial Issue of Religion in the Classroom*. Toronto: McClelland & Stewart, 1997.

Thiessen, Elmer John. *In Defence of Religious Schools and Colleges*. Montreal: McGill-Queen's University Press, 2001.

Walker, Franklin A. *Catholic Education and Politics in Upper Canada*. Toronto: J.M. Dent, 1976.

Wright, Alan, Véronique Brunet, and Marie-Jeanne Monette. "Policy Narrative for Newfoundland and Labrador." In *The Evolution of Professionalism: Educational Policy in the Provinces and Territories of Canada*, edited by Adrienne Chan, Donald Fisher, and Kjell Rubenson, 169–85. Vancouver: University of British Columbia Press, 2007.

Zine, Jasmin. *Canadian Islamic Schools: Unraveling the Politics of Faith, Gender, Knowledge, and Identity*. Toronto: University of Toronto Press, 2008.

PART A

AIMS *and* PRACTICES

CHAPTER ONE

THE JEWISH DAY SCHOOLS OF CANADA

Seymour Epstein

Introduction

While this chapter will deal primarily with Jewish day-school education in
Canada, it is important at the outset to properly define the borders of Jewish
education as it is perceived by the Jewish community. Until the enlighten-
ment in Europe, all Jewish education was religious in nature, a direct result
of the famous verse in Deuteronomy 6:7: "Impress them upon your children. Recite them when you stay at home and when you are away, when you
lie down and when you get up."[1] This commandment (*mitzvah*) to transmit
"them"—meaning the texts, values, laws, and customs—from one generation of Jews to the next, and to have study pervade all of human existence,
is the root cause of the deep passion that Jews have had for education across
the ages and throughout the world.

In the modern age this commandment has manifested itself among all
kinds of Jews: the secular of all stripes and the religious of all denominations. In Canada, while the first half of the twentieth century saw several
large Jewish secular schools thrive in Alberta, Manitoba, Ontario, and Quebec, by the end of that century most Jewish day schools were religious institutions or, at least, gave some religious instruction.

In addition to the diverse array of institutions that have been created
by Jews in their efforts to interpret the command to educate their children, another important aspect of Jewish education is that it is not solely
for young students. As implied in that verse from Deuteronomy—which

25

AIMS AND PRACTICES

requires both that the commandments are passed down to one's children and that each person continue to recite them every day—Jewish study is meant to be a lifetime pursuit, and institutions for advanced adult study exist in every viable Jewish community. These range from synagogue-based (and obviously denominational) courses to academic Jewish studies on the campuses of Canadian universities. While the latter are clearly secular and scientific in nature, the liberal sector of the Jewish community views them as a legitimate form of Jewish study. The various strands of Orthodoxy have mixed views of academic Jewish studies and maintain many of their own institutions for the observance of the study commandment: *yeshivot* (for single men), *kollelim* (for married men), and women's study groups. All of these have the purpose of both teaching Jewish traditional texts and educating toward a full observance of Jewish customs and values.

Jewish education for children and young adults exists in three different spheres:

1. day schools with a full daytime curriculum of general and Jewish studies;
2. complementary schools (once called supplementary schools, and before that, *Talmudei Torah*) with after-hours and weekend schedules and a curriculum of only Jewish studies;
3. the informal domain of youth groups, summer camps, and educational trips to Israel.

Each of these different programs exists in all of the various religious streams with curricula that are specific to each type of school.

This diversity in Jewish educational options is most evident in the subject of this chapter, the 74 day schools across Canada, situated in the cities of relatively large Jewish populations: Vancouver, Edmonton, Calgary, Winnipeg, London, Hamilton, Toronto, Ottawa, and Montreal. In Toronto, for example, it is common to find two such schools situated next to each other on one city block but with very different Jewish studies curricula due to vast ideological differences. This theme of diversity will be illustrated throughout the chapter by references to the schools, their differing curricula, and the wide spectrum of their educational objectives. The differences in ideology, religious denomination, and pedagogical style are significant and make it clear that Jewish schooling across Canada is not a single entity, but rather a multi-faceted mosaic.

The Canadian Jewish community shares many similarities with the American Jewish community to its south. In addition to shared European

THE JEWISH DAY SCHOOLS OF CANADA | EPSTEIN

historical influences and roots, its pattern of integration and assimilation into the broader community is similar. Comparisons to American schools, therefore, can help illuminate the distinctiveness of Jewish schooling in Canada. A major factor that distinguishes Canadian Jewish education from its counterpart in the much larger community of the United States is the percentage of children in day schools. In the United States, most Jewish children attending a formal Jewish school are in complementary schools, most of which are congregational (synagogue-based). Conversely, in Canada, most children enrolled in a Jewish school are in day schools, and the number of children enrolled in complementary schools is small in comparison. As an example, in the figures based on the 2001 census, approximately 34 per cent of all Jewish children in Toronto were in day schools, while the national average in the US was approximately 17 per cent, a figure significantly skewed by the high enrolment levels in the greater New York area.[2] Also, most day schools in the United States are Orthodox of one persuasion or another, while Canada has a much more diverse admixture of liberal schools that are based in the Conservative and Reform movements or are community oriented.

The reasons for this strong and diverse day-school enrolment are mostly historical, starting with the *British North America Act* and its separation by religion of public schooling in Ontario and Quebec. When the choice there was limited to one between Protestant or Catholic schools, Jews began to consider establishing private Jewish schooling, even though the establishment of Jewish day schools in Canada was a later development in line with the growth of the Jewish community. A significant post–World War II Jewish immigration to Canada from traditional communities in Eastern Europe and North Africa contributed significantly to the further growth and development of day-school education by enlarging and diversifying the Jewish communities and, therefore, making it possible to have a sufficient number of students to populate a single school in some places, and multiple schools in others.

Today, government funding of Jewish day schools in Quebec, Manitoba, Alberta, and British Columbia is an additional factor affecting the stability of Jewish day schools in those provinces. The lack of such funding in Ontario—which has the highest Jewish population of all the provinces,[3] houses 48 of the 74 Canadian Jewish schools, and provides total government funding for separate Catholic and Protestant schools[4] and a few special-interest schools—has been a constant irritant among many Ontario Jews. There has been much protest activity by Ontario parents and the orga-

AIMS AND PRACTICES

nized Jewish community regarding this issue over the past few decades, but
to no avail. Notwithstanding the relative strength of Canadian Jewish day
schools, it must be noted that only a minority of Canadian Jews opt for this
type of schooling (as mentioned above, approximately a third of the school-
age cohort in Toronto, for example), and although the Orthodox and Charedi sectors figure largely in day school enrolment, they are a minority
among the Jews of Canada.

Subject Matter and Teaching Methods in Jewish Schools

Before turning to the diversity of Canadian Jewish schools, their curricula,
methods of instruction and aims, a list of the number of schools across
Canada will illustrate the geographic scope of Jewish day schools, while a
denominational breakdown for Toronto, the largest community, will demonstrate the diversity of offerings:

Vancouver	4
Edmonton	2
Calgary	2
Winnipeg	5
London	1
Hamilton	3
Toronto	39
Ottawa	5
Montreal	13
TOTAL	**74**

Table 1.1   Jewish Day Schools in Canada

The 39 schools in Toronto can be categorized as follows:

a. community schools (10), including an arts-based school, a Montessori
   school, and a 1,400-student high school;
b. Modern Orthodox schools (3);
c. Conservative schools (2);

28

d. Reform schools (2);

e. fervently Orthodox (*Charedi*) schools (18); and

f. Orthodox schools (4).[5]

One might argue with the way in which some of the categories are delineated, but the diversity based on ideology in Toronto's community of approximately 180,000 Jews is evident.

I will now describe in greater detail the various kinds of schools that exist in Canada, along with the ideological movements behind them.

The Nature and Ideological Foundations of Jewish Schools in Canada

The very first attempt at day-school education took place in what is now Germany at the end of the eighteenth century. After Joseph II of Austria issued the *Toleranzpatent* of 1782, an edict of tolerance that granted Jews equality before the law and the right to state-sponsored education, it was determined that Jewish-German schools could be established that would teach both secular and Jewish subject matter.[6] Since then, the day-school movement has developed worldwide in every country with a substantial Jewish population. One of the fascinating aspects of the post-Communist period in Eastern Europe and the various republics of the former Soviet Union is the rapid growth of day schools in that part of the world from 1990 on. After three generations of Soviet repression of Jewish religion and culture, it was close to miraculous to see the profound interest in Jewish learning displayed by Jews who barely knew they were Jewish.[7]

In each jurisdiction where Jewish day schools exist, they have not only grown naturally from within the Jewish community but also developed some form of relationship with the general community and its government. The establishment of a Jewish school is innate to a community that has a long tradition of the priority of education, and the relationship with the general community is due to the ubiquity of public schooling in the modern period. In almost every country of the world except the United States, government ministries of education support all or part of the general studies curriculum of the school. The formulae for such support differ from country to country, but they are always an important factor in the continuing enrolment of children in such private school settings. Where such support exists, it both lowers the cost of tuition and assures a standard curriculum of general studies. It is interesting to note that in the United States, where church–state separation is the constitutional norm, there is still state aid to

Jewish schools in some jurisdictions—not in the form of curricular subsidy, but usually in peripheral domains such as special education, transportation, food, and in-service professional development.[8]

The Jewish schools in Canada differ from one another in much the same way as in other countries; however, it is important to note that the categories are somewhat fluid. In some instances they overlap, and in certain schools they have changed as the schools developed. There is no external organization that determines how a school is to be categorized, and thus different Jewish communities define the nature of their own schools. The diversity in the communities that found, support, and populate Jewish schools results in the variety of these schools, which is described next.

Secular

There were once strong secular day schools that usually taught Yiddish either instead of or together with Hebrew. The secular (usually socialist/Yiddishist) movements that created these schools are no longer mainstream ideologies, as the Yiddish language is losing its predominance among Canadian Jews: the generation of Yiddish-speaking immigrants from Europe has given way to two generations of Canadian-born, native English speakers who have less of a connection to Yiddish (since the language of many Jewish texts and of Israel is Hebrew). The socialist/Yiddishist movement and these schools are now either non-existent or better defined as community schools.

Community

These schools attempt to service a wide spectrum of the community, but mostly among the non-Orthodox sectors of the population. Some of them have very specific pedagogical environments, e.g., Montessori, arts-based, differentiated learning/multiple intelligence. There is a diverse range of religious beliefs, practices, and Jewish identity among the families who enroll their children in these schools.

Modern Orthodox

The Modern Orthodox community leads a fully observant lifestyle in that it maintains strictest adherence to **Halacha** (Jewish law), as interpreted by Orthodox rabbis. For example, men cover their heads, as do most married women, and the Sabbath and dietary laws are strictly adhered to. They differ from Charedi Jews—who will be described below—in their acceptance of modernity (television, for example) and in their more open relationship with the general population and culture. Schools that attract Modern Orthodox families develop in communities that are fairly uniform in their religious beliefs. The observance patterns are common to most families and the schools reflect that kind of unity.

Conservative

Conservative Judaism is respectful of Jewish law as interpreted by the tradition and the movement's rabbis. However, it affirms the historical development of Jewish law and is therefore open to changes that are seen as necessitated by changes in society. The Conservative Movement in Judaism has sponsored Solomon Schechter Schools across North America, named for one of the founding fathers of Conservative Judaism and its training school, the Jewish Theological Seminary of America in New York. In Canada, one such school in Montreal bears that name, while the Toronto version uses a different name, the Robbins Hebrew Academy. In these schools there is more diversity in religious observance than in Orthodox schools, with some parents choosing the school for reasons other than denominational affiliation, such as geographic location or a high level of general studies.

Reform

Reform Judaism is an outgrowth of early attempts at reform in nineteenth-century Germany. Originally, it rejected the binding nature of Jewish law, but recently it has become more traditional in its approach, and support for day schools is one illustration of that tendency. Canada was one of the first places where the Reform Movement established a day school as a significant shift in Reform doctrine, which, as stated, previously did not support parochial day-school education. Here, too, one finds great diversity of religious practice and affiliation among the parents. One can find parents in a Reform school who are active members of a Reform Temple and who identify with the school for that reason, while others may not be involved in Reform Jewish life and do not necessarily care about that aspect of the school's curriculum.

Charedi (Chasidic and Yeshivish)

Among the fervently Orthodox fundamentalist sectors of Jewish life. there are a variety of different schools catering to the particular norms of each grouping. "Charedi" is the Hebrew term used to describe all Orthodox settings to the right of Modern Orthodoxy. Its meaning refers to God-fearing Jews and is not especially precise as a descriptor since it lumps together

AIMS AND PRACTICES

very disparate groups whose differences stem from eighteenth-century Eastern Europe. Included in this category are **Chasidic** schools of many "courts" (i.e., different groups of **Chasidism** based on their geographical origins in eastern Europe, e.g., **Bobov**, Lubavitch [**Chabad**], and **Satmar**), and "**Lithuanian**"-style yeshivot, which are fervently anti-Chasidic. Due to the specificity of each setting, one finds a high level of unity of practice and belief in any one Charedi setting. Synagogue ritual, *Rebbe* (spiritual guide) reverence, and modes of dress differentiate the various groupings. On the most trivial level (at least for outsiders and especially many non-Jews, but not for the adherents), the boys in one school will all wear exactly the same black fedora, produced by one manufacturer in Brooklyn. The boys in the school down the block will sport a slightly different brim and cut of felt.

Sephardic
Sephardic Jews trace their origins to Jews who were expelled from the Iberian Peninsula at the end of the fifteenth century, and Canada boasts a significant Sephardic population, mostly of North African extraction and mostly in Montreal and Toronto. Montreal has several Sephardic schools, while Toronto has one such small setting. These are schools in which the Sephardic religious and cultural heritages are part of the curriculum. Sephardic Jews, while maintaining a traditional approach to Jewish law and practice—mostly untouched by the liberal movements of the nineteenth and twentieth centuries—do have their own liturgical, musical, and culinary traditions that are rooted in places such as North Africa, Iran, Turkey, Yemen, Iraq, and other Muslim settings.

The categories listed above do not reflect any formal distinctions made by some external body, but rather the manner by which the schools might define themselves. "Liberal," as used above, refers only to the religious ideologies of the Reform and Conservative movements; it does not necessarily reflect a liberal approach to pedagogy. There are also many exceptions in enrolment patterns. There are community schools that attempt to welcome Orthodox children, and there are some less observant families that favour a modern Orthodox setting.

In addition, a word about **Zionist ideology** is in order. Most Jewish day schools of all streams are supportive of modern Zionist thinking and the State of Israel. It is common in many schools to find the Israeli flag flying next to that of Canada. However, there are some Charedi schools that are non-Zionist in that they demonstrate the traditional Jewish ties to the land of Israel without any overt political support for the State of Israel itself. In the extreme minority, there are some Chasidic schools that are anti-Zionist in that they express overt opposition to political Zionism and the creation of the State of Israel in 1948. How Israel and Zionism are taught in any given school depends on the ideology of that institution, and here, too, diversity reigns.

Subject Matter

Most mainstream day schools provide their students with a general-studies curriculum that is based on government guidelines. In those provinces where there is ministry funding for the general-studies portion of the school, strict compliance with guidelines and standards is the norm. In Ontario, most elementary schools voluntarily follow ministry guidelines, while secondary schools granting a diploma must follow the Ontario secondary curriculum and pass inspection. In some of the Charedi schools there is divergence from the full general-studies curriculum of the province due to both time constraints and the importance of religious belief. Charedi schools tend to teach Jewish studies in the morning hours and part of the early afternoon. They eliminate any material that clashes with their belief system, which is based on a literal reading of the Hebrew Bible and its traditional commentaries. In most day schools, however, general studies play a significant part in the curriculum.

In the liberal Jewish schools—secular, community, Reform, and Conservative schools—there is an attempt at integrating general and Jewish studies where the curriculum affords such opportunities. For example, a unit on sound might be integrated in lower school with the sounds of the *shofar* (the ram's horn used in Jewish prayer ritual). Jewish history can be integrated into world history. (What was happening in Safed while Elizabeth I reigned in England?) Biology-class experiments can reflect Jewish values on animal suffering. And environmental issues can be taught in light of the biblical commandments that stress respect for the land.

The most difficult aspect of Jewish day-school curricula for an outsider to appreciate is the large scope of Jewish studies. Just in terms of relative quantity, Jewish studies range from 30 to 75 per cent of the school day, depending on ideology. I turn now to detail the content of such instruction.

Prayer

All religious day schools have prayer services as part of the school day and also teach Jewish prayer (*t'fila*) as subject matter. The various types of prayer and the amount of time dedicated to prayer vary depending on school ide-

AIMS AND PRACTICES

ology, but as much as 45 minutes a day in Charedi and Modern Orthodox settings can be devoted to actual prayer time and the study of prayer.

Hebrew Language

The complexity of this area of study, which exists in one form or another in all Jewish day schools, is difficult to understand for an outsider and is also a subject of much debate among Jewish educators. The norm of *ivrit b'ivrit* (a form of Hebrew immersion using spoken Hebrew for most Jewish studies subjects) is no longer the rule in most day schools across the ideological spectrum. Most schools are struggling with the questions of what kind of Hebrew to teach, how to teach it, and how much time to devote to this sacred language. While it is true that a contemporary Israeli speaking modern Hebrew (revived as a spoken language at the turn of the twentieth century) could have a conversation with Isaiah in biblical Hebrew or with Rabbi Judah in Mishnaic Hebrew, there are significant differences.

School ideology plays a part in this curricular debate. The general tendency is for most Orthodox schools to stress textual Hebrew for use in decoding traditional texts, and to put much less emphasis on spoken Hebrew. There are, however, variations on this theme. Some schools teach girls conversational Hebrew, while the boys spend more time on Talmudic study. Usually, the more liberal the school, the more conversational Israeli Hebrew is taught. There are still some schools that teach all or most Jewish studies in Hebrew.

The teaching of two other languages can be found in Jewish schools. First, some Charedi schools study Jewish subject matter in Yiddish because the Hebrew language is understood to be too holy for regular conversation. Second, **Aramaic** is required for intensive Talmudic study and is therefore taught in Charedi and Modern Orthodox schools.

The Bible

All day schools study the Hebrew Bible in its original Masoretic text. The most-studied books are the first five, the Pentateuch or **Torah**, but significant portions of the Prophets and Writings are studied at all levels of elementary and secondary schools. Rabbinic, medieval, and modern commentators are used in different modes by diverse religious schools. Almost all Pentateuch study is accompanied by the commentary of Rashi (a Rabbinic commentator of eleventh-century France), which is printed in a Hebrew alphabet somewhat different from the standard and therefore presents a significant learning obstacle. Some schools use translations into English, French (Sephardic schools in Montreal), or Yiddish (Charedi schools, as noted above) more than others.

The Talmud

Talmudic material from the first century BCE to around the fifth century CE is taught in most day schools. Non-Orthodox schools might limit their students to *Mishna* (the first code of Jewish law, a Hebrew text), while Orthodox and Charedi schools teach male students a great deal of *Gemara* (a later discussion of the *Mishna* in the academies of Palestine and **Babylonia**, a mostly Aramaic text). There are male secondary settings in the Charedi sector that teach the **Talmud** as the sole Jewish subject matter.

Laws and Customs

Judaism is a religion based on **Rabbinic law**, which finds its authority in biblical law but with multiple codes dating from the second century CE to the modern period. This means that any curriculum that honours Jewish law (*halacha*) and wishes to transmit it to students must incorporate legal codes as a separate exercise. In religious settings, such as the modern Orthodox, Charedi, Conservative, and Reform schools, emphasis is placed on the laws and customs of Jewish practice, while in others this occurs less often.

Calendar Cycle

The annual cycle of holidays, feasts, and fasts is an integral part of the Jewish curriculum in all types of Jewish schools. Some schools teach the celebration of special days as part of other subject areas such as the Bible, the Talmud, history, and codes, but all schools take the time before the various holidays to review the complex norms of celebration and commemoration.[9]

History

Jewish history is taught in most schools, with the exception of some Orthodox and Charedi settings. In some schools it is integrated as much as possible with world history. Its study usually begins in middle school and extends through secondary school.

Literature

In the broadest sense, Jewish literature has a span of some three thousand years. It begins with the Hebrew Bible, transcends centuries and world geography, and extends to the *belles lettres* of contemporary writers in Israel and the Diaspora. As with the other subjects, the ideology of the school

AIMS AND PRACTICES

determines what constitutes Jewish literature and what will be taught. A liberal school will teach twentieth-century secular Israeli writers, while a non-Zionist Orthodox or Charedi school will opt for observant authors.

Values

A Jewish religious school teaches values—both those originating in the biblical traditions and shared by all of human civilization, and those unique to Jewish life. They are usually integrated into the various curricular domains listed above and not taught as a separate subject.

Teaching Methods

The summary of the content of Jewish studies constitutes the "what" of the Jewish curriculum. The "how" is just as complex and equally diverse. There are traditional schools where the teaching of the Bible is the same as it was in eighteenth-century Europe or North Africa. A verse is read, translated, and memorized. There are other schools where smartboards connected to the internet are being used to bring ancient texts into the twenty-first century.

One of the major differences in approach is related to modern scientific biblical criticism. Some liberal schools take full advantage of the latest research and critical approaches to the Bible and the Talmud. In Modern Orthodox and Charedi settings, most of that critical material is considered heretical, and biblical commentary is limited to traditional sources. This curricular vantage point affects the methodology of Bible study.

Because of the cyclical nature of the annual holidays and the weekly portions of the Bible read ritually in the synagogue, there is a danger of repeating the same material year after year. To combat this problem, some schools have created a spiral curriculum that is age-specific. In each year, new material is added for each holiday and Sabbath so that a cumulative effect is achieved over the elementary years. This permits the children to mature in their appreciation of the calendar cycle as their own powers of conceptualization develop.

As mentioned above, some schools attempt as much integration of subject matter as possible, in a desire to create one world for the student rather than a divided world view of general, secular studies and Jewish religious material. This works best in those ideological settings—the four liberal types of schools—where there is a less emphatic secular–religious divide. If both general and Jewish studies are equally valued and both are open to critical scrutiny in such schools, then all subject matter can be approached in the same way. In contrast, in the more isolationist Charedi schools, the secular curriculum stands apart; it is viewed as secondary, and teachers seek to convey its lesser importance in students' lives.

A distinctive manner of Jewish teaching and learning is *chevruta*, a traditional study method for Talmudic texts. It is much like peer-mediated instruction or peer coupling in that students work on a complex text together, arguing out the various possible interpretations until they feel some level of mastery. While *chevruta* has been used for centuries in Orthodox male settings for the study of the Talmud, recent experimentation with the technique has introduced it as a learning model into liberal schools in a variety of subject areas.

All Jewish schools have some level of special education for students with learning problems. Some schools have very sophisticated programs and special resources to deal with a wide range of learning issues, while other schools are weaker in this domain. Parents of children with special needs must search for the proper setting for such students. In cities such as Montreal and Toronto, with a large variety of schools across the ideological spectrum, it is easier for such families to find a place in one of the schools, but not always possible. In smaller communities the options for special education within a Jewish school are much more limited, and consequently some parents must choose either the public schools or a non-Jewish private setting.

Summary
The two most important aspects of Jewish schooling that I have wished to convey in this section are its scope and diversity. The totality of material in the Jewish studies curriculum is overwhelmingly large when viewed as a complement to a full general-studies load and when compared to the subject content of other faith-based schools. Indeed, in **Rabbinic literature** alone, one refers to the "Sea of Talmud" to describe the amount of material that must be covered. Given the various forms of Jewish life in the modern post-enlightenment age, the different types of Jewish schooling accordingly represent a diverse spectrum. There are, therefore, neither central curricula nor syllabi in any of the Canadian cities that have multiple schools. Indeed, the large communities that boast a central agency for Jewish education (i.e., a board of Jewish education) or a central teacher-training institution (e.g., Toronto's Jewish Teacher Education Program at York University) must constantly design their programs of curricular assistance, pre-service education, and in-service professional development to suit a multiplicity of learning models and curricular objectives; and this does not occur without difficulty.

AIMS AND PRACTICES

The Outcome Aspirations of the Various Schools

Once again, it must be said that diversity will reign supreme in any discussion of the educational goals of the schools. We must return to the categories listed at the outset of this chapter, with the understanding that some of the divisions are fuzzy and that there is considerable overlap.

Secular

There are very few schools left in this category, but there are secular parents who choose a community school without specific denominational affiliation because they want their children exposed to Jewish culture, Hebrew language and literature, and Jewish history. These schools are concerned with producing a loyal Canadian citizen with a full range of general knowledge, critical skills of discernment, and the identity and literacy required of a committed member of the Jewish people. Jewish culture and peoplehood are key terms used in secular settings. The emphasis in these schools is on a cultural or national Judaism over religious Judaism.

Community

There is a duality of meaning in the use of the word "community" in these settings. These schools wish to create an alternative to traditional Orthodox schools by bringing together a variety of families who do not desire an Orthodox education for their children. As such, they are a community apart. In another sense, many of these parents are not joining synagogues of any denomination and are using the school as their primary community of Jewish affiliation. Some of these community schools have even created prayer groups at the school for Sabbath and holiday services. This is a reversal of the trend of their parents' generation. Synagogues once produced schools, and now schools are sprouting mini-synagogues. While these schools also aspire to produce loyal Canadian Jews, they have usually added liberal and pluralistic religious values and practice to their curricular objectives. Many of them have a specialization, such as an arts-based curriculum, egalitarian (gender-neutral) prayer services, more stress on modern Hebrew, or a unique pedagogy such as Montessori.[10]

Modern Orthodox

The Orthodox schools all teach general studies, but the emphasis in these settings is on learning classical Jewish texts and religious observance. Every effort is made to create an environment where Orthodox Jewish practice is the norm. In the schools that are intensely Zionistic, short-term study trips or long-term immigration to Israel is an outcome the schools would be proud of. In all Orthodox settings, though, a graduate who lives honourably as a citizen of any country and couples that with a full commitment to Jewish religious traditions and laws is a desirable outcome.

Conservative and Reform

These two liberal (i.e., non-Orthodox) movements have established day schools in Montreal (Conservative) and Toronto (both). They are products of the synagogues affiliated with these movements and aspire to raise future members of their respective religious denominations. Since the schools attract families from outside these two movements (affiliated with other Jewish groupings or not affiliated at all), there is a mix of ideologies and religious practice among the students. This mix is equally true of the teaching staff and administration. Each of the movements teaches some material about its own history and doctrine, but what distinguishes these religious, non-Orthodox schools is their desire to impart a text-critical approach to study in both general and Jewish subject matter. These schools aspire to produce a caring and concerned citizen of Canada who respects the traditions of the religion and participates in synagogue life.

Charedi

In this category of ultra-Orthodox institutions there are many variants among the different schools, which are usually small settings for that very reason. As mentioned above, the major division is between Chasidic schools and those of the **Lithuanian-Yeshiva tradition**, but beyond that there are sub-divisions that, while meaningful to each group, are hardly discernible to an outsider. These Charedi schools generally want to produce a graduate who can function in the wider society but whose first loyalty is to the very conservative and fully traditional norms of a Charedi lifestyle. Much of modernity is shunned, and every aspect of life, from dress to cuisine, is governed by their interpretation of Jewish law and custom.

Jewish law incorporates a clear directive to respect the laws of one's host country (*dina d'malchuta dina*, the law of the land is the law),[11] but even that directive is open to commentary and nuance. Loyal Canadian citizenship is not, in any way, in opposition to Charedi values, and some Charedi Jews have become very active in the political arena, but, as stated, it is not the priority value of a Charedi education.

Sephardic

One glaring difference in Quebec is that the Sephardic schools' teaching is conducted in French, since most of the families in these schools are North African in origin. The one Sephardic school in Toronto has English as its language of instruction. Of course, Hebrew is also taught and the rest of the Jewish curriculum is supplemented with Sephardic liturgy, the rulings of Sephardic rabbis, and Sephardic music. These schools are maintained in order to promote Sephardic culture, and their hope is to produce proud and knowledgeable Sephardic Jews.

The differences among the various schools are sometimes subtle but in other cases rather clear. One can see children walking to two different schools on the same street and from their dress alone identify the school they attend. Some Orthodox schools separate children by gender; all Charedi schools do. All schools have a positive relationship to Israel, but some schools celebrate Israel Independence Day and others do not (for the complex political-religious reasons mentioned above).

There is a distinction in Jewish law between ritual laws which inform the Jew's relationship with God and moral laws which govern the relationship with other human beings. All Jewish schools blend general studies, Jewish learning, and a pursuit of values in such a way that the curricular product reflects a balance of those two legal traditions that suits the ideology of each individual school.

A Minority in a Majority Culture

While I have mentioned the place of general studies and Ministry of Education curricula in the Jewish day schools, it is worth elaborating on the various attitudes to the majority Canadian culture in which the schools operate. In general, the history of Jews in Canada has been one of healthy integration into the larger society and significant contributions to that society in many spheres of Canadian life. Specifically, graduates of Jewish day schools have excelled in many professions and in business. Some have achieved great success in all three levels of government, the diplomatic corps, and the media.

As expected, the day schools reflect the society and culture that sponsor them. All day schools are supported by private tuition, even those in provinces that subsidize the general-studies instruction. For that reason the parents and governing boards of the schools determine the relationship of the school to the wider culture. As a rule (with some interesting exceptions), the more religiously liberal the school, the more open the contact with the non-Jewish majority culture. While all schools teach the three Rs, schools that are more Orthodox place greater emphasis on Jewish studies and Jewish life.

There are many illustrative examples of this, but two will suffice. As mentioned above, in the Charedi schools Jewish studies (labelled *kodesh* or sacred) are taught in the freshness of the morning hours and usually after lunch as well. General studies (labelled *chol* or secular) are taught at the end of the day. Both the overt and the hidden curriculum are obvious to all who attend; the school's priority lies in the Jewish studies, and the general-studies curriculum is of only secondary importance. At the other end of the spectrum, there are parents in some community schools who send their children specifically for the high academic level of general studies. While the Jewish content interests them, it is not the primary motivation for enrolment.

This displays, once again, the diversity of attitudes toward the majority culture found amongst the Jews of Canada and in the spectrum of day schools sponsored by that population sector. One cannot speak of a single type of "Jewish school" in Canada. Rather, one finds in Canada a rich array of schools with differing approaches to curriculum, teaching methods, and educational outcomes.

Appendix

As an appendix I provide the websites of six different schools across Canada. The reader may peruse these sites for descriptive mission statements and other material in order to compare such data with my analysis above.

1. The Calgary Jewish Academy: www.cja.ab.ca
2. King David High School (Vancouver): www.kdhs.org
3. Tiferes Bais Yaakov Daniel T. Gordon High School for Girls (Toronto): www.tiferesbaisyaakov.com
4. L'Ecole Maimonide (Montreal): www.maimonide.ca
5. Associated Hebrew Schools of Toronto: www.associatedhebrewschools.com
6. Paul Penna Downtown Jewish Day School (Toronto): www.djds.ca

In addition, the following sources, not cited directly in the chapter, provide helpful information on Jewish education:

Butovsky, Mervin, and Ode Garfinkle, eds. and trans. *The Journals of Yaacov Zipper, 1950–1982: The Struggle for Yiddishkeit*. Montreal and Kingston: McGill-Queen's University Press, 2004.

Himmelfarb, Harold S., and Sergio Della Pergola, eds. *Jewish Education Worldwide: Cross-Cultural Perspectives*. Lanham, MD: University Press of America, 1989.

AIMS AND PRACTICES

Schiff, Alvin Irwin. *The Jewish Day School in America*. New York: Jewish Education Committee Press, 1966.

Shaviv, Paul J. *The Jewish High School: A Complete Management Guide*. Toronto: Principal Press, via Createspace.com, 2009.

United Jewish Welfare Fund of Toronto. *Study on Jewish Education*. Toronto: United Jewish Welfare Fund, 1975.

Notes

1   Translation from *The Torah*.

2   The comparison is somewhat weakened by the fact that religious affiliation is not in American census data. Consequently, the Jewish populations of American cities are not measured as exactly as they are in Canada. See Charles Shahar and Tina Rosenbaum, *Jewish Life in Greater Toronto: A Survey of the Attitudes and Behaviours of Greater Toronto's Jewish Community*, and their 2001 Census Analysis Series, both at http://www.jewishtoronto.com/page .aspx?ID=160838; and Seymour Epstein and Joyce Levine, "Jewish Education in Canada," *Encyclopedia Judaica* (Farmington Hills, MI: Thomson Gale, 2006), 208–10 for the school data.

3   Shahar and Rosenbaum, *Jewish Life in Greater Toronto*.

4   In Ontario there are only a few publicly funded Protestant schools, and there exist private Catholic and Protestant schools as well.

5   In all cases, multiple campuses were counted as separate schools. The categories are more detailed than those used by United Jewish Appeal—Federation of Toronto in their unpublished school data. See sources of data in note 2 above.

6   Alex Pomson and Howard Deitcher, eds., *Jewish Day Schools, Jewish Communities* (Portland, OR: Littman Library of Jewish Civilization, 2009), 7. Note the reference to Jacob Katz's *Out of the Ghetto* in their note 21. The first day school was established in Berlin.

7   Seymour Epstein, *From Couscous to Kasha: Reporting From the Field of Jewish Community Work* (Jerusalem and New York: Urim Publications, 2009), 37–92.

8   The New York Board of Jewish Education (recently renamed The Jewish Education Project) is a source of information on such peripheral support in the State of New York. See http://www.bjeny.org.

9   These special days of the lunar calendar are numerous: Rosh haShana, Fast of Gedalia, Yom Kippur (fast), Sukkot, Shmini Atzeret, Simchat Torah, the New Moon each Hebrew month, Chanukah, Fast of Tevet, Tu b'Shvat, Fast of Esther, Purim, Passover, Counting the Omer, Holocaust Day, Israel Independence Day, Lag b'Omer, Jerusalem Day, Shavuot, Fast of Tammuz, Tisha b'Av (fast), and all the Sabbaths with their weekly portions of Bible readings.

10 See Alex Pomson and Randal F. Schnoor, *Back to School: Jewish Day School in the Lives of Adult Jews* (Detroit: Wayne State University Press, 2008), for a comprehensive study of a community school.

11 Babylonian Talmud, *Nedarim*, 28a.

Bibliography

Epstein, Seymour, and Joyce Levine. "Jewish Education in Canada." *Encyclopedia Judaica*, 208–10. Farmington Hills, MI: Thomson Gale, 2006.

Epstein, Seymour. *From Couscous to Kasha: Reporting from the Field of Jewish Community Work.* Jerusalem and New York: Urim Publications, 2009.

Pomson, Alex, and Howard Deitcher, eds. *Jewish Day Schools, Jewish Communities.* Portland, OR: Littman Library of Jewish Civilization, 2009.

Pomson, Alex, and Randal F. Schnoor. *Back to School: Jewish Day School in the Lives of Adult Jews.* Detroit: Wayne State University Press, 2008.

Shahar, Charles, and Tina Rosenbaum. *Jewish Life in Greater Toronto: A Survey of the Attitudes and Behaviours of Greater Toronto's Jewish Community.* http:// www.jewishtoronto.com/page.aspx?ID=160838

———. *2001 Census Analysis Series, Basic Demographics, Issues of Jewish Identity.* http:// www.jewishtoronto.com/page.aspx?ID=160838

CHAPTER TWO

THE DISTINCTIVENESS OF
CATHOLIC EDUCATION

Mario O. D'Souza, csb

Introduction

The distinctiveness of Catholic education is based on a detailed elaboration of the words "Catholic" and "education." Their union as "Catholic education" is the result of merging educational convictions that are informed by one's age and time, and by a faith tradition that is perennial, given that Catholic education is based "on a specific and detailed vision of the meaning of human life and of existence as a whole."[1]

The Catholic faith is secured upon its own anthropology and understanding of personhood, and the Church outlines the environment to nurture such a growth. Catholic education shares in the mission of the Church[2] and is secured upon its legal structure.[3] It affirms that human beings are created in the image and likeness of God and are invited to share eternal life, a call that begins on earth. While in *absolute ultimate terms* the aim of life is eternal union with God, personal and communal transformation through knowledge and learning and working for the common good are all secondary but necessary *ultimate aims* of Catholic education.[4] Finally, Catholic education depends upon the cooperation of the three agents: school, family, and Church.

In describing the distinctiveness of Canadian Catholic education, too much attention is paid either to its funding status or to its relationship to provincial politics and its historical evolution. Influential and important as these factors are, they cannot and do not constitute the nature, purpose, and aim of Catholic education. The universality of Catholic education is housed in the universality of both the Catholic faith and human nature. In a confessional context, faith and human nature inform educators as to the purpose and nature of education, and, in the Catholic context, this relationship between education and human nature is further informed by the Catholic faith, the Catholic intellectual tradition, and all of learning.

The use of formulaic answers in funding and historical agreements as a means to defend Catholic education are, in the context of Canadian multiculturalism and religious diversity, not convincing: funding for Catholic schools has been withdrawn in many Canadian provinces, and some have done so by abrogating minority rights.[5] The legal arrangements of history have been changed with the evolution of the Canadian socio-political landscape. Catholic educators also rely on the theological distinctiveness of the Catholic tradition. While Catholic education must be shaped by its theological identity, this identity cannot shoulder the entire responsibility in demonstrating the distinctiveness of such an education. What is needed is the rigorous articulation of a clear relationship between a Catholic philosophy of education—the wider examination of Catholic education—and a Catholic theology of education—informed by faith and doctrines—both of which attend to the distinctiveness of Catholic education, but through different lenses.

In the midst of cultural and religious diversity, public funding of Catholic education is, therefore, often politically charged. In setting aside this discussion, and by concentrating instead on the value of Catholic education *per se*, however it is funded, it is my intention to reflect upon the educational distinctiveness of such an education and the formation of future citizens. Many non-Catholic students attend Canadian Catholic schools. How does such an education educate a religiously and culturally diverse citizenry for life in common, particularly in relation to the common good?

The Canadian Context

While most of the rest of this chapter attempts to frame the discussion within a universal philosophy of Catholic education, it is worth noting some of the particularities of Canadian Catholic education. At the time of writing, full public funding of Catholic education is available in three of Canada's ten provinces—Alberta, Saskatchewan, and Ontario—and all three of its territories. In this regard, *Catholic Schools Across Canada* is a short and informative work of the political context of Catholic education in Canada.[6]

THE DISTINCTIVENESS OF CATHOLIC EDUCATION | D'SOUZA

As personhood and education are intricately linked in Catholic education, the forces that diminish personhood and those that lead to its flourishing are always in tension. A document from the Canadian Catholic School Trustees' Association weaves sin and salvation, social justice and good works, and love of neighbour together and promotes a culture that moves beyond "materialism and acquisition."[7] In an era of outcomes-based education, other educators, such as James T. Mulligan, have inquired about the effective relationship between the Church's promotion of social justice and its realization in the Catholic schools and in the lives of students: whether the Catholic school makes a difference to the common life of the three provinces and three territories that provide public funding.[8] The same educator also celebrates the features found in the best Canadian Catholic schools: holistic curricula, social capital, good collegiality, nurturing social consciousness, and compelling social vision.[9] Studies on the relationship between justice and the Catholic school affirm that the Gospel's call to serve the poor is mandatory and not optional,[10] an application that includes "ecological stewardship" and real concern for the poorest of the poor.[11] However, the Canadian context must also face issues such as the treatment of the peoples of Canada's First Nations and whether Canadian immigrants are welcomed and integrated into society.[12] While the obstacles and potential to preach the Gospel, particularly to Catholic students, may well change generationally, the Canadian context shows significant challenges and calls for a contextual commitment on the part of Catholic educators and church leaders alike.[13]

The role of the Catholic teacher is fundamental to the outcome of Catholic education.[14] Particular Canadian issues range from the debate about whether Catholic teachers should be educated in a Catholic faculty of education to ensure their catholicity, to how many non-Catholic students may be enrolled in a Catholic school. While they are not exclusively Canadian traits, Mulligan lists three challenges that face Catholic educators: "the challenge of neoconservative ideology to the vision of Catholic education," "the challenge of Catholic educators to accept the political dimension of their vocation," and "the challenge for Catholic educators to interpret postmodern culture."[15] One document on curricular applications in the Canadian context ends with a poignant question: "how will this curriculum present ways of bettering the human condition?"[16] And, again in the context of outcomes-based education, the *Ontario Catholic School Graduate Expectations* lists seven expectations that are dependent on the relationship between the teacher, the student, and the curriculum.

AIMS AND PRACTICES

The relationship between faith and culture understandably shows more Canadian particularities. Canadian society can be described as post-Christian, but both Christian and non-Christian immigrants qualify that claim in ways that are beyond the scope of this chapter. However, within the Catholic context, there is a great diversity of opinions, even when it comes to Church teachings. In the midst of an "aggressive secularism," Catholics, including those in schools, hold diverse opinions on issues such as premarital sex, whether divorced Catholics should receive the Eucharist, and the role of women in the Church, opinions that are further complicated by the fact that many young Catholics do not know their faith as taught by the Church.[17] The issue of critical inquiry and dissent[18] is one that straddles both faith and culture, as well as the teacher and the curriculum. Canadian students, like their counterparts in other Western societies, are not exempt from the tension between what the Church teaches on issues such as divorce, premarital sex, homosexuality, and women's ordination, and the positions that students hold and the critique they offer. There are those who have maintained that precisely because of provincial public funding for Catholic schools, these and related issues must be able to be critically examined, by both the teacher and the student. This critical inquiry, McDonough maintains, is what is essential to the nature of the school, which is more than an extension of the **Magisterium**.[19] The place of critical inquiry is complicated, notes McDonough elsewhere, as "Canadian teachers are trained in secular universities ... their professional training ... is incommensurable with a pedagogy that would tolerate uncritical acceptance of religious instruction."[20] Catholic education in Quebec faces its own challenges, particularly in the context of separatism. Quebec, it may be said, led Canadian secularism, and as Boudreau reminds us, the Church's *Declaration on Religious Freedom (Dignitatis Humanae)* "clearly declares that one has a right to religious freedom: a right to religion and a right from religion."[21]

Finally, diversity, unity, and education have distinctively Canadian features. The chief provider of Canadian diversity is immigration, which brings religious, cultural, and social diversity, as well as a diversity of opinion about the role of the state in the lives of citizens. Immigration, therefore, has shaped—and continues to shape—Canadian democracy. Immigration has led to a rise in the Catholic population in Canada, but, in the context of Catholic schools, this is accompanied by a tension between Catholics who hold to the traditional teachings of the Church, for example, in the areas of women's ordination and issues in sexual ethics, and their counterparts

THE DISTINCTIVENESS OF CATHOLIC EDUCATION | D'SOUZA

who have lived in Canada over many generations and are the product of their own historical and cultural evolution. Whereas it is maintained in this chapter that the universality of human nature grounds Catholic education, the particular challenges that face Canadian Catholic educators must continue to be considered alongside this understanding of human nature. And so, while answers and solutions may be distinctively Canadian, they must also be distinctively Catholic.

Personhood and Education

Catholic intellectuals have contributed to our understanding of the relationship between personhood and education. The neo-Scholastic philosopher Jacques Maritain says that the ultimate aim of education is the growth of the student as a person, a growth through "personal life and spiritual progress."[22] But he also says that the "goal" of education (which he uses interchangeably with "aim") is the "internal and spiritual freedom of the student," and liberation achieved through "knowledge and intelligence, good will and love."[23] He understands freedom as moving beyond freedom of choice to what he calls "freedom of autonomy," an internal and spiritual condition through which one grows in personhood. For Maritain, personality and freedom are intimately bound and essential to the educational process.[24] Furthermore, his use of "spiritual" is to be understood in its widest sense, including religious and other forms of knowing, as well as knowledge that is immaterial—not bound by matter—and knowledge that inspires and influences human growth and freedom. The ontological unity of the student—that fundamental unity that we each possess as a human person—is dependent upon these various strands coming together.

Thomas Groome, a contemporary religious educator, also bases his thinking on a philosophy of personhood. Among five principles that he lists that are "grounded in Catholic understanding of God and human existence," he includes "a positive anthropology of the person."[25] He also understands personhood in the context of education as "an ontological concern," saying that "Catholic education intends to inform and form the very 'being' of its students, to mould their identity and agency—who they are and how they live. In traditional philosophical terms, its intended learning outcomes moves beyond epistemological (*episteme*, knowledge) to the ontological (*ontos*, being) without leaving the former behind."[26]

The school—one of the agents of Catholic education—strives for human growth through a variety of means: the curriculum, the school environment, the teachers' role, religious practices, justice and love for others, and

AIMS AND PRACTICES

so on. The school also exists in relation to society by preparing citizens to take their place in the world through their deliberation, choices, and actions. And while there are many secondary aims: implications of knowledge, preparation for citizenship, striving for the common good, earning a living, the promotion of an integral culture, the primary aim of Catholic education is the promotion of human freedom through growth in one's personhood.[27]

Indeed, the documents of Catholic education all attest to the primacy of personhood and its incremental realization through freedom (both of student and teacher), and they do so within their historical climate such that their span from the opening and closing of the Second Vatican Council (1962 to 1965; henceforth "Vatican II") to the present shows an incremental development of what this encounter with, and ensuring of, human freedom entails. Individual freedom is never completely realized, and its relationship to education is ongoing, as is human transformation: "Education is not given for the purpose of gaining power but as an aid towards fuller understanding of, and communion with man [sic], events and things. Knowledge is not to be considered as a means of material prosperity and success, but as a call to serve and to be responsible to others."[28] In that every education is inspired by a specific conception of the human being,[29] the Catholic school implements its intellectual mandate based upon its anthropology, and safeguards this mandate by avoiding either a narrow intellectualism or a narrowing of the relationship between faith and culture. While Catholic education shares in the overall mission of the Church, it implements its particular mission according to the specific relationship between knowledge, learning, and growth in personhood.

The Catholic school is called to transform and create a Catholic culture, not an insular ghetto variety, but rather culture as a lens through which deeper and more challenging questions may be examined; thus the cultural dimension of human existence needs to be secured upon a Christian anthropology and ethics.[30] In addition, Catholic culture has a distinct set of religious beliefs, values, behaviours, and rituals,[31] all of which enhance a Christian understanding of existence.

An earlier work on education reminded Catholic educators that the Catholicity of the school is more than the fact that it is "staffed with Catholic teachers, offers facilities for the frequentation of the Sacraments, and has each day half-an-hour's doctrinal instruction sandwiched in between the other subjects of the scholastic programme." Rather, its Catholicity depends on every subject and all its activities being imbued with "the Christian appreciation of things and the Christian outlook of life." Everything that it teaches must have as a "background" and be "related to a Catholic philosophy of life."[32] It is this conviction that frames this chapter.

The Teacher and the Curriculum

The Catholic nature of the school is ensured by its teachers. It is the teacher's world view, convictions, and values that are the causal principles that make teaching a genuine human experience, so schools must do all they can to nourish the faith commitment of teachers. Thus the aim of Catholic education depends more on the person of the teacher than on subject matter and methodology.[33] This does not mean that the diversity of human learning and knowledge must in any way be compromised; quite the contrary, enhancing freedom in the context of the school is a human activity, one that is metaphysically, existentially, ethically, and religiously the fruit of human interaction and dialogue. So the teacher's own maturity—religious, intellectual, moral, and social—is essential to the student's understanding and appropriation of freedom. The teacher's maturity must be housed in a love of truth and a commitment to enduring values such as the dignity and sanctity of the human person, living a moral and spiritual life, love of one's neighbour, a personal liberation through knowledge and learning, embracing the teachings of the Church, and so on. Teaching, therefore, is a complex activity and is secured and unified in the personhood of the teacher.[34] The Catholic teacher, regardless of the subject, teaches through a particular vision and world view shaped by a Christian understanding of existence. It is with this conviction as a backdrop that one situates the claim that "it must never be forgotten that the school itself is always in the process of being created, due to the labour brought to fruition by all those who have a role to play in it, and most especially by those who are teachers."[35] Instruction, then, is never understood apart from the person of the instructor.[36] In the world of practice, Catholic teachers often wonder how their Catholicity shapes subjects other than religious education and theology. The teacher's convictions, world view, and vision of existence is enormously formative, and while Catholicity is not parachuted into the curriculum, how teachers teach creates the platform for the emergence of these convictions and values that provide an overall context for a Christian meaning of existence.

With respect to the fundamental and formative role of freedom, concerns have been raised about the teacher's freedom to allow students to critique the enduring values and truths of the Catholic faith. The Catholic documents are clear as to the role of the teacher in enabling the personal-

AIMS AND PRACTICES

ity of the student to be strengthened and to grow by a natural and chronological passage through the specific stages of mental and moral growth. So while teenagers are naturally curious about questions of sexual morality, for example, it would be harmful to isolate this curiosity either physiologically or by a reduction to a relativistic and individualistic ethic. The Catholic response, therefore, is twofold. First, faith and the demands of faith are in relation to all of life, and while the stages of life challenge particular dimensions of faith, Catholic education is directed to the education of the whole person. Second, the school's mandate is to impart a general education, one that is sensitive and responds to the formative and influential stages of the student's growth and maturity. In an age of early specialization, the school could claim that it attends to the education of the whole person, which the university cannot do because of its rigid disciplinary distinctions. One essential means of carrying out such a whole education is through the diversity of the curriculum and the unity of this diversity in the person of the teacher.

The education of the whole person is a philosophical concept as it involves the integration of dimensions that include but go beyond religion. While religion informs this process in a more direct way, other dimensions such as the emotional, aesthetic, social, civic, cultural, etc., must be included in this integration. The inner liberation of the teacher is also essential in this process. While wholeness as opposed to fragmentation or miniaturization does require the contribution of other agencies, undertaking the education of the whole person is, in fact, claiming that there will be an achievement or attainment of unity of purpose and outlook.[37] The education of the whole person is, then, a communal activity, and so wholeness is opposed to narrowness and restriction and has implications for life in the context of religious and cultural diversity.

Since John Dewey, the role of experience and education has occupied a place of prominence in educational thought. Dewey rightly points out that while experience and education are related, not "all experiences are generally or equally educative. Experience and education cannot be directly equated to each other."[38] Catholic teachers rightly speak of the importance of their students' experiences and ways of separating the liberating from the enslaving experiences. It has been maintained that there are four paths along which the Catholic teacher unifies the student's experiences: "the teacher's love of truth unifies the student's experiences"; "the teacher's knowledge unifies the student's experiences"; "the teacher's method unifies the student's experiences"; and "the teacher's worldview unifies the student's

52

experiences."[39] The unification and liberation of experience is part of the intellectual mandate of the Catholic school and realized through the systematic transmission of knowledge, and the implications of this knowledge through choices and actions. Showing the relationship between experience and truth, particularly how one experience of truth builds upon another, is the indispensable task of the teacher.

In the Canadian context, the preparation of Catholic teachers is largely self-directed; that is, teachers take responsibility for their own graduate education, usually theological in nature. There are many reasons why contemporary Catholic education relies heavily upon theology, and Catholic educational theorists continue to deliberate as to why philosophy no longer plays a unifying role in Catholic educational theory.[40] However, even Bernard Lonergan's critique of a static philosophy of education sheltering in the seeming safety of perennial truths is by no means a handing over of educational theory to relativism, individualism, or the bifurcating theories of modernism and postmodernism; quite the reverse.[41] His thoughts on a disciplined subjectivity developed in his philosophical and theological method has implications for educational theory through a personal appropriation of knowledge, interiority, intellectual, moral, and spiritual conversion, as well as a host of cognitional, epistemological, and metaphysical questions that, in the context of education, place a responsibility on the instrumental role of the teacher and the affective and experiential role of the student. The four levels of conscious or intentional operations—experiencing, understanding, judging, and deciding—shape and make demands on the freedom of teacher and the student alike.[42]

The instrumental role of the teacher has implications for how one understands the purpose and nature of the curriculum. The Catholic documents recognize the "autonomy" and "methodology of individual subjects"; indeed "these disciplines are not to be seen as simply subservient to faith."[43] The unity of the curriculum is founded upon truth: truth of the individual subjects and their truth in relation to the dynamic purpose of knowing and learning, with implications for living, choosing, and acting. The diversity of the curriculum is what unites the student's experience of learning and knowing. Unfortunately, educators often worry more about the structure and content of the curriculum than they do about the implications it has for the enhancement of liberation and freedom. Imparting information is only one part of institutional education, a fact that emerges in particularly high relief when one observes that the amount of information currently available to students is now enormous. What is often lacking is a means of arranging,

AIMS AND PRACTICES

prioritizing, and evaluating this information and recognizing its potential either to liberate or to enslave. It is a human task to assist students in distinguishing what is true, good, and human from their opposites. There is also a concern in the Catholic documents as to how students are assisted in grappling with the meaning of life in the face of technological and scientific innovations. The ideals of these documents must therefore by applied to the challenges and questions faced by students in Canadian Catholic schools. The Catholic philosopher of education Terence McLaughlin warns of the dangers of "edu-babble"—which he defines as "imprecise and platitudinous rhetoric"[44]—when Catholic educators choose catchy phrases from Catholic documents, such as "the school should be based on the values of the Gospel," and thus give the impression that complex and challenging matters have been settled.[45] The application of the documents needs more attention than merely an adherence to what sounds right.

The human quality of education calls for breaking down the walls of indifference and individualism, as well as responding to the other challenges that accompany the evolution of a multi-racial and multi-religious society. The Catholic documents are attentive to the diversity and humanizing role of the curriculum, urging educators that "there is no separation between time for learning and time for formation, between acquiring notions and growing in wisdom."[46] Knowledge also has a communal and interpersonal dimension, and the communal nature of the curriculum and its incremental building upon each stage of intellectual, spiritual, moral, and social growth is imperative to the Christian vision of existence. However, much needs to be done in educating teachers as to *why* there is a diversified curriculum and *how* that diversity is essential for the unity and integrity of the student as one who knows and learns, but, more importantly, as one who chooses, acts, and decides. The diversity of the created order, the reality and experiences of the sensory world—which is after all a major source of our knowledge, though not the only means of our knowing—is what is expressed in a diversified curriculum.

Therefore, while the absurdity of a *Catholic mathematics* or *Catholic physics* is too obvious, what is often not obvious to Catholic educators is why mathematics and physics are indispensable to the curriculum of the Catholic school; without them the school would not be Catholic.[47] The curriculum is an ever-growing edifice, but not as an intellectual abstraction or form of snobbery encouraging the juggling of ideas and opinions that are unrelated to life. This does not mean that simplistic and constant relationships are sought after when teaching abstract and theoretical knowledge.

Rather, understanding why the humanizing and liberating nature of the curriculum is essential to the student's growth in freedom is to understand why institutional education is composed of diverse ways of knowing, and to understand how and why mathematical, scientific, literary, historical, and religious knowing are different and how they are nevertheless related in the one knowing subject: the student. All this, therefore, confirms why education—knowing, learning, choosing, and acting—must begin with experience but be completed in reason. Because of its humanizing quality, the curriculum has an intrinsic hierarchy of values and knowledge built into it. The humanities, the liberal arts (particularly their philosophical disposition), theology, and religious education have a leading role to play in showing why such hierarchies are intrinsic to the curriculum.

Institutional education is of course much more than the systematic organization of the curriculum, but such an education is primarily intellectual in nature. This is a claim that often does not seem to sit well with Catholic educators, worrying either that it sounds elitist and exclusive or that it reduces education to a narrow intellectualism. Either extreme is genuine cause for concern. The intellectual nature of Catholic education, however, arises from its philosophical anthropology—an understanding of the human person that includes but is wider than religious beliefs—but this nature is not narrowly reducible to acquiring knowledge intellectually. The intellectual mandate of Catholic education exists in relationship with other bodies of knowledge as well as other ways of knowing and how they have implications for growth in one's personhood. In fairness, much needs to be said to situate the claim that human persons reveal themselves most fully through a life of reason, a revelation that includes ontological, spiritual, and communal dimensions. However, this much at least must be said: while all knowing and learning is not to be reduced to an intellectual variety or to intellectualism, all knowing does need the distinguishing and uniting power of reason to differentiate the different kinds of knowing and the different ways of coming to know, as well as how they are all unified in the one knowing student. It is also worth acknowledging that not everything can be learned through formal classroom instruction: one cannot take a course in wisdom, or being sympathetic, or being charitable. However, the student should be able to understand that growing in wisdom, sympathy, and charity (unquestionably characteristics of Catholic education) have more to do with the intuitions and experiences gained through the informal curriculum than through the organized learning in the formal curriculum. But the knowledge that comes through wisdom, sympathy, and charity has a place

AIMS AND PRACTICES

in the context of the school and is structured through organized and systematic bodies of knowledge and systems of learning: hence the claim that "while *sanctity* is the aim of Christian *education* ... *learning* is the end of the Catholic *school*."[48] Learning and freedom are interdependent, and the intellectual mandate of the Catholic school must show *why* and *how* this is so.

Faith and Culture

Catholic religious education, which really was born after Vatican II, has been shaped by the Catholic theological tradition.[49] It would seem, then, that the decline of a "Catholic *philosophy* of education" and the ascent of a "Catholic *theology* of education"—marked since the close of Vatican II— has been shaped by this theological tradition housed in "the internalization of individualized Christian conviction."[50] While religious education has been shaped by Catholic theology, scripture, ethics, and social teachings, it has also been shaped by disciplines that are not specifically Catholic, such as psychology and educational, social, and political theories, and that have possibly conflicting approaches to personhood. For its part, the institutional Church has insisted on the systematic and orderly imparting of religious knowledge, and the *Catechism of the Catholic Church* (1992) shows how doctrinal, moral, ecclesial, social, and spiritual teachings can be contained in one systematic text and based on a hierarchy of truths and values. However, this containment did not sit well with all, particularly with those uncomfortable with the introduction of a formal relationship between religious education and the *Catechism,* criticisms that came even before its promulgation.[51]

Many factors contribute to the school's environment; what is of importance to the Catholic school is students' moral and spiritual life as shaped by this environment. While an integrated curriculum has its role to play, the moral and spiritual life of students is the particular focus of religious education, which in the Catholic tradition is never apart from catechesis and the wider field of evangelization. Catechesis is defined as an education of children, the young, and adults in the faith, but "especially the teaching of Christian doctrine ... in an organic and systematic way, with a view to initiating the hearers into the fullness of Christian life."[52] For its part, evangelization "means bringing the Good News of the Scriptures into all the strata of humanity, and though its influence transforming humanity from within and making it new."[53] While values and truths are not limited to religious education, the latter does have a specific role in their cultivation of the former in the context of faith. Faith after all is a gift, but it needs nurture and the structure of teaching.

THE DISTINCTIVENESS OF CATHOLIC EDUCATION | D'SOUZA

One of the recurring themes in the Catholic documents is the synthesis between faith and culture. Since Vatican II, the Church has emphasized the relationship between the personal and the communal nature of faith. Culture, of course, has been transformed from the older categories of "high" and "low" to culture as the very condition of one's existence; it is now the stage of students' choices, actions, and deliberations. While parents and the Church have responsibilities for educating in this relationship between faith and culture, especially the interior and mysterious life of faith, the school must enhance this relationship through the particularity of its educational mandate. So, while liturgical celebrations, prayers, and other rituals are part of the Catholic school, they must stand in relation to the education of the whole person.

Church documents elaborate on the importance of faith becoming a culture and the transmission of faith through culture.[54] But culture as the expression and realization of one's personhood is now immensely elastic. While religious education must take historical, social, economic, and political factors into account, the Church teaches that students, irrespective of context, must possess certain universal traits of faith and belief that are secured in Revelation and on its anthropological, moral, ecclesial, doctrinal, and social teachings. Catholics, however, given contemporary diversity, are no longer held together in a seamless web of belief and practice, and they are often faced with cultural choices that leave them—as it does believers of other faiths—anxious, fearful, disoriented, and confused, so that understanding culture as a set of values and truths that inform a common way of life becomes an increasingly daunting task that tests the synthesis between faith and culture. Furthermore, one cannot presume that teachers are educated in the relationship between faith and culture and that they will come out in favour of this synthesis. If education is all that is undertaken to enhance a student's personhood through freedom and liberation, then teachers must grapple with the Catholic understanding of freedom and liberation in their own lives. The teacher's witness to the Catholic faith, particularly its moral, doctrinal, and social teachings, is what gives life to what may otherwise seem an abstract phrase: synthesis between faith and culture. The moral life requires both a disposition and information. But one is always *invited* to live this life through personal sanctity and holiness and a concern and love for others. The Christian faith is not an abstraction; it is the personal affirmation of certain historic events, and responding to them historically in the living of one's life. So in spite of the wider social and cultural context of religious education, Catholic education is not simply a "human activity but a genuine Christian journey toward perfection."[55]

AIMS AND PRACTICES

In the Catholic school, faith and morals are inseparable, and the mysterious life of faith and the largely observable life of morals are part of the manifestation of the ever-growing and shaping of the student's personality. The school must teach students "primarily ... how to think." So while the core of morality is reason as it influences action, the core of religion is love.[56] Morality and faith are not, of course, the exclusive jurisdiction of the Catholic school. However, the school must show the relationship between reason and love, a relationship that is recognized in all the activities and concerns of the school. Wisely, however, are teachers reminded that they never really reap the fruits of their labour in the immediacy of the school, for the student's liberation and freedom, while observable and measurable in some ways, is ultimately hidden in the mysterious yet ever-growing life of faith and belief in relation to personality.

The Church insists that religious education, at any stage, cannot exist apart from catechesis and evangelization, and that an effective and faithful religious education cannot be imparted apart from its doctrinal, moral, ethical, and social teachings, all of which are secured upon hierarchies of truths and values essential to the coherence and structure of the faith. For its part, religious education, shaped as it is by an intellectual diversity, is naturally exploratory in nature and understandably interested in discovering the relationship of faith, belief, and culture. This tension between religious education on the one hand and the Church's teachings on the other has been documented.[57] It is said that the Church's Magisterium has been compromised in favour of "modern social sciences and ... fashionable new secular educational theories." Indeed, it is maintained that in the post-conciliar period (i.e., since Vatican II), "Catholic professional religious educators ... have failed to teach the Catholic faith properly, and how they have trained others to do the same, is a long, complicated, and rather depressing history."[58]

The Catholic school, whatever its political and economic relationship to the state or province, is an arm of the Catholic Church, and while its primary intellectual nature is secured upon pedagogical and systematic methods, its ultimate relationship to the Church cannot be disputed. However, even though the student's growth in the life of faith and belief are not limited to intellectual categories, growth in such a life must be governed by the intellectual mandate of the school. Put simply, the Catholic student should be able to understand and articulate the content and nature of the Catholic faith—scriptural, doctrinal, moral, and social—and to live it through the synthesis of faith and culture. Our age of religious individualism sug-

THE DISTINCTIVENESS OF CATHOLIC EDUCATION | D'SOUZA

gests that Catholic students appear to be less anxious to be able to articulate the precepts and doctrines of their faith.[59] A similar lack of intellectual and systematic knowledge in other subjects of the curriculum would not be tolerated.

What would be a parallel aim for non-Catholic and non-Christian students in Catholic schools? Given that Canadian Catholic schools do not offer these students religious instruction according to their tradition—similar to Catholic schools in Islamic countries, for example, which offer religious instruction to Muslim students as well—this parallel aim would be realized more indirectly through citizenship education and in making students aware of their responsibilities in living in a religiously and culturally diverse society.

Today, the relation of the Catholic school to faith and culture is undoubtedly complicated by shifts from a classical notion of culture secured upon immutable and permanent truths to a (post)modern notion in which culture is considered more empirically and as being in process. The older form of culture was equated with certain ideals associated with the liberal arts. The tension stems from the fact that while the Catholic faith teaches enduring and immutable truths, it is now the case that human individuation, the particularity of history, and culture "in process" are seen as necessary filters for faith and belief. And while Lonergan shows how this classical notion of culture still informs Christian doctrine and how the modern notion of culture should emphasize the responsibilities of the person as the one who knows and appropriates faith, belief, and truths, thus escaping the charge of individualism and relativism,[60] there remains the difficulty that such appropriation and responsibility for one's life of faith and morals—admitting, of course, that such a life never exists apart from divine grace—presumes a context and a knowledge of what needs to appropriated and how it is to be carried out. Faith is much more than intellectual knowledge or the schemas of theologians and religious educators. But recalling that the purpose of the school is to enable students how to think—as well as to understand the limitations of reducing everything to thought, which itself requires thinking—the Catholic school must enable its students to understand the content and structure of the Catholic faith and its relationship to the moral life and its realization through deliberation, choices, and actions. For its part, the creativity and exploratory nature of religious education should be celebrated and its scholarship encouraged, particularly as our understanding of culture has changed so much and continues to change, all of which influences the life of faith and morals.

AIMS AND PRACTICES

Thus, while the Catholicity of the school is not reducible to religious education, an occasional celebration of the sacraments, praying, or the celebration of other religious rituals, the school would be seen to have failed if its Catholic students were unable to articulate the nature and content of their faith, its place and role in the curriculum, its role in their intellectual, moral, and spiritual conversion, and its shaping of their choices and actions. Religious education, therefore, can run the danger of being rendered a soft discipline and fail to be intellectually rigorous, a failure detrimental to the synthesis between faith and culture. And though Catholic religious education cannot and must not shoulder the entire responsibility of exhibiting the distinctiveness of Catholic education more broadly, it does hold a place of primacy in showing the relationship between faith and culture and the synthesis of this relationship in the curriculum and everything else that constitutes the environment of the Catholic school.

Diversity, Unity, and Education

Defining the common good in the face of cultural liberalism, pluralism, moral and religious diversity, and democracy is challenging, but it cannot be ignored. The common good is more than a collection of private goods; while it certainly has a material dimension, it is also moral and social in nature and always related to human beings as persons.[61] The end goal of the state is the common good of its citizens, "which is not only a collection of advantages and utilities, but also rectitude of life, an end good in itself ... the intrinsically worthy good."[62] The contingency of history prevents the common good from being fully realized in any age, but it remains a source of human perfection and growth. In a pluralist context, terms like the "common good," "human person," "human development, and "human perfection" will rarely find universal agreement, but achieving even a general agreement has enormous implications for the growth of human society. In Vryhof's words, "If we can agree on some non-negotiables—respect for others, the sanctity of life, the importance of the public good, honesty and fair dealing, stewardship of the environment, promotion of community, both local and worldwide—we could be far along the road toward a genuinely democratic pluralism."[63]

In Canada, the realization of human personhood is usually relegated to the religious and the cultural, thus encouraging a divorce between the economico-political and the religio-cultural spheres; this runs the danger of promoting "common goods," rather than *the* "common good."[64] The common good has material, moral, and intellectual dimensions, but if human

60

THE DISTINCTIVENESS OF CATHOLIC EDUCATION | D'SOUZA

flourishing is relegated to the private spheres of religion and ethnic culture, then even the constricted liberal depiction of the common good as life bound by economic and political union will be compromised, leading to the further miniaturization of human beings.

All religions have encountered strains in educating their adherents in living faithful lives amidst a variety of diversities. One can sympathize with religious educators who promote rejecting plurality in favour of inwardly centred orthodox practices. However, while education and democracy have a natural relationship, pluralist democratic societies encounter strains and often appear to be divided when even the most general expressions of the common good have been introduced as fruit of this relationship. In the midst of diversity, particularly religious diversity, there is a pressing need for religious educators to educate their adherents about the implications of life in a democratic society, particularly in relationship to citizenship. The aim is to re-widen the narrowing of society beyond the secular and material categories of capitalism. However, more is needed than the obvious acknowledgment of religious differences; there is a need to recognize the contribution of religions to the common good of political society.

A great deal has been written on citizenship education and its implications for religious education.[65] While the actions, choices, and decisions of interest to religious educators of different faiths may well be diverse, each tradition has a responsibility to prepare its adherents to take their place as citizens in political society: "education in pluralism extends beyond the local group and presents ideas of justice and fairness as proper expectations for all members of the society, including those whose beliefs and values are shaped by religious traditions that are considerably different from one's own."[66] The religious educator must form students who look on religious plurality as a feature of modern freedom and not just as an accidental characteristic of the pluralist state. For their part, political leaders cannot acknowledge the diversity of the state and, at the same time, isolate religious diversity to the periphery of society. The citizen as a person is more than a political animal; citizens are also called to transcend the narrow confines of society. Thus the education of persons is more than the education of citizens bound in economic and political relationships.

An earlier document recognizes the charge that Catholic schools may seem to fail in forming "convinced, articulate Christians ready to take their place in social and political life."[67] In fairness, this document and other Catholic educational documents referred to in this chapter present a convincing case as to how the Catholic school must emphasize the preparation

AIMS AND PRACTICES

of students as future citizens, particularly in working for the common good. In affirming the Catholic school as a service to the Church, society, and to the common good, these documents point to the breadth of Catholic education. What is interesting is how these documents have grown in their insistence on the need to transform the "temporal order," and how this transformation is viewed as a good and an end in itself. That transformation, however, is seen in wide terms based on an anthropology that transcends political and social theories that are anxious to isolate religious beliefs and practices. Thus, Catholic education works for the transformation of the social order and for the citizen's contribution in working for the common good, achieved through moral, intellectual, and social means.

The *Pastoral Constitution on the Church in the Modern World*, for example, lays the foundation to attain such a good: "The social order and its development must constantly yield to the good of the person, since the order of things must be subordinate to the order of persons and not the other way around.... The social order requires constant improvement: it must be founded on truth, built on justice, and enlivened by love: it should grow in freedom toward a more humane equilibrium."[68] The Catholic school's commitment to the common good is secured on this foundation. While the school must distinguish "work" as a particularly human characteristic, the worker's "vocational identity" is one that involves the whole person, and through work it must contribute to "elevating unceasingly the cultural and moral level of society."[69] The citizen contributes to the common good as a person, and persons enrich the common good, not limiting it to material good or a collection of private goods bound in political and economic union. Thus "fellowship," "cooperation," "dialogue," and "peace" must form part of the vocabulary of the Catholic school, as must "charity," "forgiveness," and "love." Indeed, the concept of *tolerance*, so often heard in the context of Canadian pluralism, seems incompatible with a plurality of persons striving for the common good. Such striving requires more than a tolerance of the Other; it requires "fellowship."[70]

While acknowledging the power of religious identity, Amartya Sen warns against the "singular classification" of religious identity: "a person's religion need not be his or her all-encompassing and exclusive identity."[71] This has interesting implications for Canadian Catholic education, particularly as the number of non-Catholic students attending Catholic schools is significant. The Catholic school is well poised in preventing human miniaturization through the singular classification of religious identity, and it does this through the Catholic understanding of the common good so well developed in papal **encyclicals** (since *Rerum novarum* in 1891), and secured

THE DISTINCTIVENESS OF CATHOLIC EDUCATION | D'SOUZA

upon the nature and dignity of the person, the transformation of the social order as an end in itself, life in community as a source of moral, intellectual, and social perfection, and temporal unity in spite of religious diversity.

Education is in some ways observable through choices, actions, and decisions, and thus there are those who have rightly related the common good to the moral life. From the Catholic perspective, this is carried out by relating issues of social justice and a striving for the common good to personal morality and moral formation, suggesting that such an ethic could be related to three foundational virtues: "solidarity, compassion, and hospitality."[72] The virtues, of course, are never realized in vacuum; they need a "viewpoint, a more complex worldview that gives a fuller account of human experience."[73] In the case of the Catholic school, the world view and account of human experience are undoubtedly Catholic, but the Catholic position on education can unite a diverse religious student body through its mandate to teach students how to think, and it is able to do so without the charge of proselytizing or demeaning other faiths.

There is no implication that other religious traditions are unable to offer such a denominational system as an effective educational model to respond to Canadian religious diversity. The purpose here has been to speak of the *distinctiveness* of Catholic education and its contribution amidst religious diversity. Religious traditions understand human freedom in different ways. In claiming that human freedom is the fundamental aim of Catholic education, such an education has a naturally integrating and unifying ability in maintaining that it strives for human freedom in enabling students how to think. To be able to think about unity amidst diversity without losing one's own religious identity or one's responsibility to the common good is a particular form of human freedom, one that Catholic education is well poised to deliver.

Conclusion

The nature of Canadian Catholic education is usually circumscribed in the language of faith and religious education. And while it is beyond the scope of this chapter to address the implications of such circumscription, it has been my attempt to present a certain Catholic educational philosophical universality that is usually associated with *a holistic education* or terms that are usually associated with Catholic positions on education: *an integral education* and *the education of the whole person*.

The phrase *the education of the whole person* seems to be a favourite among Catholic educators, and for good reason, but its implications and implementation require a wider stage than the language of faith or religious

63

education. As stated previously, while the *absolute ultimate aim* of such Catholic education is eternal union with God, there are also *ultimate aims* that enjoy their own independence, autonomy, and imperative for fulfillment in the school. The school must teach students primarily how to think, and this ability is governed by the fundamental intellectual mandate of the Catholic school. The different realms of knowledge, including, of course, the knowledge of faith and belief, all fall under this intellectual mandate. It is this diversity of knowledge and the diversity of ways of knowing that are the strengths of the Catholic school, secured upon a specific anthropology. The Catholic school draws attention to the student's social, moral, intellectual, and religious obligations acquired through knowing and learning as well as through their integration. Yet there are many objections to such a unified conception of education. The Catholic position on education may not be able to convince all these critics, but it does possess a world view and intellectual principles that house its pedagogical practice, one that is defensible even amidst diversity that often seems ungrounded and without ultimate aims.

Notes

1 Terence McLaughlin, "Distinctiveness and the Catholic School: Balanced Judgment and the Temptations of Commonality," in *Liberalism, Education and Schooling: Essays by T.H. McLaughlin,* edited by David Carr, Mark Halstead, and Richard Pring (Exeter: Imprint Academic, 2008), 201.

2 The Congregation for Catholic Education [All documents from this Congregation are henceforth abbreviated as CCE], *The Catholic School,* 4–5.

3 Cardinal Zenon Grocholewski, "The Catholic School According to the Code of Canon Law." *Catholic Education: A Journal of Inquiry and Practice* 12, no.2 (2008): 148–59.

4 Vatican Council II, "*Gravissimum educationis* / Declaration on Christian education," in *Vatican Council II: The Basic Sixteen Documents, 575–591,* ed. A. Flannery (Dublin: Dominican Publications, 1996), §1.

5 Fagan, *The Loss of Constitutional Rights in Education in Newfoundland and Labrador.*

6 Canadian Catholic School Trustees' Association, *Catholic Schools across Canada: Into the New Millennium,* ed. John H. Flynn (Toronto: CCSTA, 2003).

7 Canadian Catholic School Trustees' Association, *Build Bethlehem Everywhere: A Statement on Catholic Education* (Nepean, ON: CCSTA, 2002), 12.

8 James T. Mulligan, *Catholic Education: Ensuring a Future* (Ottawa: Novalis, 2005), 289. See introduction, page 5.

9 Mulligan, *Catholic Education: Ensuring a Future*, 311–12.

10 Thomas Oldenski, *Liberation Theology and Critical Pedagogy in Today's Catholic Schools: Social Justice in Action* (New York: Garland, 1997), 36.

11 John B. Kostoff, *Auditing Our Catholic Schools: A Process of Discernment, Discussion, and Action* (Toronto: Pearson, 2010), 70, 5.

12 Institute for Catholic Education, *Project Report: Catholic Education in the Separate School System of Ontario* (Toronto: ICE, 1990), 109, 141.

13 See James T. Mulligan, *Evangelization and the Catholic High School: An Agenda for the 1990s* (Ottawa: Novalis, 1990), 90–105.

14 See Dennis Murphy, *Called to Teach: The Catholic Teacher as Witness* (Toronto: Catholic Register, 2003).

15 James T. Mulligan, *Catholic Education: The Future Is Now* (Ottawa: Novalis, 1999), 163–68.

16 Institute for Catholic Education, *Writing Curriculum for Catholic Schools: A Framework*, introduction by Joan Cronin (Toronto: ICE, 1996), 8.

17 Dennis Murphy, *Catholic Education: A Light of Truth* (Toronto: Catholic Register Books, 2007), 15

18 See Leonard A. Kennedy, *The Catholic School in An Age of Dissent* (Toronto: Ave Maria Press, 2002).

19 Graham McDonough, "The Sacred and the Secular: Is There a 'Crisis of Faith' in Separate Schools?" *Our Schools, Our Selves* 17, no. 3 (2008): 112.

20 Graham McDonough, "Contextualizing Authority for the Religious Teacher," *Religious Education* 103, no. 1 (2008): 50.

21 Spencer Boudreau, *Catholic Education: The Quebec Experience* (Calgary: Detselig Enterprises, 1999), 39.

22 Jacques Maritain, *Education at the Crossroads* (New Haven, CT: Yale University Press), 15.

23 Maritain, *Education at the Crossroads*, 15, 11.

24 Jacques Maritain, *The Education of Man: The Educational Philosophy of Jacques Maritain*, ed. and intr. Donald and Idella Gallagher (Westport, CT: Greenwood Press, 1962), 160–79.

25 Thomas Groome, "What Makes a School Catholic," in *The Contemporary Catholic School: Context, Identity, and Diversity*, ed. Terence McLaughlin, Joseph O'Keefe, and Bernadette O'Keefe (London: Falmer Press, 1996), 108. I understand positive anthropology to mean human beings created in the image and likeness of God, and moved by grace and choosing the good, the virtuous, and the holy, to strive to live out God's will in this life, and thus inheriting eternal life.

26 Groome, "What Makes a School Catholic," 121.

27 Mario D'Souza, "The Christian Philosophy of Education and Christian Religious Education," *Journal of Educational Thought* 34, no. 1 (2000): 15–17.

28 CCE, *The Catholic School on the Threshold of the Third Millennium* (Rome, 1997), 18.

29 CCE, *Educational Guidance in Human Love: Outlines for Sex Education* (Rome, 1983), 9.

30 Pontifical Council for Culture, *Toward a Pastoral Approach to Culture* (Boston: Pauline Books and Media), 2.

31 Andrew B. Morris, "By Their Fruits You Shall Know Them: Distinctive Features of Catholic Education," *Research Papers in Education* 13, no. 1 (1998): 92.

32 Edward Leen, *What Is Education?* (New York: Sheed and Ward, 1947), 79, 80, 81.

33 CCE, *The Catholic School*, 14.

34 Mario D'Souza, "The Preparation of Teachers for Roman Catholic Schools," *Paideusis: Journal of the Canadian Philosophy of Education Society* 9, no. 2 (1996): 5–19.

35 CCE, *Lay Catholics in Schools: Witnesses to Faith* (Rome, 1982), 41.

36 Wolfgang Brezinka, *Beliefs, Morals, and Education: Collected Essays in the Philosophy of Education*, trans. J.S. Rice (Aldershot: Averbury, 1994).

37 McLaughlin, "Distinctiveness and the Catholic School," 51.

38 John Dewey, *Experience and Education* (New York: Collier Books, 1938), 25

39 D'Souza, "The Preparation of Teachers for Roman Catholic Schools," 9–14.

40 Terence McLaughlin, "The Distinctiveness of Catholic Education," in *The Contemporary Catholic School: Context, Identity, and Diversity*, ed. Terence McLaughlin, Joseph O'Keefe, and Bernadette O'Keefe (London: Falmer Press, 1996), 136–79; John Elias, "Whatever Happened to a Catholic Philosophy of Education?" *Religious Education* 94, no. 1 (1999): 92–110; Christopher Meehan, "Catholic Sixth Form Colleges and the Distinctive Aims of Catholic Education," *British Journal of Religious Education* 24, no. 2 (2002): 123–39; and Mario D'Souza, "Some Reflections on Contemporary Canadian Catholic Education," *Interchange* 34, no. 4 (2003): 364–81.

41 Bernard Lonergan, *Topics in Education*, ed. Robert Doran and Frederick Crowe (Toronto: University of Toronto Press, 1993).

42 Bernard Lonergan, *Method in Theology* (New York: Seabury Press, 1972), 14–15.

43 CCE, *The Religious Dimension of Education in a Catholic School* (Rome, 1988), 26.

44 Terence McLaughlin, "Distinctiveness and the Catholic School," 209.

45 McLaughlin, "The Distinctiveness of Catholic Education," 138–39.

46 CCE, *The Catholic School on the Threshold of the Third Millennium*, 4.

47 Maritain, *The Education of Man*, 136.

48 Lawrence Lynch, *Intellectual Curiosity in Catholic Schools* (Toronto: English Catholic Education Association of Ontario, 1957), 9.

49 Peter Hobson and Louise Welbourne, "Modal Shifts and Challenges for Religious Education in Catholic Schools Since Vatican II," *Christian Education Journal* 6, no. 1 (2002): 55–71; Gabriel Moran, "Religious Education after Vatican II," in *Open Catholicism: The Tradition and Its Past: Essays in Honor of Gerard S. Sloyan*, ed. David Efroymson and John Raines (Collegeville, MN: Liturgical Press, 1997), 151–66; and Graham Rossiter, "Perspectives on Change in Catholic Religious Education Since the Second Vatican Council," *Religious Education* 83, no. 2 (1988): 264–76.

50 Brian J. Kelty, "Toward a Theology of Catholic Education," *Religious Education* 94, no. 1 (1999): 12.

51 Thomas J. Reese, ed., *The Universal Catechism: Reflections and Responses* (New York: Harper and Row, 1990).

52 Pope John Paul II, *Catechesis in Our Time* (Boston: St. Paul Books and Media, 1979), 16.

53 Pope Paul VI, "On Evangelization in the Modern World," in *The Catechetical Documents: A Parish Resource* (Chicago: Liturgy Training Publications, 1975), 163.

54 Pontifical Council for Culture, *Toward a Pastoral Approach to Culture.*

55 CCE, *The Religious Dimension of Education in a Catholic School*, 23.

56 Maritain, *The Education of Man*, 116.

57 Michael J. Wrenn, *Catechisms and Controversies: Religious Education in the Postconciliar Years* (San Francisco: Ignatius Press, 1991).

58 Michael Wrenn and Kenneth Whitehead, *Flawed Expectations: The Reception of the Catechism of the Catholic Church* (San Francisco: Ignatius Press, 1996), 42, 45.

59 Anthony Bryk, Valerie Lee, and Peter Holland, *Catholic Schools and the Common Good* (Cambridge, MA: Harvard University Press, 1993), 333–34; and Christian Smith and Melinda Lundquist Denton, *Soul Searching: The Religious and Spiritual Lives of American Teenagers* (New York: Oxford University Press, 2005), 146.

60 Lonergan, *Method in Theology*, 301–2.

61 Jacques Maritain, *The Person and the Common Good*, trans. John Fitzgerald (Notre Dame, IN: Notre Dame University Press, 1966), 29–30.

62 Jacques Maritain, *Scholasticism and Politics*, trans. Mortimer Adler (London: Geoffrey Bles, 1945), 56.

63 Steven Vryhof, "A System Where Everyone Wins: The Legitimacy of Faith-Based Schools in a System of Choice," *Educational Horizons* 83, no. 2 (2005): 139.

AIMS AND PRACTICES

64 Karl Hostetler, "The Common Good and Public Education," *Educational Theory* 53, no. 3 (2003): 348.

65 Jacqueline Watson, "Educating for Citizenship: The Emerging Relationship Between Religious Education and Citizenship Education," *British Journal of Religious Education* 26, no. 3 (2004): 259–71; and Robert Jackson, *Rethinking Religious Education and Plurality: Issues in Diversity and Pedagogy* (London: RoutledgeFalmer, 2004).

66 Walter Feinberg, *For Goodness Sake: Religious Schools and Education for Democratic Society* (New York: Routledge, 2006), 156.

67 CCE, *The Catholic School*, 9.

68 Vatican Council II, "*Gaudium et spes* / Pastoral constitution on the Church in the modern world," in Vatican Council II: *The Basic Sixteen Documents*, ed. A. Flannery (Dublin: Dominican Publications, 1996), 191–92.

69 CCE, *Lay Catholics in Schools*, 15.

70 Jacques Maritain, *Ransoming the Time*, trans. Harry Binsee (New York: Gordian Press, 1972), 116.

71 Amartya Sen, *Identity and Violence: The Illusion of Destiny* (London: Allen Lane, 2006), 14.

72 Christophe Vogt, "Fostering a Catholic Commitment to the Common Good: An Approach Rooted in Virtue Ethics," *Theological Studies* 68, no. 2 (2007): 394–417.

73 Vryhof, "A System Where Everyone Wins," 135.

Bibliography

Boudreau, Spencer. *Catholic Education: The Quebec Experience.* Calgary: Detselig Enterprises, 1999.

Brezinka, Wolfgang. *Beliefs, Morals, and Education: Collected Essays in the Philosophy of Education.* Translated by J.S. Rice. Aldershot: Averbury, 1994.

Bryk, Anthony, Valerie Lee, and Peter Holland. *Catholic Schools and the Common Good.* Cambridge, MA: Harvard University Press, 1993.

Canadian Catholic School Trustees' Association. *Catholic Schools across Canada: Into the New Millennium.* Edited by John H. Flynn. Toronto: CCSTA, 2003.

———. *Build Bethlehem Everywhere: A Statement on Catholic Education.* Nepean, ON: CCSTA, 2002.

Catholic Church, *Catechism of the Catholic Church.* Ottawa: Publications Service, Canadian Conference of Catholic Bishops, 1994.

The Congregation for Catholic Education (CCE). *The Catholic School on the Threshold of the Third Millennium.* Rome, 1997.

———. *The Religious Dimension of Education in a Catholic School.* Rome, 1988.

———. *Educational Guidance in Human Love: Outlines for Sex Education*. Rome, 1983.

———. *Lay Catholics in Schools: Witnesses to Faith*. Rome, 1982.

———. *The Catholic School*. Rome, 1977.

Dewey, John. *Experience and Education*. New York: Collier Books, 1938.

D'Souza, Mario. "The Christian Philosophy of Education and Christian Religious Education." *Journal of Educational Thought* 34, no. 1 (2000): 11–28.

———. "The Preparation of Teachers for Roman Catholic Schools: Some Philosophical First Principles." *Paideusis: Journal of the Canadian Philosophy of Education Society* 9, no. 2 (1996): 5–19.

———. "Some Reflections on Contemporary Canadian Catholic Education." *Interchange* 34, no. 4 (2003): 364–81.

Elias, John. "Whatever Happened to a Catholic Philosophy of Education?" *Religious Education* 94, no. 1 (1999): 92–110.

Fagan, Bonaventure. *The Loss of Constitutional Rights in Education in Newfoundland and Labrador: The Roman Catholic Story*. St. John's: ADDA Press, 2004.

Feinberg, Walter. *For Goodness Sake: Religious Schools and Education for Democratic Society*. New York: Routledge, 2006.

Grocholewski, Zenon, Cardinal. "The Catholic School According to the Code of Canon Law." *Catholic Education: A Journal of Inquiry and Practice* 12, no. 2 (2008): 148–59.

Groome, Thomas. "What Makes a School Catholic." In *The Contemporary Catholic School: Context, Identity, and Diversity*, edited by Terence McLaughlin, Joseph O'Keefe, and Bernadette O'Keefe, 107–25. London: Falmer Press, 1996.

Hobson, Peter, and Louise Welbourne. "Modal Shifts and Challenges for Religious Education in Catholic Schools Since Vatican II." *Christian Education Journal* 6, no. 1 (2002): 55–71.

Hostetler, Karl. "The Common Good and Public Education." *Educational Theory* 53, no. 3 (2003): 347–61.

Institute for Catholic Education. *Ontario Catholic School Graduate Expectations*. Toronto: ICE, 2003.

———. *Writing Curriculum for Catholic Schools: A Framework*. Introduction by Joan Cronin. Toronto: ICE, 1996.

———. *Project Report: Catholic Education in the Separate School System of Ontario*. Prepared for the Board of Directors. Participating staff: B. Blishen, R.B. Robinson, F. Eaton, and B. Roland. Toronto: ICE, May 1990.

Jackson, Robert. *Rethinking Religious Education and Plurality: Issues in Diversity and Pedagogy*. London: RoutledgeFalmer, 2004.

AIMS AND PRACTICES

John Paul II, Pope. *Catechesis in Our Time*. Boston: St. Paul Books and Media, 1979.

Kelty, Brian J. "Toward a Theology of Catholic Education." *Religious Education* 94, no. 1 (1999): 5–23.

Kennedy, Leonard A. *The Catholic School in an Age of Dissent*. Toronto: Ave Maria Press, 2002.

Kostoff, John B. *Auditing Our Catholic Schools: A Process of Discernment, Discussion, and Action*. Toronto: Pearson, 2010.

Leen, Edward. *What Is Education?* New York: Sheed and Ward, 1947.

Leo XIII, Pope. *Rerum Novarum. Encyclical Letter of His Holiness Pope Leo XIII on the condition of the working classes*. Boston: Daughters of St. Paul, 1891/1942.

Lonergan, Bernard. *Topics in Education*. Edited by Robert Doran and Frederick Crowe. Toronto: University of Toronto Press, 1993.

———. *Method in Theology*. New York: Seabury Press, 1972.

Lynch, Lawrence. *Intellectual Curiosity in Catholic Schools*. Toronto: English Catholic Education Association of Ontario, 1957.

Maritain, Jacques. *Education at the Crossroads*. New Haven, CT: Yale University Press, 1943.

———. *The Education of Man: The Educational Philosophy of Jacques Maritain*. Edited with an introduction by Donald and Idella Gallagher. Westport, CT: Greenwood Press 1962.

———. *The Person and the Common Good*. Translated by John Fitzgerald. Notre Dame, IN: University of Notre Dame Press, 1966.

———. *Ransoming the Time*. Translated by Harry Binsee. New York: Gordian Press, 1972.

———. *Scholasticism and Politics*. Translated by Mortimer Adler. London: Geoffrey Bles, 1945.

McDonough, Graham. "Contextualizing Authority for the Religion Teacher." *Religious Education* 103, no. 1 (2008): 48–61.

———. "The Sacred and the Secular: Is There a 'Crisis of Faith' in Separate Schools?" *Our Schools, Our Selves* 17, no. 3 (2008): 107–17.

McLaughlin, Terence. "Distinctiveness and the Catholic School: Balanced Judgment and the Temptations of Commonality." In *Liberalism, Education and Schooling. Essays by T.H. McLaughlin*, edited by David Carr, Mark Halstead, and Richard Pring, 199–217. Exeter: Imprint Academic, 2008.

———. "The Distinctiveness of Catholic Education." In *The Contemporary Catholic School: Context, Identity, and Diversity*, edited by Terence McLaughlin, Joseph O'Keefe, and Bernadette O'Keefe, 136–79. London: Falmer Press, 1996.

Meehan, Christopher. "Catholic Sixth Form Colleges and the Distinctive Aims of Catholic Education." *British Journal of Religious Education* 24, no. 2 (2002): 123–39.

Moran, Gabriel. "Religious Education after Vatican II." In *Open Catholicism: The Tradition and Its Past: Essays in Honor of Gerard S. Sloyan*, edited by David Efroymson and John Raines, 151–66. Collegeville, MN: Liturgical Press, 1997.

Morris, Andrew B. "By Their Fruits You Shall Know Them: Distinctive Features of Catholic Education." *Research Papers in Education* 13, no. 1 (1998): 87–112.

Mulligan, James T. *Catholic Education: Ensuring a Future*. Ottawa: Novalis, 2005.

———. *Catholic Education: The Future Is Now*. Ottawa: Novalis. 1999

———. *Evangelization and the Catholic High School: An Agenda for the 1990s*. Ottawa: Novalis, 1990.

Murphy, Dennis. *Called to Teach: the Catholic Teacher as Witness*. Toronto: Catholic Register, 2003.

———. *Catholic Education: A Light of Truth*. Toronto: Catholic Register Books, 2007.

Oldenski, Thomas. *Liberation Theology and Critical Pedagogy in Today's Catholic Schools: Social Justice in Action*. New York: Garland, 1997.

Paul VI, Pope. "On Evangelization in the Modern World." In *The Catechetical Documents: A Parish Resource*, 157–99. Chicago: Liturgy Training Publications, 1975.

Pontifical Council for Culture. *Toward a Pastoral Approach to Culture*. Boston: Pauline Books and Media, 1999.

Reese, Thomas J., ed. *The Universal Catechism: Reflections and Responses*. New York: Harper and Row, 1990.

Rossiter, Graham. "Perspectives on Change in Catholic Religious Education since the Second Vatican Council." *Religious Education* 83, no. 2 (1988): 264–76.

Sen, Amartya. *Identity and Violence: The Illusion of Destiny*. London: Allen Lane, 2006.

Smith, Christian, and Melinda Lundquist Denton. *Soul Searching: The Religious and Spiritual Lives of American Teenagers*. New York: Oxford University Press, 2005.

Vatican Council II. "*Gaudium et spes* / Pastoral constitution on the Church in the modern world." In *Vatican Council II: The Basic Sixteen Documents,* edited by A. Flannery, 163–282. Dublin: Dominican Publications, 1996 [original work published 1965].

———. "*Gravissimum educationis* / Declaration on Christian education." In *Vatican Council II: The Basic Sixteen Documents, 575–591,* edited by A. Flannery. Dublin: Dominican Publications, 1996 [original work published 1965].

Vogt, Christopher. "Fostering a Catholic Commitment to the Common Good: An Approach Rooted in Virtue Ethics." *Theological Studies* 68, no. 2 (2007): 394–417.

Vryhof, Steven. "A System Where Everyone Wins: The Legitimacy of Faith-Based Schools in a System of Choice." *Educational Horizons* 83, no. 2 (2005): 125–42.

AIMS AND PRACTICES

Watson, Jacqueline. "Educating for Citizenship: The Emerging Relationship Between Religious Education and Citizenship Education." *British Journal of Religious Education* 26, no. 3 (2004): 259–71.

Wrenn, Michael J. *Catechisms and Controversies: Religious Education in the Postconciliar Years.* San Francisco: Ignatius Press, 1991.

Wrenn, Michael and Kenneth Whitehead. *Flawed Expectations: The Reception of the Catechism of the Catholic Church.* San Francisco: Ignatius Press, 1996.

CHAPTER THREE

BETWEEN IMMIGRATING AND INTEGRATING: THE CHALLENGE OF DEFINING AN ISLAMIC PEDAGOGY IN CANADIAN ISLAMIC SCHOOLS

Nadeem A. Memon

Introduction

The initiation and establishment of Islamic schools[1] in Canada has a relatively short history. The earliest school and those established soon after can all be traced back to a movement that began in the late 1970s and early 1980s. The first school, founded in Mississauga, Ontario, has been followed by schools founded in suburbs of other major Canadian cities: Vancouver, Montreal, Calgary, Halifax, and Ottawa. In 2010, there were over 60 full-time Islamic day schools across the country, with close to half in Ontario alone. In fact, Toronto houses one of the largest concentrations of Islamic schools across North America.[2]

Amidst the relatively rapid growth of Islamic schools in Canada, one challenge has been establishing some form of concerted effort or collaboration between schools. To date, and despite the concentration of schools in Toronto for instance, there is no organization or association of schools with any degree of oversight. All schools are, therefore, privately administered, either individually owned and operated or through community organizations such as mosques. Though some schools have articulated a vision because of a need to distinguish themselves among competitors, most schools operate with a limited sense of educational vision. For many Islamic schools, purpose and pedagogy are defined by sincere and committed individuals who rely on their personal schooling experience and their adaptation of what are deemed best practices in other schools (public and faith-

73

AIMS AND PRACTICES

based). The lack of administrators and, in some cases, even teachers who are certified educators has meant that the amount of energy dedicated to defining the basis upon which school aims will be defined has been limited. In many ways, the growth of, and the hurdles in establishing and defining, Islamic schools mirror the trajectory of most faith-based schools: humble beginnings, simplistic frameworks, and disparate aims.

Canadian Islamic schools have not been alone in their struggle to define themselves. The growth of Islamic schools in Canada is intertwined with the evolution of schools south of the border. The earliest Islamic schools are connected through the shared history of national, cross-border organizations such as the Muslim Students' Association and the Islamic Society of North America (ISNA), two early organizations that were established to serve North American Muslim communities.[3] As a result, the purpose and pedagogy of Islamic schools in Canada have been arguably shaped by the aims and rationales of more transnational discourses in the Canadian Muslim diaspora related to decolonization, immigration, and revival.

The aim of this chapter is to explore the challenges in defining an Islamic pedagogy or, put another way, the conception of education in Islam in the context of Islamic schools in Canada. The challenges faced by Canadian Islamic schools will be contextualized within the factors alluded to in the title: immigrating and integrating. Each of these factors will be explored in relation to the aims and curriculum of early Islamic schools.

To begin, it is necessary to contextualize the development of the first Islamic school in Canada with global trends in education within the Muslim world. In 1977, coinciding with the conception of the first school in Canada, the groundbreaking First World Conference on Muslim Education was held in Mecca, Saudi Arabia. The conference admittedly had little direct effect on the decision to establish Islamic schools in Canada, yet it certainly captures the global Muslim discourse of Islamic education in the time period. North American Muslim scholars, activists, and those whom I refer to as "visionaries" of Islamic schooling were undoubtedly aware of, if not influenced by, this conference. I begin this chapter, therefore, with one of the few well-conceptualized frameworks of what defines education within the Islamic tradition in order to situate the problems and promises of Islamic schools in Canada.

Historical Method

The research described in this chapter draws on a larger North American oral history project conducted with 24 Islamic school teachers, administrators, and visionaries.[4] Pioneers in Islamic schooling were selected based on their involvement with the earliest schools and identified through speaking with community members. The voices presented in this chapter are largely from the interviews conducted with Canadian Muslims who established the earliest schools and, in some cases, Americans who have influenced the development of Canadian Islamic schools. Interviews were conducted between 2007 and 2009.

Defining Education in Islam

To understand the challenges and yet appreciate the common sense of purpose often subconsciously held by advocates of Islamic schooling, I will employ the definition of education in Islam defined by Naquib Al-Attas at the First World Conference on Muslim Education. Al-Attas, an Indonesian scholar, has arguably made one of the most significant contributions to Islamic philosophy in contemporary Islamic studies. Notably, he split his graduate studies between McGill University and the University of London, which influenced his conception of **Islamization**. Al-Attas is one of a handful of international Muslim immigrants who spent their years of graduate studies in North America initiating, debating, and forming perspectives on the discourse of what is now known as the Islamization of Knowledge.[5] Within this discourse, Al-Attas is also one of the few Muslim scholars to have attempted to articulate an Islamic philosophy of education. Most Muslim scholarship on education provides pedagogical insights in relation to the purpose of teaching and learning, the method of teaching, the curriculum, theories of child development, and the student-teacher relationship, but few have attempted, whether in the past or the present, to articulate a framework that considers both the purpose of education and its implications for teaching and learning.[6]

In his short treatise entitled *The Concept of Education in Islam*, Al-Attas begins by emphasizing the importance of reflecting on meaning and purpose in the formulation of a system of education and its methodology.[7] On this point, generally four Islamic terms are most often referenced to describe the purpose and process of education in Islam: *ta'lim* (direct instruction), *tarbiyah* (nurturing wholeness), *tazkiyah* (personal development), and *ta'dib* (comportment).[8] From among those who have reflected on pedagogical principles in Islam one will most often find the terms used

AIMS AND PRACTICES

interchangeably and arbitrarily. However, the term *ta'lim* is often reserved solely for direct instruction and used in educational contexts to refer to students in the process of learning. The term *tazkiyah* is less commonly used with reference to education but has been employed to define an aspect of education. The two terms that are most often used to define the purpose of education in Islam, then, are *tarbiyah* and *ta'dib*, of which Al-Attas is resolute that the latter is more accurate.[9]

Al-Attas defines education as "recognition and acknowledgement, progressively instilled into man, of the proper places of things in the order of creation, such that it leads to the recognition and acknowledgement of the proper place of God in the order of being and existence." "Proper place" refers to both the ontological domain of human beings in relation to the world and the theological domain that entail the religious and ethical aspects of everyday living.[10] Two aspects of his definition are particularly important to defining an Islamic pedagogy. First, based on Al-Attas's theorization elsewhere and the secondary literature produced by those who have studied his writings, I gather that teaching knowledge in relation to putting things in their "proper places" is manifested in many ways. In relation to human relationships it is about adhering to ethical norms in social behaviour. It manifests as respect, humility, and love for one's parents, families, communities, neighbours, teachers, and so on. In relation to the natural world, proper place is about maintaining and cultivating the natural environment and being conscious of personal actions and choices that can harm nature. Similarly, intellectually and spiritually, proper place is defined by recognizing one's ultimate purpose and essence. And the list could go on of the ways that "putting things in their proper place" manifests itself in every aspect of living and learning.[11]

What must be highlighted from Al-Attas's conception of education is that action is essential to knowledge. In the examples given above, it is insufficient to know or understand that something is ethically objectionable. The example of cultivating our natural environment, being conscious of the ways our life choices may cause harm to it, requires ethical action on the part of the individual. To differentiate between knowledge and education, Al-Attas emphasizes that an education must include recognition of the proper place of knowledge in relation to the order of creation and must lead to action (*'amal*). For instance, if an individual does not act ethically on what they have learned, then it would not be an education in the whole sense of the word.[12]

The second aspect that is explicit in Al-Attas's conception of knowledge is the emphasis placed on the order of existence. The purpose of education (in its proper place) is then to recognize one's place in relation to one's station and condition in life with respect to oneself, as well as one's family, community, and society. This means, according to Al-Attas, that one must recognize and acknowledge one's place in the human order, which must be understood as arranged hierarchically and legitimately based on the Qur'anic criteria of intelligence, knowledge, and virtue and must act accordingly in a praiseworthy manner.[13] For the young this manifests as respect for their elders; for the lay it manifests as recognition of scholars; and for all human beings it manifests as recognition of their servitude to God and their ultimate state of helplessness in relation to life and death.

The two aspects of recognition—knowledge (*ilm*) and acknowledgement or action (*'amal*)—are captured in the Islamic conception of *'adab* (comportment) and therefore in the process of *ta'dib* (cultivating of *'adab*). *Ta'dib*, Al-Attas would argue, defines the purpose and content of education in Islam. The purpose of education is not simply to produce good citizens but to cultivate human beings both spiritually and in relation to societal responsibilities.[14]

Returning to Al-Attas's initial proposition that *ta'dib* encompasses the other concepts used to define education in Islam, namely *tarbiyah* (nurturing wholeness), I discern that he then employs the latter to define the method of teaching and learning. If *ta'dib* defines the purpose and content, *tarbiyah* defines methods of instruction. *Tarbiyah* is often defined by its similarity to the Latin definition of *educare*—to bring out, develop, nurture, and foster. In numerous treatises on education in Islam, both medieval and contemporary, the term *tarbiyah* has been developed to articulate principles of child development, instructional methods, methods of learning, and student–teacher relationships.[15]

Through the overarching conceptualization of *ta'dib*, Al-Attas provides a framework for the purpose, content, and methodology of an Islamic pedagogy. Although what Al-Attas conceptualizes is not necessarily definitive—as other educational theorists might place their emphasis elsewhere—for the objective of understanding the problems and promises of Islamic schools in particular, his framework serves well as a starting point both theoretically and historically.[16]

A framework that defines an Islamic pedagogy is relevant here in order to appreciate what Canadian Islamic schools are striving for. Many of the

AIMS AND PRACTICES

sentiments expressed in Islamic school mission statements, in school phi-losophies, and in the rationalization of those who have pioneered many schools are evident in Al-Attas's theorization. What this illustrates is that the principles of education in Islam are embedded in foundational Islamic beliefs.[17] Although many Islamic school pioneers may not have verbalized or codified a statement of purpose or reflected about the ways in which the principles of education in Islam would alter their administering of schools, there is general consensus on the aims of education among those who have envisioned full-time schools. This is not to say that all Islamic schools will have similar objectives or methods, but instead that each will draw on the tradition dynamically to create what they conceive of as an Islamic educa-tion. The richness of the tradition is in its diverse interpretations and imple-mentations within the principles of an Islamic pedagogy alluded to above. What will be discussed in the rest of the chapter are the challenges and promises of Canadian Islamic schools—challenges related to actualizing a framework, sense of vision, and distinct pedagogy and promises that have arisen from the struggle of grappling with the nature of Islamic pedagogy in Canada that employs contemporary educational practices and methods.

The Idea of Islamic Schooling

The earliest Islamic schools in Canada were closely related to the wave of Muslim immigrants who often came primarily for graduate studies and to build professional careers. Coming to Canada for graduate studies con-nected this particular cadre of Muslim immigrants to fellow Muslims south of the border who were active in establishing national networks and orga-nizations, namely the Muslim Students' Association (MSA) and later the Islamic Society of North America (ISNA).

With the MSA and ISNA serving as the catalyst for the earliest Muslim immigrant–established Islamic schools in Canada and United States, a number of factors challenged and strengthened the potential for defining an Islamic pedagogy in Islamic schools. First, many Muslim immigrants who came to pursue graduate studies came simply for that reason, and with no real intentions to make North America their permanent home. Second, for those who did intend on establishing roots in North America, separate, faith-based schooling was not a high priority, for two reasons: (1) establish-ing places of prayer and national organizations for the propagation of Islam was of utmost priority, and (2) the vast majority of early immigrants consid-ered cost-free (i.e., taxpayer-supported) public schooling to be of a higher

78

standard than what was available "back home" and a good way for their children to integrate into society. The third challenge posed to the development of early Islamic schools was the gendering of schooling. Among the Muslim educators I interviewed who immigrated in the 1960s and 1970s, the task of child rearing and concerns over education were most often relegated to women.[18] In the early days of the MSA, for example, women spearheaded the education committee, but there was minimal recognition of their contribution to the overall agenda of the MSA.

When the idea of establishing a full-time school in Toronto began to take shape in the late 1970s, curriculum concerns were paramount. What to teach was more important than how to teach. Some of this study's interviewees spoke of their experience on university campuses in the late 1960s where they would discuss, with their Christian and Jewish colleagues, matters of religious schooling and the potential for separate Islamic schools.[19] One participant commented that at that stage of the development of religious schooling in North America, discourses around religious education emphasized curricular content over pedagogical aims and principles. For many in the Muslim community who were concerned about preserving their faith tradition, this translated into the task of creating spaces for teaching rudimentary aspects of Islam. In the United States, for example, this concern was manifested in the development of age-appropriate teaching materials about Islam in English. And in relation to the schooling of children "back home" in the Middle East or South Asia, such a curriculum project was daunting in itself. What developed as a result were weekend and evening schools for children, often held in mosques or individual homes, where a parent or community leader would teach children the recitation of the **Qur'an** and basic beliefs and practices related to the five pillars of Islam.[20]

For many early Muslim immigrants to Canada it was their early experience with weekend schools and summer programs from which the idea of a full-time Islamic school evolved. For the pioneers whom I interviewed, establishing full-time schools seemed like the next logical step forward. One educator recollected the impact that those years of teaching at a weekend Islamic school program had had on her with respect to the potential for the development of formal Islamic schooling: "It's amazing that from that experience I began to say, okay I have an undergraduate degree in teaching and now I have a child and I want good Islamic education. And I started talking about lesson plans and I started talking about Islamic schools, thinking

AIMS AND PRACTICES

about why the Catholic schools were fulltime [and] why are we just doing weekend schools?" For most early pioneers of Islamic schooling the rationale seemed obvious: If there are successful weekend school programs and a growing demand, they asked, then why not develop day schools similar to those of other faiths? It was a question that led to the inevitable movement to create Canadian Islamic schools.

Supplementary (i.e., weekend, evening, and summer) school initiatives in Toronto in particular made a significant impact on Muslim communities south of the border, drawing the attention and support of the MSA and ISNA. These began as an initiative to expand local mosque-based programs into city-wide Islamic educational programming. In the late 1970s, Jame Mosque coordinated funding and support to teach Arabic to Muslim children as part of the Heritage Language Program. The half-day summer camp then expanded into an optional full-day program offering both Arabic language classes and Islamic studies. The summer program garnered significant interest, and its successful operation refined the administrative capabilities of a handful of Muslim educators. It also attracted the interest of ISNA, whose education committee was considering the initiation of two full-time Islamic schools as pilot projects. Toronto, as a result, became one of the two.

To School or Not to School Separately—Differences of Perspective
To ensure the viability of the Toronto pilot project and to determine the amount of seed money that would be granted, the MSA education committee suggested conducting a survey to gauge the level of interest and determine what Muslim parents would want from an Islamic school. The survey was intended to gather data about how many parents were interested in sending their children to an Islamic school, how many teachers were willing to teach in one, and what sorts of concerns, questions, and hesitations parents had. In the words of one my participants, "that's when we found divergent opinions about what parents wanted out of the school."[21]

From the outset some parents were adamant that Islamic schools were a bad idea. From their schooling experiences back home, the term "Islamic school" conjured images of traditional *madaris* (sing. *madrassa*: Qur'anic schools). In Southeast Asia in particular, *madaris* have been socio-politically marginalized and supported by a relatively small number of citizens. A schooling system that was once heralded across the Muslim world for its rigour and applicability, not solely to religious leadership but also to scientific and industrial work, had now lost its prestige. The contemporary reality

80

in places such as the South Asian Subcontinent is that children are sent to *madaris* as a last resort and often when they are deemed uneducable in the secular sciences.[22] For some early Canadian Muslim immigrants, then, the idea of an Islamic school raised serious concerns. One of my participants described the tension that existed in the early 1980s:

> At that time the [South Asian] Subcontinent Muslim community didn't want to have an Islamic school because they used to think of the *madrassa* and schools for the orphans, you know, people voiced it, we don't want this. If we have these types of schools our children will be *mullas* [religious scholars] and won't be academics and so on. That was there at that time. So we struggled with people from the inside and the outside.[23]

This depiction perhaps oversimplifies the range of opinions that existed. Indeed, there were parents in Toronto who aspired to establish *madaris* for the cultivation of religious leaders through the memorization of the Qur'an and study of the Islamic sciences. However, these parents were also dissatisfied with the concept of an Islamic school, arguing that its religious teachings were far too superficial. Nevertheless, Canadian Muslims who desired *madaris* did indeed establish them, and they did so in tandem with the development of full-time day schools by others in the community.

The voices of resistance from within the Toronto community were from those who feared that Islamic schools would isolate rather than integrate their children as Muslims in a new land. Establishing separate schools was tantamount to forfeiting the very privileges that colonial schooling awarded those from decolonized parts of Muslim majority countries.[24] Islamic schools, some feared, would reinforce the very religious and cultural practices that would highlight their differentness. At the same time, some parents wanted the rigour and strict code of conduct that they were accustomed to in education systems from back home. Canadian Muslim immigrants who came on student visas for graduate studies or for professional positions had likely graduated from British schools or Convent schools in their country of origin. Memories of the "colonial classroom," where classrooms were relatively unadorned and controlled by a strict code of conduct, and where the teaching of religion (most often Catholicism) was present but limited, described effective schooling for some.[25]

The impact of Canadian Muslim immigrants' education, therefore, played a significant role in shaping the development of early Islamic schools. The relatively innovative idea of an Islamic school elicited a vari-

AIMS AND PRACTICES

ety of opinions, interpretations, fears, and aspirations. Many parents who feared that their children would not be academically competitive if they were to attend an Islamic school opted to enroll their children for the primary years and then transfer them to public schools prior to high school. One of my participants captured the sentiment best when he said, "For us, secular education is very important, but so is religious [Islamic] education. We don't want to be deficient in regards to secular education but at the same time we want our children to have their moral code."[26] Others, who felt Islamic schools were underdeveloped and wanted the rigour and moral values with which they were raised in Convent Schools, sent their children to publicly funded Catholic schools.[27] Between each group of parent voices, the challenge that remained was over this very distinction: what distinguishes the secular from the religious, and how would an Islamic school negotiate the tension between them?

For those who were committed to the development of an Islamic school, the challenge was daunting. Parents committed to the idea had varied conceptions of the purpose of an Islamic school. There were those parents who were weary of the public system. Some who had attended public schools in Canada either had a negative experience of social or cultural discrimination or were taught curricula that misrepresented Islam and Muslims. Many of the issues cited by Muslim parents that served as rationale for taking their children out of secular public schools are similar to the concerns expressed by most faith-based school supporters. Issues such as teaching evolution, sex education (in particular the acceptability of premarital sex and homosexuality), and textbooks that are either devoid of or misconstrue religious perspectives were and continue to be among the points of contention for Islamic school parents, as well as all parents who support faith based schools.[28]

From the inception of the earliest Islamic schools until today, parents who dissent based on curricular issues have tended also to be the ones who have used the language of Islamization, or the insistence of integrating an Islamic world view into the existing ministry-mandated curriculum. Many of the issues listed above serve as the areas of their discontent. The aim of an Islamic school for these parents, then, is to create a learning environment conducive to teaching from an Islamic perspective or at least one that does not counter the religious and cultural values nurtured at home. One participant who enrolled his children in the first Islamic school in Canada expressed the overarching fear "that if you throw them [our children] out [into public schools] without the proper guidance about the religion, they might completely get lost, lose their culture, their religion...."[29]

BETWEEN IMMIGRATING AND INTEGRATING | MEMON

For many parents, the crux of the concern is beyond the formal curriculum. The school ethos and values—in particular the acceptability of values and behaviors related to gender relations—was and continues to be one of the driving forces behind establishing faith-based schools. Concerns over either marriage outside the faith or promiscuity, and, as a result, the protection of girls in particular, have been cited as a rationale for the establishment of many faith-based schools, including Islamic schools.[30] For some parents, the purpose of an Islamic school is not as much concerned with curricular integration as it is with the transference of religious values and practices. The education in the foundational teachings of Islam (prayers, fasting, and daily etiquette), along with a school environment that enforces the adherence to these values, is imperative.

The complexity of demands and expectations that were placed on early Islamic schools was overwhelming. One scholar of the immigrant Muslim experience in North America refers to the complexity as a "cacophony of voices" holding a range of beliefs related both to social integration, assimilation, or isolation, and the role that schools ought to play in the formation of a Muslim identity.[31] The challenge for the earliest Islamic schools was in accommodating the diverse demands. This inclusion had to accommodate those parents who knew little about the purpose of Islamic schooling but supported it simply out of fear of what impact the public school might have on their children,[32] or those parents for whom faith was not even a primary marker of their identity but who felt Islamic schools could reform delinquency.[33] And then there were those parents who ranged from wanting Islamic schools to raise the next generation of *ulema* (religious scholars) to those who wanted to preserve and protect faith values and practices.

Although diverse, each of the expectations of Islamic schools mentioned above is rooted in the conception of *adab*. As one prominent American Muslim scholar, who is also among the few who have questioned the purpose and vision of Islamic schools in North America, has emphasized, "The Islamic community is one rooted in the concept of *adab*...."[34] Whether or not it was articulated conceptually in the way that Al-Attas propounded, the need for an Islamic education to nurture moral behaviour served as the core objective of early Islamic schools. Granted, even within the objective of nurturing *adab* there remains a range of perspectives and interpretations about whether certain behaviours are morally grounded or culturally determined, and given the extent to which behaviours ought to be encouraged or enforced, the focus on *adab* still had implications for the curricular development of Islamic schools.

What to Teach? Developing Curriculum for Islamic Schools

The challenge in defining the purpose and objectives of Islamic schooling is captured in the diversity of voices discussed above. For the first pilot Islamic school in Canada, formally opened in 1982, the present-day ISNA School in Mississauga, Ontario, this range of expectations and limiting of objectives had a significant impact on the development of school curriculum. In pursuing community and, in particular, parental support, most early Islamic schools lacked an opportunity for serious deliberation over purpose and pedagogy. Quite frankly, the varied expectations stunted possibility in pedagogy, and what resulted was a curriculum that was starkly similar to a public school. In trying to appease the largest number of parent supporters, especially those who were concerned whether their children would receive an education commensurate to that in public schools, the aspect of faith in most early Islamic schools remained appended to, as opposed to integrated into, the curriculum. The following overview of the curriculum in faith-based schooling in general will frame the curricular challenge in Islamic schools in particular.

There are generally four areas, methods, or steps that define the trajectory of formal and informal curriculum development in faith-based schools. These are: (1) establishing terms of reference, (2) understanding faith-based education as a separate subject-specific task, (3) permeating the school environment, and (4) integrating faith perspectives into the public secular curriculum.[35] There have been attempts at expanding beyond integration in other faith-based schools, but given the infancy of Islamic schools in Canada, these first four categories will suffice for this analysis.[36]

The initial step of establishing terms of reference sets the groundwork for any curriculum-development initiative. In the case of Islamic schools in Canada, or across North America for that matter, this process has never taken place largely because there is to date no overarching institute or accrediting body that oversees the establishment of disparate privately funded schools, either provincially or nationally. Arabic concepts that define the purpose and process of education in Islam, as discussed earlier in relation to Al-Attas, are often employed in Islamic school mission statements but are rarely defined, described, or conceptualized in relation to contemporary Islamic schooling.[37] In the absence of a thorough deliberation and conceptualization of what terms such as *ta'dib* or *tarbiyah* may look like in the practice of Canadian Islamic schools, the curricular approaches of most early Islamic schools have, as a result, relied more heavily on teaching Islam as a separate subject and as a symbolic permeation of the school environment.

Prior to even the establishment of the first Islamic schools by ISNA in Chicago and Toronto, curricular initiatives had been established to support the education of Muslim children in North America. During the initial growth of weekend and after-school Islamic educational programs in the late 1970s, IQRA Education Foundation was established in Chicago by two Muslim educators in order to develop curricular materials for teaching Islam. This initiative relates to the category of religious studies as a separate course of study or a subject-specific task. This meant that early Islamic schools adopted the public secular curriculum almost in its entirety, with the exception of particular content-related exclusions, and then appended courses on Islamic studies to the list of ministry-mandated subjects. Most schools across North America, therefore, relied on the Islamic studies textbook series developed by IQRA Education Foundation during the 1980s and 1990s. At the time when IQRA's work first began there was a dearth of educational material in English about Islam for primary-school children. IQRA sought to fill that void by creating curricular materials for teachers: textbooks, skill books, teacher/parent guides, enrichment books, and educational aids that would organize and package foundational Islamic teachings in a way that was accessible for schools. The early textbook series included teaching Arabic, Qur'anic studies, *Seerah* (the life of the Prophet Muhammad), fundamental aspects of *'aqida* and *fiqh* (beliefs, practices, and guidelines for everyday living), and *akhlaq* (character). The IQRA model soon became the default route for the majority of early Islamic schools attempting to define the "Islamic" in their schools. And for many, if not most, parents, this was sufficient. Since the wide dissemination and use of IQRA materials in many Islamic schools there has been a plethora of similar attempts (most often taking place in the United States) to develop curricular materials for teaching Islamic studies.[38]

Apart from appending Islamic studies onto a mandated provincial curriculum, the other major curricular approach for early Islamic schools was the permeation of Islam into the school environment. Consistent with other faith-based schools, Islamic schools attempted to create a school culture and environment that reinforced religious beliefs, values, traditions, and practices.

For those parents concerned about their children being influenced by commonly held values and lifestyles that ran counter to a religious world view, such permeation in school policies and environment created a controlled environment. The overarching rationale of early immigrants who supported the idea of Islamic schooling as alternatives to public schools was

AIMS AND PRACTICES

quite simply preservation and protection, as discussed earlier. Adopting and adapting to a new culture produced anxieties for some around cultural norms in North American society. The acceptance of dating and premarital sex in secular public schools, for example, was viewed as the most dangerous of lifestyle choices that justified the need for Islamic schooling for many. Such lifestyles, it was feared, not only countered the ethical code of Islam but would lead to the breakdown of the family through inter-religious marriages and sexual promiscuity.[39] Speaking to the urgency of protecting children, the first principal of Mississauga's ISNA School recalled the early days of Islamic schooling:

> The community suffered much within the public school in many ways, our norms, our traditions, our values. Usually we have a high level of protection for our children. And then they go to the public school and are subjected to things that Muslim families actually see as quite shocking. Like using bad words, using drugs, obscenity. And this is why, I say, this [the Islamic school] is an environment that is protected to allow children to learn.[40]

However, it is common knowledge that whether public or Islamic, the level of "protection" of children from social realities is relative. Students in Islamic schools are equally enticed by social norms and trends that shape and at times challenge their sense of personal identity.[41] But a significant segment of Muslim immigrants—in particular, those who supported the establishment of Islamic organizations and schools—were influenced by the contemporary discourses of Islamic conservatism.[42] In relation to permeating the school environment with an Islamic ethos, such conservatism often translated into imposing particular interpretations of Islamic beliefs through school policies. What has become normative in most Islamic school environments is, therefore, an Islamic dress code, segregation of classes (in some schools), and reprimanding students for behaviours deemed sacrilegious. All of this exists alongside daily congregational prayers and school walls decorated with Islamic teachings from the Qur'an and prophetic tradition.

Aside from permeating the school environment with an Islamic ethos, the development of Islamic studies course materials for elementary and secondary school students has to an extent been a tangible result of the past 30 years of Islamic school growth. From IQRA to newer attempts, textbooks and teaching aids for imparting basic beliefs and practices of Islam have evolved with more effective instructional tools for student interest.

86

These textbook series have also filled an important and urgent void for the day-to-day function of Islamic schools. However, for many Muslim educators in the field, both Islamic studies textbooks and a permeated school environment remain superficial appendages that are insufficient in defining an Islamic pedagogy. As one Canadian Islamic school principal said in an interview, "apart from that [basic religious education], it's just a regular school."[43]

As schools began to blossom across major cities in Canada and the United States, the discourse also began to shift. Muslim educators who initiated many of the early schools, along with a growing number of teachers in the field, began to question whether Islamic schools were "Islamic" enough—or, more accurately, whether what defined Islamic schools at the time (permeation and appended religious studies) was the extent of an Islamic school's potential. The conservative discourse that monitored beliefs also began to shift toward thinking about schools as transformative spaces where faith practice would be appealing.[44] The conceptions of "being Muslim" shifted, for example, from teaching children rudiments of faith to community service and character education. All of these shifts encouraged new considerations for Islamic school curriculum from one that appended religious studies to one that integrated and infused it.

The critique of some Muslim educators was that the initial curricular attempts in Islamic schools reflected the immigrant experience and the impact of colonial schooling alluded to earlier. One educator described the early model of Islamic schools as one that "thrived from the secularization of Muslim education from the colonial period." He elaborated by stating,

> That's what they [immigrant Muslims] all knew in their home countries. You have the Western subjects and then you have Islam added on to it. You have the Islamic sciences but you don't have time for that of course so you put a little bit of Qur'an, a little bit of *fiqh* [Islamic law], a little bit of *seerah* [history of the early period of Islam], and you call it Islamic studies—none of which is based on pedagogy. So you have a secularized framework and a watered down content and you expect to do miracles—none of it based on pedagogy—none of it.[45]

The challenge for Islamic schools has been to redefine form and structure in relation to pedagogical principles that, outside of the First World Conference, have not been seriously deliberated. The Council of Islamic Schools in North America (CISNA) initially attempted such a project but has largely been dormant, outside of school accreditation, since its inception in the late 1980s.[46] As a result, there have been a few notable attempts, largely in the United States and one in Canada, to "rewrite the curriculum of every subject so that Islamic knowledge/thinking is integrated into every subject."[47]

The Inadequacy of Initial Curricular Attempts— Toward Integration

The challenge in developing an integrated curriculum is twofold: first, the term *integration* is complex in itself and can be interpreted in a multitude of ways; second, it requires a re-writing of an entire curriculum—a project that is difficult due to a lack of funding and resources, in particular in an Islamic school community that lacks an overarching body to bring together disparate schools and smaller organizations.

On the first issue of the multiple meanings of integration, I borrow an example from literature on Jewish day schools that illustrates the numerous ways in which teachers understand the task of integration. I synthesized the following eight approaches from an article by Jon Levisohn, who writes about Jewish education in America or interpretations of what integration means to teachers:

1. the development of faith-based practices and language throughout the school environment, as discussed earlier;
2. making connections through similarities between views held in religious studies with those in social and political studies, e.g., the American Revolution and the founding of the State of Israel;
3. the study of prominent religious figures, intellectuals, achievements, and contributions to civilization;
4. comparing contemporary political and social debates with classical conceptions in traditional sources: e.g., biblical, Rabbinic, medieval, and modern thought;
5. training religious studies teachers to teach outside of formal religious studies and into other subject areas so that students have model teachers who integrate subject areas;
6. to teach about political and cultural schisms from within the larger diaspora of religious communities, in order to understand the development of differences;
7. "add and stir" approach to integration, where bits of religious content are simply "appended" to existing curriculum;
8. teaching through guiding questions and self-exploration into the role of religious communities.[48]

BETWEEN IMMIGRATING AND INTEGRATING | MEMON

For faith-based schools, the above analysis illustrates the number of ways in which religious beliefs and the historical struggles, contributions, and cultures of a particular people can be integrated into existing school curricula. Some teachers see the task as relying more heavily on language, others on cultural identity and history, and yet others see integration related to the lived practice of religious tenets. The challenge for faith-based schools, Islamic schools in particular, that have yet to develop an integrated curricular framework for all schools, is balancing between various haphazard attempts at integration that depend on a handful of lead teachers. The absence of a framework is what one Jewish education scholar, Alex Pomson, has labelled "weak integration" because there is no epistemological synthesis across disciplines.[49] Students as a result receive disconnected meanings and messages about their identity that are again dependent on the training, commitment, and conviction of the teacher.

The challenge of curricular integration was also on the minds of many Islamic school pioneers. In fact, some have been calling for a *tawhidic* curriculum, one that is unified by an Islamic epistemology of *tawhid* (the Oneness of God), since the 1990s when it was still unpopular in the minds of Muslim parents.[50] As described earlier in the contextualization of the development of early Islamic schools, many Muslim immigrants who supported the first Islamic schools were not keen on any attempt to radically alter the conventional curriculum. They entered with the assumption that the public secular "curriculum is basically sound, needing only a bit of infusion of Islamic ideas here and there."[51]

The challenge for Islamic school visionaries has, therefore, been the task of moving beyond both weak integration and the appendage of Islamic studies as separate subject areas. To address these challenges, a number of curricular initiatives have been founded, including one in Edmonton by the first publicly funded Islamic school in Canada that calls for an "epistemic correction of knowledge."[52] These initiatives are distinct from the curriculum organizations such as IQRA discussed above in that an attempt is made to first identify an Islamic world view and then to adapt conventional learning outcomes into a faith-based framework. From such an approach, it is insufficient to begin a class on rain or the water cycle, for example, with a verse from the Qur'an. Rather, the water cycle would be introduced and explained to students in relation to its physical, natural, and spiritual significances as interrelated and interdependent to a God-centred, or *tawhidic*, way of knowing the world.[53] The approach of the Edmonton-based Muslim Education Foundation (MEF) is based on three primary concepts: *tawhid* (Oneness of God), *risalah* (prophecy), and *ma'ad* (the Return). The aim of

AIMS AND PRACTICES

the MEF is to develop an education model that allows children to understand existence and their own place through a deeper understanding of the
various levels of existence from an Islamic world view. Developments like
the MEF and many others in the United States represent a drastic shift in
the curricular approaches in Islamic schooling. What began as superficial
attempts at appending are now beginning to be more holistic and thematic
ways of integrating, and in fact, in cases like MEF, are initiating new frameworks that are epistemologically grounded in an Islamic world view. These
developments, which are embedded within concerted critiques of the quality and uniqueness of Islamic schooling, are, however, representative of a
significant level of introspection that pervades the field today.

Returning Full Circle: Questioning the Purpose of Islamic Schooling

The fact that Islamic schools have survived, if not significantly grown, in a
post-9/11 era of media misrepresentations, public scrutiny, and politically
charged Islamophobia must be contextualized.[54] Prior to and since 9/11,
Islamic schools have become deeply introspective. What began for many
early Canadian Muslim immigrants as a fear, distrust, and anxiety about a
new life in a new land has become insufficient to define the aims and objectives of Islamic schooling. As many schools have become more established
and now attract a second and third generation of Canadian Muslims as
teachers and students, contextualizing this growth within a post-9/11 era
has meant a renewed voice that questions whether these schools are isolat-
ing or civically integrating young Muslims.

Over the past decade in particular there has been a growing number of
voices that question the purpose and pedagogy of Islamic schools. Replicating curriculum from public and other faith-based institutions is not an
alternative vision; nor is simply "protecting" children a rationale worthy of
the work of Islamic schools. One of the participants in my study, a director of an Islamic school, told me, "we have to be clear why we started this.
And if we say that we started this school to protect our children that's a fall-
back position. I didn't start this school to protect them...."[55] Reiterating the
voices of those parent supporters who send their children to Islamic schools
with academic preparatory expectations rather than nurturing a sense of
faith-consciousness, he continued, "Why are we here? When they [parents]
come and ask me what our standardized test scores are, how many of our
kids are going to Harvard? I say wait a minute, you know, why are we here?
Are we here just to replicate another Prep school? I don't think so. If we are

BETWEEN IMMIGRATING AND INTEGRATING | MEMON

not here to offer an alternative vision of the human being, of life, then replicating what already exists is shameful."[56]

Another Islamic school pioneer mirrored the same sentiment, emphasizing the need for introspection and thinking anew: "I think that's why every school has to periodically if not regularly ask the question, 'Why are we here? Why is this Islamic school here....? What's the point? What are we doing?'"[57] The need for rethinking the purpose and pedagogy of Islamic schools has come from two overarching concerns: first, the recognition that current practices in Islamic schools are relatively conventional—implementing a comparatively untouched secular public-school curriculum with an external Islamic ethos;[58] and second, a concern that what is integrated from an Islamic world view is approached in a manner that is stale, irrelevant, and decontextualized.[59]

Although most of the voices of school pioneers and researchers are American, arguably much of the discourse about change and introspection has its roots in Canada. For example, a landmark conference for Islamic schools and Muslim educators alike sparked new conversations and levels of consciousness about the education of Muslim children and, more importantly, the vision of education in Islam. The *Beyond Schooling: Building Communities That Matter* conference held in 2001 at the Ontario Institute for Studies in Education (OISE) at the University of Toronto garnered international interest from Muslim educators who were encouraged to rethink the purpose of schooling and the potential of Islamic education. Similar to the landmark World Conference on Muslim Education in 1977, the *Beyond Schooling* conference in many ways served as the catalyst for new discourses and conceptualizations of the aims of Islamic schooling by encouraging a deeper engagement with educational philosophy. From the establishment of the first Islamic schools in the late 1970s to the deliberation over curricular approaches since, the trajectory of growth for Islamic schools in many ways has now made urgent a discourse about the purpose and pedagogy of Islamic schools.

Notes

1 This chapter focuses on full-time Islamic day schools (K–12) that follow a ministry-mandated curriculum. There are also evening and weekend supplementary programs to teach Islam, as well as traditional *madrassa* schools that teach the Islamic sciences more formally. For more information on the latter, see Nadeem Memon, "From Mosques to Madrassas: Muslim Communities in Canada in Search for Preservation and Renewal," in *Islam in the Hinterlands:*

Muslim Cultural Politics in Canada, ed. Jasmin Zine (Vancouver: University of British Columbia Press, 2012).

2 Ontario Ministry of Education: Private Elementary and Secondary Schools shows that there were 46 Islamic schools in Ontario alone in 2010 (http://www .edu.gov.on.ca/eng/general/elemsec/privsch/). Data on the number of Islamic schools in the rest of the country are circumspect. However, informal data gathered by Canadian Muslim associations such as the Muslim World League show the existence of 47 schools across Canada, with 33 in Ontario (http://mwl canada.org/canada/schools.htm). I draw my data on the assumption that the information on the Ontario Ministry of Education site is far more up to date. If that assumption holds, there are 13 more schools in Canada than the MWL site shows at minimum, totalling at least 60 Islamic schools across the country.

3 In the United States, the earliest Islamic schools have their roots in the Nation of Islam and can be traced back to the 1930s. Known as Sister Clara Muham- mad Schools since the late 1970s, these schools in many ways preceded the establishment of full-time day schools by the MSA or the ISNA. Among immi- grant communities, the first full-time day schools are attributed to the ISNA; however, even in the 1970s there were Muslim communities across North America that were in the process of establishing schools and were not con- nected to ISNA. Although the ISNA considers itself to be representative of all diverse Muslim communities, not all Muslim communities consider them- selves a part of or represented by the ISNA. See Nadeem Memon, "From Protest to Praxis: A History of Islamic Schools in North America," Ph.D. Dissertation, Ontario Institute for Studies in Education, University of Toronto, 2009, for a more detailed historical account.

4 Memon, "From Protest to Praxis."

5 The Islamization of knowledge movement is rooted within the discourse of Islamic revivalism and popularized in the field of education, in particular in the late 1970s after the First World Conference on Islamic Education in Mecca in 1977. The Islamization of Knowledge movement called for a revamping of higher-education institutions in the Muslim world that would recognize the primacy of an Islamic world view in all subject areas. There was, however, dis- tinctions between the ways in which Muslim intellectuals understood the pro- ject of Islamization. See Ali Zaidi, "Islam, Modernity, and the Human Sciences: Toward a Dialogical Approach," Ph.D. dissertation, York University, 2007.

6 Seyyed Hossein Nasr, *Traditional Islam in the Modern World* (London: Kegan Paul International 1987).

7 Muhammad Naquib Al-Attas, *The Concept of Education in Islam: A Framework for an Islamic Philosophy of Education* (Kuala Lumpur, Malaysia: International Institute for Islamic Thought and Civilization 1999), 12.

8 These Arabic terms hold multiple meanings and can be translated differently. The simple translations provided are the commonly used translations from contemporary literature on Islamic education.

9 Al-Attas, *The Concept of Education in Islam*, 12.

10 Al-Attas, *The Concept of Education in Islam*, 19–21.

11 Al-Attas, *The Concept of Education in Islam*, 47–49.

12 Al-Attas, *The Concept of Education in Islam*, 19

13 Al-Attas, *The Concept of Education in Islam*, 26–27.

14 Al-Attas, *The Concept of Education in Islam*, 22.

15 Nasr, *Traditional Islam in the Modern World*; Imam Al-Zarnuji, *Instruction of the Student: The Method of Learning*, 2nd ed., trans. G.E. von Grunebaum and Theodora M. Abel (Burr Ridge, IL: Starlatch, 2003).

16 It should be noted that Al-Attas's theories and the concept of Islamization are far more complex and contested than what I have presented here. There are a handful of Muslim scholars who have debated and articulated divergent positions on Islamization, and there are equally a number of scholars who have challenged the conception of Islamization in its entirety. For a deeper analysis of the issue of Islamization and its positions, see A.H. Zaidi, "Muslim Reconstruction of Knowledge and the Re-enchantment of Modernity," *Theory, Culture, and Society* 23, no. 5 (2006): 69–91; Bassam Tibi, "Culture and Knowledge: The Politics of Islamization of Knowledge as a Postmodern Project? The Fundamentalist Claim to De-Westernization," *Theory, Culture & Society* 12, no. 1 (1995): 1–24.

17 Whether overarching "principles" of education from within the Islamic tradition can be determined is also debatable. Principles of Islamic education that are articulated by Muslim scholars and educators are considered by some to be contextual and cultural interpretations, and by others to be definitive truths. See Farid Panjwani, "The 'Islamic' in Islamic Education: Assessing the Discourse," *Current Issues in Comparative Education* 7, no. 1 (2004): 19–29.

18 Phone interview: Freda Shamma, 17 March 2009.

19 Phone interview: Tasneema Ghazi, 24 April 2008.

20 Jame Mosque in Toronto was among the first to begin a formal educational program for children. Abdalla Idris Ali, who emigrated from Sudan to pursue a doctorate at the University of Toronto, was one of the first teachers at the evening and weekend school and soon was appointed as its educational director in the late 1970s.

21 Personal interview: Abdalla Idris Ali, Kansas City, 25 February 2008.

22 Robert W. Hefner and Muhammad Q. Zaman, eds., *Schooling Islam: The Culture and Politics of Modern Education* (Princeton, NJ: Princeton University Press, 2007).

AIMS AND PRACTICES

23 Personal interview: Abdalla Idris Ali, Kansas City, 25 February 2008.

24 Many Canadian Muslims who immigrated from parts of South Asia and the Middle East that were once colonized (by the British in particular) brought with them the schooling experiences from what are often called "colonial schools," i.e., schools established by the British in India, for example. Parents who sought to establish Islamic schools, therefore, often relied on their own schooling experiences, which reflected conventional practices/models in Western secular educational pedagogy such as the limiting of religious studies to a single subject.

25 Jasmin Zine, *Canadian Islamic Schools: Unraveling the Politics of Faith, Gender, Knowledge, and Identity* (Toronto: University of Toronto Press, 2008), 288–94.

26 Personal interview: M.D. Khalid, Toronto, 25 September 2007.

27 Personal interview: Abdalla Idris Ali, Kansas City, 25 February 2008.

28 Kent Greenwalt, *Does God Belong in Public Schools?* (Princeton, NJ: Princeton University Press, 2004), 1–3.

29 Personal interview: M.D. Khalid, Toronto, 25 September 2007.

30 Lois Sweet, *God in the Classroom: The Controversial Issue of Religion in Canada's Schools* (Toronto: McClelland and Stewart 1997), 75–76.

31 Aminah Beverly McCloud, "Islam in America: The Mosaic," in *Religion and Immigration: Christian, Jewish, and Muslim Experiences in the United States*, ed. Yvonne Y. Haddad, Jane I. Smith, and John L. Esposito (New York: Altamira Press 2003), 159.

32 Phone interview: Seema Imam, 18 December 2007.

33 Personal interview: Abdalla Idris Ali, Kansas City, 25 February 2008.

34 Hamza Yusuf, "Foreword," in *The Instruction of the Student and the Method of Learning*, by Imam Al-Zarnuji, original translation by G.E. Von Grunebaum and Theodora M. Abel (Burr Ridge, IL: Starlatch, 2001), vii.

35 Institute for Catholic Education, *Curriculum Matters: A Resource for Catholic Educators* (Toronto: Institute for Catholic Education 1996), 22–26.

36 Jon Levisohn, "From Integration of Curricula to a Pedagogy of Integrity," *Journal of Jewish Education* 74 (2008): 264–94.

37 Memon, "Social Consciousness in Canadian Islamic Schools?"

38 Other curricular textbook series include *Goodword Islamic Studies* materials, *The Right Path, Hurry to Faith, Al Amal,* and the most popular of the new textbook series, *I Love Islam.*

39 Lois Sweet, *God in the Classroom: The Controversial Issue of Religion in Canada's Schools* (Toronto: McClelland and Stewart 1997), 75.

40 Personal interview: Abdalla Idris, Kansas City, 25 February 2008.

41 Zine, *Canadian Islamic Schools,* 288–94; Loukia K. Sarroub, *All American Yemeni Girls: Being Muslim in a Public School* (Philadelphia: University of Pennsylvania Press), 2005.

42 Memon, "From Protest to Praxis," 177–204.

43 Personal interview: Abdalla Idris Ali, Kansas City, 25 February 2008.

44 Phone interview: Dawud Tauhidi, 7 February 2008.

45 Phone interview: Bilal Ajieb, 25 January 2008.

46 Noura Durkee, "Primary Education of Muslim Children in North America," *Muslim Education Quarterly* 5, no. 1 (1987): 53–81.

47 Freda Shamma, "The Curriculum Challenge of Islamic Schools in America," in *Muslims and Islamization in North America: Problems and Prospects,* ed. Amber Haque. Kuala Lumpur, Malaysia: Amana Publications 1999.

48 Levisohn, "From Integration of Curricula to a Pedagogy of Integrity," 265–72.

49 Pomson, "Knowledge That Doesn't Just Sit There: Considering a Reconception of the Curriculum Integration of Jewish and General Studies," *Religious Education* 96, no. 4 (2001): 543.

50 Dawud Tauhidi, *The Tarbiyah Project: A Renewed Vision of Islamic Education* (Canton, MI: Tarbiyah Institute, 2006).

51 Shamma, "The Curriculum Challenge for Islamic Schools in America," 286.

52 Elma Harder, *Concentric Circles: Nurturing Awe and Wonder in Early Learning* (Sherwood Park, AB: Al-Qalam Publishing, 2006), xv.

53 Harder, *Concentric Circles,* xvi.

54 Memon, "From Protest to Praxis," 7.

55 Personal interview: Dawud Tauhidi, Canton, Michigan, 7 February 2008.

56 Personal interview: Dawud Tauhidi, Canton, Michigan, 7 February 2008.

57 Personal interview: Afeefa Syeed, Chicago, 12 April 2008.

58 Michael Merry, *Culture, Identity, and Islamic Schooling: A Philosophical Approach* (New York: Palgrave Macmillan, 2007), 60.

59 Amjad Hussain, "Recent Western Reflections on Islamic Education," *Religious Education* 103, no. 5 (Oct./Dec. 2008): 585.

Bibliography

Al-Attas, Muhammad Naquib. *The Concept of Education in Islam: A Framework for an Islamic Philosophy of Education.* Kuala Lumpur, Malaysia: International Institute for Islamic Thought and Civilization, 1999.

Al-Zarnuji, Imam. *Instruction of the Student: The Method of Learning.* 2nd ed. Translated by G.E. von Grunebaum and Theodora M. Abel. Foreword by Hazma Yusuf. Burr Ridge, IL: Starlatch, 2001.

AIMS AND PRACTICES

Durkee, Noura. "Primary Education of Muslim Children in North America." *Muslim Education Quarterly* 5, no. 1 (1987): 53–81.

Greenwalt, Kent. *Does God Belong in Public Schools?* Princeton, NJ: Princeton University Press, 2004.

Harder, Elma. *Concentric Circles: Nurturing Awe and Wonder in Early Learning.* Sherwood Park, AB: Al-Qalam Publishing, 2006.

Hefner, Robert W., and Muhammad Q. Zaman, eds. *Schooling Islam: The Culture and Politics of Modern Education.* Princeton, NJ: Princeton University Press, 2007.

Hussain, Amjad. "Recent Western Reflections on Islamic Education." *Religious Education* 103, no. 5 (Oct./Dec. 2008): 579–85.

Institute for Catholic Education. *Curriculum Matters: A Resource for Catholic Educators.* Toronto: Institute for Catholic Education, 1996.

Levisohn, Jon. "From Integration of Curricula to a Pedagogy of Integrity." *Journal of Jewish Education* 74 (2008): 264–94.

McCloud, Aminah Beverly. "Islam in America: The Mosaic." In *Religion and Immigration: Christian, Jewish, and Muslim Experiences in the United States,* edited by Yvonne Y. Haddad, Jane I. Smith, and John L. Esposito. New York: Altamira Press, 2003.

Memon, Nadeem. "From Mosques to Madrassas: Muslim Communities in Canada in Search for Preservation and Renewal." In *Islam in the Hinterlands: Muslim Cultural Politics in Canada,* edited by Jasmin Zine. Vancouver: University of British Columbia Press, 2012.

———. "From Protest to Praxis: A History of Islamic Schools in North America." Ph.D. Dissertation, Ontario Institute for Studies in Education, University of Toronto, 2009.

———. "Social Consciousness in Canadian Islamic Schools?" in *The Education of Muslim Minority Students: Comparative Perspective,* edited by M. McAndrew, J. Ipgrave, and A. Triki-Yamani, special issue, *Journal of International Migration and Integration (JIMI)* 11, no. 1 (2010): 109–17.

Merry, Michael. *Culture, Identity and Islamic Schooling: A Philosophical Approach.* New York: Palgrave Macmillan, 2007.

Nasr, Seyyed Hossein. *Traditional Islam in the Modern World.* London: Kegan Paul International, 1987.

Panjwani, Farid. "The 'Islamic' in Islamic Education: Assessing the Discourse." *Current Issues in Comparative Education* 7, no. 1 (2004): 19–29.

Pomson, Alex. "Knowledge That Doesn't Just Sit There: Considering a Reconception of the Curriculum Integration of Jewish and General Studies." *Religious Education* 96, no. 4 (2001): 528–45.

Sarroub, Loukia. *All American Yemeni Girls: Being Muslim in a Public School.* Philadelphia: University of Pennsylvania Press, 2005.

Shamma, Freda. "The Curriculum Challenge for Islamic Schools in America." In *Muslims and Islamization in North America: Problems and Prospects,* edited by Amber Haque. Kuala Lumpur, Malaysia: Amana Publications, 1999.

Sweet, Lois. *God in the Classroom: The Controversial Issue of Religion in Canada's Schools.* Toronto: McClelland and Stewart, 1997.

Tauhidi, Dawud. *The Tarbiyah Project: A Renewed Vision of Islamic Education.* Canton, MI: Tarbiyah Institute, 2006.

Tibi, Bassam. "Culture and Knowledge: The Politics of Islamization of Knowledge as a Postmodern Project? The Fundamentalist Claim to De-Westernization." *Theory, Culture & Society* 12, no. 1 (1995): 1–24.

Yusuf, Hamza. "Foreword," in *The Instruction of the Student and the Method of Learning* by Imam Al-Zarnuji, original translation by G.E. Von Grunebaum and Theodora M. Abel. Burr Ridge, IL: Starlatch Press, 2001.

Zaidi, Ali. "Islam, Modernity, and the Human Sciences: Toward a Dialogical Approach." Ph.D. dissertation, York University, 2007.

———. "Muslim Reconstruction of Knowledge and the Re-enchantment of Modernity." *Theory, Culture, and Society* 23, no. 5 (2006): 69–91.

Zine, Jasmin. *Canadian Islamic Schools: Unraveling the Politics of Faith, Gender, Knowledge, and Identity.* Toronto: University of Toronto Press, 2008.

PART B

FAITH *and* CITIZENSHIP

CHAPTER FOUR

JEWISH EDUCATION, DEMOCRACY, AND PLURALISTIC ENGAGEMENT

Greg Beiles

In his book *For Goodness Sake: Religious Schools and Education for Democratic Citizenry,* Walter Feinberg foregrounds the paradoxical challenge of liberal democratic pluralism: how do we allow for the reproduction of diverse communities without which there can be no pluralism, while at the same time ensure the values, attitudes, and dispositions that are necessary to sustain liberal democracy? Many would argue that pluralism is one of the necessary values of a healthy liberal democracy. At the same time, the reproduction of the unique discursive community risks creating isolated groups with diminished commitment to the public good; it may even permit the establishment of communities that promote anti-liberal, anti-democratic attitudes. Feinberg focuses on this issue in the context of religious schooling, where "the educational problem is to find a way to respect religious teachings while reproducing in each generation the values, attitudes, and dispositions guaranteed by and for a liberal democracy."[1] This chapter is a case study of how a Jewish elementary and middle school takes up this challenge by striving to nurture, within the context of a Jewish religious education, the dispositions and values required for pluralistic, democratic citizenship.

The Toronto Heschel School is an interdenominational Jewish Day School. The school has approximately 280 students (as of 2009) from Junior Kindergarten to grade eight. One of the core founding principles of the Heschel School is to provide a safe space for interdenominational pluralism.

According the school's mission statement, "The mandate of the School is to draw its students from a wide range of Jewish observance.... The School's philosophy is based on religious pluralism, understanding and mutual respect." For the past thirteen years I have been associated with the school as a teacher, curriculum developer, and teacher trainer. In many ways my view of the school is that of an insider, a "believer" with regard to its educational mission and pedagogical methods. At the same time, I came to the project of religious education as an outsider and retain some ambivalence about it. My own upbringing was very secular, and only nominally Jewish. I attended diverse, multicultural, multi-ethnic public schools, and I have deeply ingrained instincts about the importance of universal public education. I identify as a Canadian who believes strongly in multiculturalism, diversity, and liberal democracy.

Because of my involvement with the school, I cannot claim to undertake a dispassionate analysis of its work. Rather, I invoke for my method William E. Connolly's notion of "critical responsiveness"—that is, to work from within a tradition or community while maintaining a critical perspective vis-à-vis its limitations and possibilities.[2] In order to maintain some objectivity, I have attempted to limit my own observations and impressions of the school. The data I have collected derive from curriculum documents, interviews with key administrators and educators, and samples of student work provided to me by other teachers.

To elucidate and clarify criteria for what counts as democratic pluralism I draw upon the work of two scholars. The first is Feinberg, whose aforementioned book takes up directly the questions of religious education in relation to liberal pluralistic democracy. The second is Connolly, who advocates a rich plurality of diverse metaphysical perspectives within public discourse. Feinberg and Connolly complement each other well, in the sense that the former outlines classic criteria for liberal democracy, while the latter seeks to reform and enrich liberalism by exploring the "visceral register of subjectivity and intersubjectivity"[3] that is at play in pluralist discourse and practices. In this chapter, I integrate the more formal criteria for liberal democratic pluralism articulated by Feinberg, with Connolly's attention to viscerality and intersubjectivity in pluralistic encounters. I explore how The Toronto Heschel School addresses these criteria for pluralistic democracy within the context of religious education. These criteria, based on an integration of the criteria expressed by Feinberg and Connolly, comprise the following: (1) respect for democratic institutions and processes; (2) opportunities for engagement among individuals with diverse meta-

JEWISH EDUCATION, DEMOCRACY, ENGAGEMENT | BEILES

physical positions; (3) recognition of contingencies in our own tradition in order to respect the beliefs of others and to seek opportunities for renewal within our own tradition; (4) nurturing complex identities through a recognition of the inter- and intrasubjective processes through which identity is formed; (5) cultivation of "arts of the self" as part of inter- and intrasubjective relations; and (6) a sense of moral autonomy that is attuned to its own visceral and infrasensible dimensions.

Ultimately, a faith-based school can meet the demands of liberal democracy if it is able to cultivate among students an identity that is at once grounded in its own traditions while at the same time oriented toward the intersubjective requirements of democratic engagement.

Democratic Process and Culture

One of the main ways in which The Toronto Heschel School nurtures democratic habits of mind is by finding *and emphasizing* correlations between democratic institutions and processes in secular society with democratic gestures and impulses in the Jewish religious tradition. The school accomplishes this in large part through its civics curriculum,[4] which integrates Jewish sources with experiential learning about democracy. The formal curriculum in this area begins in grade five, with an introduction to democracy through a study of rights and responsibilities. Students begin by considering the rights, responsibilities, and privileges each of them has in their home. They then look at two "rights" documents: the United Nations Declaration of the Rights of the Child, and excerpts from the Canadian Charter of Rights and Freedoms. Students explore the content of these documents by ranking and debating the relative importance of each of the prescribed rights. These sources are then juxtaposed to sources from the Torah, primarily 'Aseret Hadibrot—the Ten Commandments. As students readily discover, the Ten Commandments is not a list of rights, but rather a list of responsibilities. Students compare the responsibilities found in the Torah with rights they have discovered in the other two documents. They discuss questions such as these: Do all responsibilities have corresponding rights? Which comes first, rights or responsibilities? Can you have rights without responsibilities? Can you have responsibilities without rights? While the discussion is more or less open-ended, one of the stated goals of the curriculum is that students recognize that without the communal acceptance of responsibilities it would not be possible to sustain rights. These abstract ideas are brought home to the students through practical analogies. For example, if students want the right to a full recess, they will have to take responsibility for being prepared to go outside on time. The capstone activity of the unit is for the students to generate their own classroom Bill of Rights and Responsibilities. Once it is drafted, this document is posted in the classroom instead of the traditional list of "class rules." The Bill of Rights and Responsibilities is referred to throughout the school year as issues that it addresses arise.

Before starting to draft their Bill, students are introduced to two key concepts that structure their process. First, they learn that Canada is a constitutional monarchy, and that the Governor General is the representative of the crown. An analogy is made between the Governor General and the classroom teacher, who represents the principal of the school and therefore must ultimately sign off on the students' Bill. This analogy helps students understand the role of the Governor General in Canadian government and, at the same time, provides true accountability and limits for their own Bill. The list that the students derive will have to be consistent with the broader philosophy of the school and, of course, the law of the land. Teachers point out to students that this reflects a well-known Talmudic concept that the law of the land takes precedence over internally derived religious law.[5] Next, students are introduced to the notion of consensus democracy by learning about the Iroquois First Nations, who used consensus-based decision-making processes. A study of Iroquois democracy expands the definition of Canadian government beyond the traditional study of the parliamentary system and opens the way for a deeper exploration of intercultural perspectives on democracy. As the year progresses, students learn to use different forms of democratic decision making—including simple majority, "first past the post" plurality, and party voting. However, their Bill of Rights and Responsibilities—as a "constitutional" document—must be developed with the agreement of everyone: a full consensus.

To discuss their ideas and achieve a consensus, students learn how to use a discursive process in which they rotate roles as a chairperson, keeper of the speakers' list, and recorder. As teachers who have been involved with this unit report, the process of reaching consensus is seldom easy, and students learn that democracy (especially consensus democracy) is a system that requires considerable patience, forbearance, extra-parliamentary lobbying (i.e., some cajoling and debating at recess), and, ultimately, compromise.

The learning outcomes of the grade five civics program are manifold. Students learn about forms of procedural democracy by actually engaging in democratic process. They learn about some of the formal structures and

JEWISH EDUCATION, DEMOCRACY, ENGAGEMENT | BEILES

institutions of Canadian democracy by making analogies between these institutions and democratic practices in the classroom. Most importantly, they practice the habits of mind required for democratic culture: listening to one another, waiting their turn to speak, respectful debate, flexibility, and willingness to compromise. The use of experiential pedagogy, in which the outcome of learning is directly relevant to students' classroom experience, generates a level of critical engagement and a sense of personal and collective agency. These aspects of the unit satisfy the exposure to democratic process and practice in citizenship that Feinberg holds as so important. The use of discussion and debate in the context of an authentic political project practises the agonistic respect among constituents advocated by Connolly. From the point of view of Jewish education, the civics curriculum helps students experience Judaism in a dynamic, non-dogmatic, and non-exclusive way: they experience their Jewish learning as a process in which Jewish sources are used creatively in relation to other systems, and for a real-life purpose.

In grade five, then, students spend their year-long civics course learning the basics of democracy, democratic systems, and protocols for democratic decision making. By the time they reach Junior High (grades six to eight), students at The Toronto Heschel School are expected to be able to use these protocols in weekly class meetings to discuss, vote on, and carry out *tikkun olam* (social justice) projects. The scope of the projects is structured by the Talmudic idea that the obligation for social justice starts locally, first with one's own community.[6] As the youngest Junior High cohort, the grade six students are obliged to devise a *tikkun olam* project that pertains to the school community itself. Since the grade six science curriculum focuses on earth sciences, this project is usually oriented toward an environmental-awareness project within the school. In grade seven, the scope of the project is expanded to the larger Jewish community, with a particular focus on Israel. By grade eight, students are required to conceive of a project that goes beyond the Jewish community. This structure allows students to appreciate the wisdom in the Jewish concept of care for those in closest proximity— after all, it can be more challenging to care for those close to you than it is to send money to a distant and abstract other; at the same time, students learn that it is not sufficient to care only for your own, and that the concentric circles of care must be expanded.

The use of democratic process in the context of a social-justice project is not accidental. The idea for the civics program at The Toronto Heschel

FAITH AND CITIZENSHIP

School was initially inspired by the moral development research of Lawrence Kohlberg. Kohlberg and his colleagues discovered that progress
toward higher stages of moral development[7] was accelerated in societies with democratic values and decision-making systems.[8] Based on their
conclusions about moral development, Kohlberg and his colleagues developed their Just Community School project[9] in which high-school students
participated in democratic forums empowered to make decisions about
school policy and functioning. For The Toronto Heschel School students,
the scope of their decision-making process is less broad, focusing primarily on their social-justice projects. This more limited scope makes sense,
because the students are much younger than those who participated in
Kohlberg's projects. The idea that democratic process should be directed
toward social action also reflects a traditional Jewish idea that moral action,
not only merely cognitive moral process, is incumbent upon us. This idea
is rooted in the biblical concept of *na'aseh venishma'*—"first we do, then we
understand"—a perspective on cognition that suggests that action shapes
ethical development. The use of democratic process for the purpose of
executing a moral project is, therefore, an integration of two pedagogies
of moral development: the Kohlbergian insight that democratic process
stimulates the ethical point of view, and the Judaic notion that moral action
stimulates moral consciousness.

The use of Kohlberg's research and model for school-based democracy
exemplifies the willingness of The Toronto Heschel School staff to incorporate secular pedagogies into their teaching and to seek ways to integrate
these approaches with traditional Jewish sources and methods. From the
point of view of Moreh E,[10] a grade eight civics teacher, there may even be
correlations between democratic process and religious experience:

> I can reflect personally from teaching this unit that there is an element of
> something going on that's spiritual or holy when kids positively engage in
> the democratic process. It is almost a real act of holiness when you are trans-
> formed from a classroom into an ideal way that humans should be interact-
> ing, which involves listening and true understanding and really engaging
> with the democratic process without being obsessed with the product.

Moreh E's experience of the democratic process as a holy or religious experience correlates with texts that the students study in preparation for their
civics class. At the beginning of the year, before engaging in the democratic
process, the Junior High students spend some time studying Jewish texts

JEWISH EDUCATION, DEMOCRACY, ENGAGEMENT | BEILES

that pertain to the issue of democracy and democratic culture. The first text students study is the well-known debate between Rabbi Eliezer and the other sages over the ritual status of a particular oven.[11] Rabbi Eliezer claims that the oven is not susceptible to ritual impurity, whereas the sages contend that it is. To support his claim, Rabbi Eliezer invokes various miraculous events, such as the uprooting of a carob tree, the reversal of the flow of a river, and the collapse of the walls of *Beit Hamidrash*—the house of learning. Each of these miracles takes place, except for the collapse of the walls, which tilt diagonally out of respect for both sides of the argument. Despite his success in invoking miracles, the sages resist Rabbi Eliezer's claim to authority. Finally, Rabbi Eliezer says,

> "If the Law agrees with me, let it be proved from heaven." Sure enough, a divine voice cried out, "Why do you dispute with Rabbi Eliezer, with whom the Law always agrees?" Rabbi Joshua stood up and protested: "The Torah is not in heaven! [Deut. 30:12]. We pay no attention to a divine voice because long ago at Mount Sinai You wrote in your Torah at Mount Sinai, 'After the majority must one incline'" [Ex. 23:2].

The radical conclusion of the rabbis is that no person can claim unique access to divine truth. Using a common trope of Rabbinic exegesis, the **Talmud** cites biblical passages to substantiate key ideas: once the Torah was revealed to humanity at Mount Sinai, its interpretation became a matter of human discourse, and majority rule is applied in deciding matters of legal dispute. By studying this text as an introduction to their civics course, students learn that there are valid correlations between democratic process and Rabbinic tradition. Not all Jewish schools would emphasize such correlations, nor would they bring this provocative text to the attention of their students. The Toronto Heschel School does so explicitly to help students see correlations between Jewish values and the values of democratic pluralism.

Both Feinberg and Connolly repeatedly emphasize that democratic procedure is necessary but not sufficient for a rich, multi-vocal discourse. For Connolly, in particular, the cultivation of certain dispositions or "relational arts" is necessary for pluralistic discourse to flourish. The importance of cultivating these democratic habits of mind is not lost on The Toronto Heschel School teachers. As part of their preparation for democratic discussions, the students study a text from the Mishna (a second century C.E. legal text) and its commentary (Tosefot Yom Tov) that speak to the kinds of motivations and discursive habits that are necessary for successful discourse and social action:

FAITH AND CITIZENSHIP

Rabbi Yochanah Hasandlar said: "Every gathering which is convened for Heaven's sake will end up with success; every gathering which is not convened for Heaven's sake will not end up with success."[12]

The criterion for success is not whether the gathering was for a sacred or secular cause but what motivation guides the conveners. Even if a gathering has no direct connection with a mitzvah it will be blessed with success if its organizers were motivated by a desire to serve Heaven through it. On the other hand, even if the gathering is convened for the purpose of a mitzvah it is doomed to failure if its organizers are motivated by a desire for honor or anything else not for Heaven's sake.[13]

The gist of these sources is that when a group comes together to plan and implement a project, even if the project is for the purpose of fulfilling a religious commandment, the project will fail if the participants have the wrong attitude. While the correct attitude is only alluded to through the phrase "for the sake of heaven"—that is, for a higher purpose—one clearly stated obstacle to success is the desire for personal honour. When discussed with the students, the "desire for personal honour" serves as shorthand for any kind of selfish behaviours that could hijack or derail democratic process. To draw students' attention to attitudes and skills required for effective democratic process, and to create procedures to help reinforce these attitudes and skills, a list of Protocols for Democratic Discussion are discussed and posted in the classroom:

1. Be prompt and prepared.
2. Allow one person to speak at a time.
3. If you wish to speak, signal to have your name put on the Speakers' list.
4. Express your own opinions and ideas. Try not to speak for others.
5. Stay on topic and connect your ideas to what others have said.
6. If you think you can help someone clarify an idea, check with him or her first.
7. "Share the air time"—avoid repeating your idea once you have expressed it.
8. Express opinions without being judgmental.
9. Take turns in different "roles." Try each of the roles at least one time in the year.
10. Avoid arguing for the sake of arguing.[14]

Several mechanisms are put in place to help students become conscious of how they participate in the discussions with these protocols in mind. Dur-

JEWISH EDUCATION, DEMOCRACY, ENGAGEMENT | BEILES

ing each discussion one or two students play the role of observers, whose job it is to record how successful the group was in adhering to the protocols. At the end of the discussion, the observers report their notes to the class. In addition, each student receives a self-assessment rubric at the beginning of the year, and at various points throughout the year. The rubric allows students to chart their own progress vis-à-vis democratic habits of mind and the Protocols for Democratic Discussion. The civics teachers use the same rubric for their assessment of the students, and the report-card mark for Civics is based on a combination of the teacher and student assessments on these democratic habits of mind. As students progress through the Junior High civics program, they are expected to become increasingly mature in their use of democratic process and increasingly self-aware of their own development vis-à-vis the democratic habits of mind. This goal of metacognitive development speaks to critical thinking and self-reflection that for Feinberg are essential cognitive processes for mature liberal citizenship.

Through the civics curriculum at The Toronto Heschel School, democratic and discursive habits are substantiated by Jewish texts and ultimately serve the purpose of fulfilling the mitzvah of *tikkun olam*. As a result, democratic arts of liberalism and "relational arts of the self" are incorporated into a Judaic telos. This reflects an ancient cultural strategy of Judaism, i.e., to utilize intellectual and cultural techniques of the cultures among which Jews found themselves, within a framework of Jewish values and metaphysics. This geometry of integration avoids the need to adopt the metaphysical assumptions of liberalism, while at the same time nurtures within Judaism those very inclinations that are required by liberal, democratic society. To be sure, these inclinations are already present in Jewish sources—provided one wishes to foreground such sources. This does not mean, however, that Judaism equals liberalism; rather, at the level of discursive practice, and at what Connolly calls the "infrasensible" level of subjective and intersubjective relations, important correlations can be discovered between the two systems.

Complex Identity

Both Connolly and Feinberg stress how important it is that religious and cultural groups recognize the contestability and contingency of their own traditions. Feinberg notes that "the commitment to pluralism requires a certain ability to distance oneself from one's primary commitment, to grant a certain contingency (if not to one's own beliefs, then to the fact that one holds them rather than some other set) and to allow that regardless of 'the truth' of one's own beliefs, others have an equal right to hold conflicting beliefs."[15] For Connolly, awareness of contingency in one's own tradition generates an attitude of "critical responsiveness" that opens up space within one's own world view for innovation and change.[16] In Jewish education, the study of Jewish history is commonly regarded as the ideal vehicle for cultivating pride, attachment, and identity. For this reason, historical events are often presented as uniform and one-dimensional narratives. One wouldn't expect the teaching contingency to be at the top of the agenda in a Jewish history class. Yet at The Toronto Heschel School an exploratory approach to the study of history is employed to help students realize that Jewish responses to historical events are complex, diverse, and contingent on various factors, including influences from other cultures.

Morah D teaches a grade seven history course called Ancient Civilizations, which explores the intersections between the history of the ancient world and Jewish history. Two units in Morah D's class integrate this study of Jewish history with reflections on Jewish identity. The first unit is called The Meaning of Exile and Return. It examines the period in Jewish history known as the **Babylonian** Exile (c. 587 BCE), during which the people of Judea were conquered by the Babylonians and sent into exile in Persia. In addition to learning about the relevant historical events, personages, and geography, students are asked to read and reflect on biblical source texts that give clues about how the people experienced and interpreted the meaning of their exile. Students read the lamentations of Amos (5:16–24), Isaiah (58:1–3), and Psalm 137, which mourn the loss of the Judean homeland. Students compare this view of loss with the pragmatic advice of the prophet Jeremiah, who tells the exiles to "build houses, dwell in them, plant gardens, and eat of them," to settle in the land of exile, and rebuild their lives there (29:5–7). By studying these diverse sources, students recognize that ancient Jews expressed multiple responses to the same historical event. At a broader level, the very process of studying primary sources, rather than relying exclusively on secondary glosses, helps students understand that historical narratives are constructed. In this unit, students also learn how Babylonian culture influenced Judaism, and how traces of these influences remain visible, for instance, in the Persian names of some Jewish months. The students appreciate that the exile and the encounter with Babylon was not merely a minor setback in an otherwise uninterrupted and uniform national development; rather, it was an event that transformed the Jewish people in significant ways. The unit exposes the students to an historical example of what Connolly calls "the politics of becoming"—the process by which suffering and cultural displacement lead to new possibilities and cultural innovation.[17]

As a summative assignment for the Exile unit, each student receives a blank cut-out in the shape of a human form, referred to as their "exile person." On one side of the human form, each student uses drawing or mixed-media collage to represent his or her impression of the experience of exile. On the back, each student attaches an "Artist Statement" that describes the artistic and thematic choices of the collage. In the work samples that Morah D showed me, many students chose to divide the forms up into several sections in order to express the diversity of responses they had learned. The following excerpt from one student's work demonstrates her understanding of multiple dimensions of historical experience:

> In the top left corner I expressed the feeling of hope. On the journey that was taken the Jews had to have hope in order to survive …. In the top right corner, I expressed the feeling of being frightened…. During the walk from Israel to Babylon, they did not know what was in the near future and did not know if they would survive…. In the bottom left corner, I expressed the feeling of relief. I believe that the Jews were relieved after they settled in Babylon and were reassured that everything was alright…. On the shirt of the Jew there are many different shapes that somehow fit together in some shape or form. In my interpretation, I think that this represents the Jews and Babylonians because they came from completely different backgrounds, believed in different Gods and spoke different languages. As they got to know each other and after they had lived together for a while, they began to incorporate each other's customs and everyday lives into their own. The Jews started to speak the Aramaic language and used it through the calendar; they become friends and learned many other things from one another.

This activity is, of course, an act of imaginative interpolation: historical fiction. Certainly, there is a good dose of historical naivety in this twelve-year-old's representation of the events. Nevertheless, it is evident that this student has developed an appreciation of the complexity of emotions, relationships, and influences involved in historical encounters. Her understanding of history is not one in which complexity has been suppressed or ignored in order to foreground a singular historical narrative.

The exercise also operates very much at the visceral level by providing students with evocative primary texts and giving them the opportunity to explore and express their ideas through the arts. I was particularly struck

FAITH AND CITIZENSHIP

by one piece of work that expressed this viscerality. For her project, a student whom I refer to as "C" named her "exile person" Rivka. She was one of the few students to actually give her person a name. C glued a number of clothes pegs onto Rivka's body. The clothes peg on the head held a bunch of words cut out of newspapers. These, wrote C, represent Rivka's thoughts: "She is holding on to her thoughts because she knows that if she lets go of her thoughts and beliefs, she will also let go of herself. Just like how in Psalm 137 the Jews swore not to forget Jerusalem." C goes on to explain:

> Another one of the pins [holds] ribbons forming a Magen David [Star of David]. The Magen David represents Judaism. Rivka is still trying to hold onto her Judaism even though she is not around all Jewish people. I put this pin in her stomach because that's where I believe Judaism and hope are…. The last pin has a tube attached to it representing exile. The point of the tube is pointing into the centre of Rivka to show that all of her emotions are being put there because of the exile. When someone squeezes the tube, the tube will suck up what it's put into and when they let go it all goes out. This motion represents the exile that the Babylonians did to the Jews…. The tube is the centre of Rivka.

One cannot pass over C's remarkable statement that Judaism and hope are "in the stomach" without recalling Connolly's discussion of the "infrasensible." Connolly defines the infrasensible as the realm of "visceral modes of appraisal," or "proto-thoughts" from which "conscious thoughts, feelings, and discursive judgments draw part of their sustenance."[18] Connolly believes that sources of consciousness are dispersed across the body in networks with infrasensible nodes. The stomach is one such node: "This infrasensible centre stores thought-imbued feelings of sadness, anxiety, happiness, disgust, anger, and revenge to be activated under certain circumstances."[19]

C's artist statement exemplifies what is evident in much of the student work: the grade seven Exile project allows students to exercise infrasensible modes of awareness as part of their study of Jewish history. The project also requires students to represent their ideas in two modes, artistic and written, and has them translate the infrasensible into conscious ideas and communicable forms. Translation of visceral, infrasensible experience into narrative discourse is a common strategy for shaping identity; and infrasensible experience can easily be shaped into unitary, unequivocal ideational narratives. However there is something else going on in this grade seven class. By studying diverse primary texts that expose different responses to historical events, students seem able to imagine and express infrasensible experience in a nuanced and complex way. If the goal of teaching Jewish history is to teach Jewish identity, then students come away from this project understanding that "being Jewish" is a complex process involving layers of emotion, change, and dynamic relations with the non-Jewish world.

The question Feinberg compels us to ask is whether this realization of the complexity of one's own identity translates into an understanding of the complexity of the identity and of the experience of others, and, thereby, into an "imaginative connection" with them. When I posed this question to Morah D, she responded,

> We try to downplay the isolationist aspect of Judaism; I don't want these kids leaving the halls of Heschel and to be shocked by the fact that there are other cultures; they need to know that they are a Jew in the world. They need to see themselves as influenced by others; that Judaism is a process and that it didn't spring out of nothing. I would hope that the students learn that that other cultures are important and that they too come from a process, complexities, have a history, literature, may have influenced us and we may have influenced them at some point in our history.

My sense from reading student work is that there are indeed transferable lessons being learned. One student, for example, concluded her Artist Statement with the following remark: "This project has taught me why I shouldn't take my life for granted. I have a family, a house and I am not forced to work all day. So the next time you hear about families being split up and exiled from their homes don't turn off the radio or change the topic. Because would you like to lose everything? I know I wouldn't." Not only has this student made a personal connection with this historical event, but she appears to have derived from it a categorical ethical imperative that transcends the particularity of the historical event. For her, identification with the Jews of the exile serves as a source for broader empathy.

Through the Exile project Morah D helps students recognize that Judaism is a process involving complex emotions and relations. In the second unit of the course, Morah D uses Jewish history as a way to tackle head on the issue of secular vs. Jewish identity. The Jewish encounter with Greek culture, known as the "Hellenistic Period" (c. 300 BCE–70 CE), is the perfect historical context for exploring this tension. Once again, Morah D offers the students the opportunity to analyse primary source evidence of diverse

Jewish responses to a historical event. One of the sources is an image of a Jewish gravestone engraved with Greek lettering above a **menorah** and images of birds and trees. The juxtaposition of Greek lettering with Jewish symbols and pagan nature symbols sparks inquiry into the level of Jewish adoption of Hellenistic culture. Students then read and compare two Rabbinic texts that evince different perspectives on the boundaries of cultural integration. In the first text (Mishna Avodah Zara 3:4), a Greek interlocutor named Proclos asks Rabban Gamliel why he would bathe in a bathhouse decorated with a statue of Aphrodite when Jewish law prohibited idol worship. "Rabban Gamliel replied, 'I cannot answer [questions related to the Torah] in a bathhouse.' When Rabban Gamliel came out, he said to him, 'I did not come into her domain; she has come into mine.'"

In the second text (Talmud Menachot 99b) a student, who is already diligent in the study of the Torah, asks Rabbi Ishmael if he is permitted to study Greek wisdom. Rabbi Ishmael replies by quoting a verse from the Torah: "The Book of the Torah shall never leave your lips and you shall mediate upon it day and night. Go find a time that is not day and not night, and in it you may study Greek wisdom."

Students analyse and compare the two texts along with the gravestone image. They consider the prescriptive messages of each source, and they debate whether the sources present diverse or overlapping evidence concerning Greek influence on Jewish life. Students learn the concepts of assimilation, acculturation, and integration in order to discuss Jewish responses to Hellenistic influence. Morah D helps the students recognize that each of these concepts is relevant to Jewish identity today, and that there is a palpable analogy between the ancient Jewish encounter with Greek culture and modern Jewish encounters with secularism.

Morah D develops this analogy by asking the students to create a poster-size Venn diagram explicating the relationships and tensions between religion and secularity in their own identity. On one side of the diagram, students represent, through drawing or collage, secular activities that they enjoy or participate in. On the other side of the diagram, students represent their Jewish activities and values. In the overlapping section of the diagram, students represent those activities and values that they deem to be both "Jewish" and "secular." As always, students are asked to write an artist statement describing their work. The elements that students choose to represent on the "Jewish" of their Venn diagram are not surprising: studying the Torah, attending **bar and bat mitzvah** celebrations, attending syn-

JEWISH EDUCATION, DEMOCRACY, ENGAGEMENT | BEILES

agogue, keeping **kosher**, Jewish holidays, prayer, and Jewish food. On the "secular" side of the diagram the students depict sports, television, movies, magazines, clothing, and secular school subjects such as math or science. Most interesting are the elements that students choose to place in the middle of their diagram—those activities that they deem to be both "secular" and "Jewish." Represented here are activities such as summer camp, dance, singing, friends, the internet, sports, music, and, interestingly, The Toronto Heschel School itself. One student placed "hockey" in the overlap. He explains: "I play hockey four times a week which does not seem very Jewish. I still included the Hockey Canada symbol in the middle of my Venn diagram because when I play hockey I feel very close to God."

A student who placed summer camp in the middle wrote, "at camp we have many secular activities like water skiing, sports and nature but we all celebrate **Shabbat** together each Friday night." One student chose to glue an image of a *kippah* decorated with Mickey Mouse. She explains: "I have put a Mickey Mouse *kippah* to symbolize how much the Jewish people in Canada have assimilated but still keep our own traditions.... Walt Disney wanted [his] stories to live on forever and that is how we keep our religion, through stories." This student identifies a universal technique—storytelling—as an analogy for a Jewish cultural process. At The Toronto Heschel School, both students and teachers regularly make use of analogies between Judaism and cultural forms drawn from their secular environment. Most often, these analogies seem to serve the purpose of deepening an understanding of Judaism.

Ultimately, what interests Morah D in this project is not so much what ends up on which side of the Venn, but the process by which students make their choices. The project is not just about representing identity, but about bringing to consciousness the processes through which identity is constructed. The projects engage students in making Jewish meaning out of their lives. Simultaneously, students realize that others may make different choices, and therefore different kinds of meaning. Most importantly, students experience identity as a dynamic, nuanced, process that involves choices, often viscerally charged ones.

Metaphysics and Limitations

When education is able to nurture in students a strong sense of autonomy in making ideational choices, it satisfies at least one key element of liberalism articulated by Feinberg:

FAITH AND CITIZENSHIP

For the most part children develop their initial conception of the good from their parents and other significant adults, but liberalism requires that they not be destined to live out this conception and that they have opportunities to reflect upon and revise it. The skills involved in critical reflection, viewed as the capacity for reflecting upon, choosing, and revising one's conception of the good, are viewed as an essential component of autonomy. Without this capacity a child is fated to life a life chosen by other people and by chance alone.[20]

When students realize that activities and ideas may belong to multiple categories, or may flow between categories, as in the Venn diagram activity, their sense of identity becomes more dynamic and fluid. Connolly valorizes this kind of fluid or "mobile" identity. Reflecting on his favourite muse, Nietzsche, he writes: "Things are mobile at bottom, rather than still or fixed. This experience of the mobility of things has profound, corrosive effects upon winter conceptions of nature, divinity, identity, truth, and ethics that have prevailed in the West."[21]

However, one must certainly wonder whether this Nietzschean mobility can be reconciled with a Jewish metaphysic that posits certain positive elements—God, the Torah, and the created universe. Moreover, we must consider how a community that seeks to sustain itself in its creativity balances the need for boundaries with openness to critical reflection and innovation. To address these questions I turned to Dr. R., the founding Judaic studies principal of The Toronto Heschel School.

Dr. R. takes a God-centric view of Judaism. She states that while "Judaism is a broad category that includes religion, identity, culture, and art, ... God sits at the centre of any and all discussion." She hastens to add that "the outcome of that discussion is personal"—so personal, in fact, "that we have no right to inquire too deeply of another person's spirituality or understanding of God." Throughout our conversation, Dr. R. emphasized that the Judaic discussion provides tremendous room for interpretation, innovation, and participation: "Through traditional skill of Jewish text study we don't just study what has been said before—the greats [i.e., the traditional scholars]; that is only the foundation to teach the child to do the same thing with their ideas. [Children's] ideas are not just tolerated but needed."

At the same time, Dr. R. describes particular structures and traditions through which this hermeneutic process takes place: "Part of finding their unique voice is to study with a partner [chevruta] to create a safe space between them to explore their unique voice until they feel comfortable with

JEWISH EDUCATION, DEMOCRACY, ENGAGEMENT | BEILES

it. From the safety and foundation of community they hone their unique idea within the discipline of the tradition."

I asked Dr. R. if there are any boundaries or limits to the hermeneutical process:

> There are no boundaries to the questions. But the answers have to be within the boundaries. For example, if an adolescent were to come and say she believed in God, but now after [she learned about] the Holocaust she asked, "Is God a sadist?" The worst thing to do would be to shut down that question. There shouldn't be any fear in asking a question or hearing a question. Now, in terms of answers, from a theological perspective God can't be a sadist. So now we have to start searching ... searching for an answer.
>
> Sometimes when there is a question we give an answer like, "Wow, I don't know, let's take a look, someone in the twelfth century asked the same question." So we're connecting the child to the process, to Judaism, we're showing a child that this process has worked because 900 years ago the same question that [he or she has just] asked; we're all in the same sphere looking for answers; that is the human challenge.

Dr. R.'s comments echo a sentiment I hear often from the teachers at The Toronto Heschel School: that Judaism is a process, and that the pedagogical objective is to engage students in that process.

I wanted to push the issues of boundaries further, so I asked Dr. R. if are there any principles that would define the limits of inquiry of this process. Her answer reflects the three categories of relationships recognized by Rabbinic theology: the relationship with God, the relationship with others, and the relationship with self:

> In terms of our relationship with God, the boundary is that there is only one God—and that God is a non-physical and infinite being. In our relationship with other people—the boundary is the preservation of the dignity of the other person; in my relationship with myself, it is to remember that I am created in the image of God and therefore must respect myself and treat myself with that in mind.

Dr. R. emphasizes the two essential elements of a Jewish metaphysic: the unity of God, and the creation of all human beings in the image of God. The affirmation of a unique, infinite God is the proposition that all phenomena in the world are somehow connected. This means that the primary task

FAITH AND CITIZENSHIP

of learning is discovering—often anew—these connections. This search for connection underpins much of the pedagogy at The Toronto Heschel School. It is what allows Moreh E to juxtapose Jewish texts that gesture at democratic process with Kohlberg's secular Just Community Schools process. It is also what opens the way for Morah D's students to wonder what fits in the overlapping circle of their Jewish–secular Venn diagram, and to discover analogies between historical and contemporary tensions in the formation of identity. Ultimately, a metaphysic of interconnectivity provides a framework from within the Jewish tradition that allows diverse sources of knowledge and culture into the educational discourse. This framework encourages students to recognize correlations between self and other, and to see themselves and others as part of an interrelated process of historical becoming. Students develop a more nuanced and dynamic understanding of their own identity and of the identity of others. This leads to a sense of moral autonomy that is not free-wheeling, but rather is imbued with a deep sense of culture, community, and history.

The other aspect of the Jewish metaphysic—the assertions that all human beings are created in the image of God—affirms, *a priori*, the fundamental dignity of the self and the Other. This affirmation is also a validation of difference. The Talmud (Sanhedrin 38a) marvels at the diversity of humanity, of which each distinct individual is nevertheless created in the image of God. Difference here is not an unhinging or dissolution that gives way to a completely mobile and fluid universe. The createdness of the universe, and of the very distinctiveness of each individual within the universe, means that configuration and form matter. The dialogical process of Judaism weaves threads of connection between differently configured nodes. Creativity is initiated not in the mobility of subjectivities, but in the connections made between configured, dignified interlocutors. The process is ultimately limited by two injunctions: first, not to destroy the metaphysical supposition of connectivity and coherence, which validates the effort to seek connections and knowledge; and second, to affirm the fundamental dignity of all persons, and thereby legitimate each person's participation in the discursive process. This is why, in the debate between Rabbi Eliezer and the sages, the walls of the Beit Midrash refused to collapse: for the Beit Midrash—the house of learning—represents both the connectivity of discourse and the community of interlocutors. The Toronto Heschel School strives to be this kind of Beit Midrash, and in doing so it nurtures liberal pluralistic values within a distinctly Jewish framework.

118

Notes

1 Walter Feinberg, *For Goodness Sake: Religious Schools and Education for Democratic Citizenry* (New York: Routledge, 2006), xxi.

2 William Connolly, *Why I Am Not a Secularist* (Minneapolis: University of Minnesota Press, 1999).

3 Connolly, *Why I Am Not a Secularist*, 33.

4 The Toronto Heschel School, *Democratic Citizenship: A Curriculum for Civics* (unpublished curriculum document, 2003).

5 "The law of the land," or *dina malkutah dina*, is the Talmudic principle formulated by Samuel, leader of the Jewish community of Persia (c. 242 CE). It accommodates Jewish law to the civil "law of the land," giving precedence to the latter where the two conflict.

6 "[Given a choice between giving money to] the poor of your city and the poor of another town—the poor of your own town have prior rights" (Babylonian Talmud, *Bava Metzia* 71a [Trans. Rabbi Dr. H. Freedman, ed. Rabbi Dr. I. Epstein (London: Soncino Press, 1960)]).

7 Defined by the greater reversibility and reciprocity of point of view in responding to ethical dilemmas. See Lawrence Kohlberg, *Essays on Moral Development*, 2 vols. (San Francisco: Harper and Row, 1981/1984).

8 Kohlberg, *Essays on Moral Development*.

9 F. Clark Power, Ann Higgins, and Lawrence Kohlberg, *Lawrence Kohlberg's Approach to Moral Education* (New York: Columbia University Press, 1989).

10 All names are pseudonyms.

11 Babylonian Talmud, *Bava Metzia*, 59b.

12 Mishna, *Pirkei Avot*, 4:11 (Bar Ilan Responsa. Spertus College).

13 Tosefot Yom Tov, cited in Greg Beiles and Eli Savage, *Democratic Classroom Communities* (Toronto: Lola Stein Institute, 2009), 3.

14 Beiles and Savage, *Democratic Classroom Communities*, 3.

15 Feinberg, *For Goodness Sake*, 103.

16 Connolly, *Why I Am Not a Secularist*, 58.

17 Connolly, *Why I Am Not a Secularist*, 51.

18 Connolly, *Why I Am Not a Secularist*, 27.

19 Connolly cites Nietzsche's "We think with our stomachs"; *Why I Am Not a Secularist*, 175.

20 Feinberg, *For Goodness Sake*, 95.

21 Connolly, *Why I Am Not a Secularist*, 53.

FAITH AND CITIZENSHIP

Bibliography

Beiles, Greg, and Eli Savage. *Democratic Classroom Communities*. Toronto: Lola Stein Institute, 2009.

Connolly, William. *Why I Am Not a Secularist*. Minneapolis: University of Minnesota Press, 1999.

Feinberg, Walter. *For Goodness Sake: Religious Schools and Education for Democratic Citizenry*. New York: Routledge, 2006.

Kohlberg, Lawrence. *Essays on Moral Development Volume I: The Philosophy of Moral Development, Moral Stages and the Idea of Justice*. San Francisco: Harper & Row, 1981.

———. *Essays on Moral Development Volume II: The Psychology of Moral Development, the Nature and Validity of Moral Stage*. San Francisco: Harper & Row, 1984.

Power, F. Clark, Ann Higgins, and Lawrence Kohlberg. *Lawrence Kohlberg's Approach to Moral Education*. New York: Columbia University Press, 1989.

The Toronto Heschel School. *Democratic Citizenship: A Curriculum for Civics*. Unpublished curriculum document, 2003.

CHAPTER FIVE

CANADIAN CATHOLIC SCHOOLS: SACRED AND SECULAR TENSIONS IN A FREE AND DEMOCRATIC SOCIETY

J. Kent Donlevy

Introduction

Canada's Catholic schools derive their raison d'être from the teachings of the Catholic Church and their legal legitimacy from, among other things, being designated as Catholic schools by Catholic bishops. Within those schools the values of respect for the Other, fairness,[1] the common good,[2] and democracy[3] are taught and promoted to both students and staff alike.

Under Canadian law, those same values are either directly or indirectly promoted and protected under provincial and federal human rights legislation and under the Canadian Charter of Rights and Freedoms. Notwithstanding the mutual acceptance and promotion of the values by Catholic schools and the secular society, tensions have arisen between individuals supported by the state and various Catholic institutions, associations, or representatives of the Catholic Church (which I refer to below as Catholic entities) with respect to the interpretation of those values and their application in particular circumstances. Those tensions have risen to the point of litigation in what this chapter names the sacred–secular divide, indicating apparently incommensurate positions in what the Canadian Charter of Rights and Freedoms calls a free and democratic society.

This chapter asks the following questions: What are examples of the differences between the sacred and secular divide with respect to the four values? What is the nature of those differences? How do those differences affect the nature, purposes, and raison d'être of Catholic education?

FAITH AND CITIZENSHIP

Part I of this chapter provides the litigious background for the four values, while Part II provides a theoretical analysis of them while shedding new light on their importance to Catholic education.

Part I

Social Tension: Catholicism's Values and Canada's Secular Values

What is good, true, and just in religion will not always comport with the law's view of the matter, nor will society at large always properly respect conscientious adherence to alternate authorities and divergent normative, or ethical commitments. Where this is so, two comprehensive worldviews collide.[4]

A combination of civil litigation cases and human rights disputes have illustrated the sacred–secular tension in the interpretation and application of the four values. In this chapter, one case and several human rights disputes are presented in brief as examples of these tensions that have arisen in Canadian society. The Hall case, and the following human rights disputes, demonstrate tension between the Catholic Church and secular society with respect to the meaning and application of the four values: Smith and Chymyshyn; *Catholic Insight*; the Corcoran dispute; and the claims launched against the Catholic Bishop of Calgary, Frederick Henry.

What have been the issues at stake, in terms of the four values stated above, in those examples? Is the negative characterization of the actions of Catholic entities and persons correct? It is to those matters that I now turn.

The Civil Litigation Case: Marc Hall

Mr. Hall, a gay Catholic high-school student from Whitby, Ontario, as a member of a marginalized, persecuted social group ostensibly merely sought to share an important occasion, his school's prom, with someone he cared for—a desire supported by the Ontario English Catholic Teachers Association.[5] The school board claimed, among other things, that to allow Mr. Hall to attend the dance with his friend would implicitly suggest that the Catholic school board approved of homosexual relations. Therefore, Mr. Hall's request was denied—a decision not supported by the Court on an injunctory application. It could easily appear to the public that in this case Catholic schools—regardless of what they profess—actually act contrary to the values of respect and fairness, not exhibiting care to those most vulnerable in its institution. Politically one can understand why the Catholic school board would have few supporters in the public square and why it faced such as persuasive hurdle in the courts. I have argued elsewhere that the Hall case was wrongly decided, but suffice it to say for the purposes of this chapter that the argument accepted by the Court on an interlocutory application was in favour of Mr. Hall.[6]

Beyond the Hall case, four human rights disputes, three argued before provincial human rights commissions and one before the Canadian Human Rights Commission, highlight the secular–sacred divide between the Catholic application of the above four values and that of the secular quasi-judicial bodies. Although these disputes do not involve Catholic schools, they highlight the same arguments that swirl around Catholic schools in dealing with similar issues, as will be discussed later in this chapter.

The Human Rights Disputes

The Smith and Chymyshyn Dispute

In the Smith and Chymyshyn human rights dispute, Tracey Smith and Deborah Chymyshyn sought to rent a hall, run by the Knights of Columbus (a fraternal men's organization dedicated to the Catholic faith) and owned by the Archdiocese of Vancouver, for their wedding reception.[7] That request was denied by the Knights, who claimed, among other things, that the religious beliefs of the Catholic Church on same-sex marriage constituted a *bona fide* exception to the legally prohibited act of discrimination. The Knights' argument did not prevail, as the British Columbia Human Rights Tribunal found, among other things, that,

> [150] the Knights ... were entitled to hold and act on their core religious beliefs; however, in doing so, they had to respect the rights of the complainants to have access to a public space to celebrate their same-sex marriage, a right that is constitutionally protected. In these sensitive and difficult circumstances, people must approach these issues with respect even in the face of disagreement.

Ms. Smith and Ms. Chymyshyn could certainly claim that the Knights had acted without regard to the values of respect for the Other, fairness, and contrary to the democratic will of the majority in Canada as that will was expressed in law. The Knights, on the other hand, may well have asked who

FAITH AND CITIZENSHIP

could have foreseen that the Charter and human rights legislation might be used, in the opinion of some, as a sword for what could be called the "tyranny of a secular minority against a religious minority."

The *Catholic Insight* Dispute

In the *Catholic Insight* dispute, the values of respect and understanding of the Other were put in the spotlight concerning an online magazine service offered to Catholic readers.

In February 2007, Rob Wells, a member of the Pride Centre of Edmonton, filed a nine-point complaint with the Canadian Human Rights Commission, alleging, among other things, that *Catholic Insight*, a conservative pro-Catholic online magazine, "targeted homosexuals as being a powerful menace, made negative generalizations about them, portrayed them ... as dangerous or violent by nature."[8]

The magazine responded that it found the allegation "unfounded and made with the intent to harass." It stated further that "[t]he Catechism of the Catholic Church has made clear that persons with same-sex attraction must be accepted with respect, compassion and sensitivity and that every sign of unjust discrimination in their regard should be avoided."[9]

On July 4, 2008, the action was dismissed by the Commission after great financial expense had been incurred by the magazine.

The Corcoran Dispute

On or about June 17, 2009, Jim Corcoran filed a complaint with the Ontario Human Rights Tribunal against the Catholic Bishop of Peterborough and others, for an alleged breach of his human rights.[10] In essence, Mr. Corcoran believed that he had been discriminated against due to his sexual orientation, which he claimed had disconcerted several members of the local Catholic Church community, as he was an altar server and was being considered for a further position in the Church. His claim alleged that he had been advised that he was no longer welcome as an altar server nor would he be considered for further duties at the altar.

Mr. Corcoran could well claim that—if the facts were as he believed them to be—he had indeed been treated with a lack of respect and fairness, and contrary to the common good, both within the Catholic community and in the wider Canadian society. Although the local bishop has responded to the allegations made against him, this matter has not yet been resolved.

The Bishop Henry Disputes

In the city of Calgary, the local Catholic Bishop, the Most Reverend F.B. Henry, wrote his January 2005 Pastoral Letter entitled "On Same-Sex Marriage," which triggered more than mere controversy, as two complaints were sent before the Alberta Human Rights Commission. Norm Greenfield and Carol Johnson each argued that Bishop Henry's comments had contravened Section 3(1) of the Alberta Human Rights, Citizenship and Multiculturalism Act.

Part of the Pastoral Letter reads as follows: "Since homosexuality, adultery, prostitution and pornography undermine the foundations of the family, the basis of society, then the State must use its coercive power to proscribe or curtail them in the interests of the common good."[11] But were Bishop Henry's words actually contradictory to the Church's espoused appreciation for the stated values, and if not, were they only another example of a disingenuous attitude on the part of the Church to those values?[12]

One is left with this question: "How is it possible that both the Catholic Church's view and the secular view, as articulated in legal institutions, can espouse the same values yet arrive at differing conclusions in these circumstances?" It is to that question that I turn in Part II.

Part II

Catholic Schools and the Four Areas of Interpretive Contestation

This chapter has proposed that the four values of respect, fairness, the common good, and democracy, are reflected explicitly or implicitly in provincial codes of human rights, the federal human rights code, as well as the Canadian Charter of Rights and Freedoms, and that the view of Catholic entities is that they too espouse those values. The differences seem to be derived from four main spheres: philosophy, anthropology, politics, and law.

The Philosophical Divide

I take the position that the values of the secular culture are encapsulated as the rights and freedoms expressed in Canadian law, and those values within that context do not acknowledge the existence or relevance of a deity to the matters before the courts or human rights adjudicatory bodies. In that sense, the secular view is distinctly different from the Catholic view of existence, which presupposes and is based upon the existence of a revealed and personalized deity. Within Catholicism there are, of course, many schools of thought with respect to philosophical understandings and ways to view the world and humanity's place within it. It is beyond the scope of this chapter to delve into that ocean, but it is fair to say that, while recognizing the diversity of views on many matters, the Vatican accepts the existence of certain timeless truths and rejects the philosophical currency of nihilism, syncretism, and religious relativism. Moreover, because the Catholic Church accepts that there are timeless spiritual truths about humankind, including what its creator expects of humankind, it sees human choice as free but bounded by the responsibility to act in accord with what is revealed by God and espoused by His Church—the Catholic Church.

The idea of timeless truths and expectations of responsibility emanating from a creator and not a particular community or society or peer group is a significant difference between the curriculum and pedagogy in public and Catholic schools. Indeed, Catholic schools are bound to evangelize the youth in teaching them the truth as understood and taught by the Church.[13] As McLaughlin states with respect to Catholic education, "[the] Catholic faith must be presented in its entirety under the guidance of the Magisterium ... respecting the hierarchy of truths ... and ensuring integrity of content.... There is therefore a persistent need to discern the essential features of the Christian message which is to be transmitted to pupils...."[14]

Can there be honest, sincere, dissent on any of these issues within the Catholic Church? Yes, of course. The Church takes a strong stand in favour of freedom of conscience.[15] But the provision of Catholic education to Catholic youth, the guardianship and stewardship of an organ of the Church remaining in the hands of believers in the Catholic faith, and the adherence of the Catholic school to being a community of faith are paramount to the evangelization of Catholic youth. In that respect, it is the local Catholic bishop who is responsible under canon law for the faith within the school.[16] Within the context of the Catholic world view and philosophy, its teachings and how they are played out within Catholic schools give evidence that Catholic schools honour and embrace the values of respect for the Other, fairness, furthering the common good in a diverse society, and the democratic ideal. Indeed, from the Catholic school position, the raison d'être of Catholic schools requires no less.

This having been said, what does it mean for Catholic schools?

Catholic Schools: Their Nature, Mission, and Justification
The philosophical divide is important for Catholic education, because the Catholic Church takes the position that the nature of Catholic education is

essentially spiritual, as it is guided by the Holy Spirit, grounded in the Gospel of Jesus Christ, and seeks through evangelization to draw the young to God the Father and thus to salvation. Therefore, by its essence it draws upon the divinely granted sacramentality of the human being as the tool to fulfill its nature. Catholic education is, as Himes suggests, a "divinely planned paideia."[17] Its purpose is the evangelization of its youth through its mission. As the Sacred Congregation for Catholic Education states, "The specific mission of the school ... is a critical, systematic transmission of culture in the light of faith and the bringing forth of the power of Christian virtue by the integration of culture with faith and of faith with living."[18]

The Sacred Congregation notes further that part of that mission of transmission is to be fulfilled by a synthesis of culture and faith, and a synthesis of faith and life. The first is reached by integrating all the different aspects of human knowledge through the subjects taught, in the light of the Gospel, while the second is reached in the growth of the virtues characteristic of the Christian.[19]

The philosophy of the Church gives meaning and purpose to the very idea of the Catholic school; furthermore, the truths taught by the Church, which it believes to be timeless, illuminate and give substance to the mission of the Catholic school. As the Congregation for Catholic Education states,

> The Catholic school finds its true justification in the mission of the Church; it is based on an educational philosophy in which faith, culture and life are brought into harmony. Through it, the local Church evangelizes, educates, and contributes to the formation of a healthy and morally sound life-style among its members.[20]

In summary, Catholic schools must teach in accord with the beliefs and values of the Catholic Church and the Church's interpretation of those values, regardless of the pressures from the wider secular society, as the nature, mission, and justification of those schools rests upon such compliance. Because secular society's values—as expressed in law—do not assume an interpretation through the belief of a deity, a conflict between differing interpretations and applications appears, arguably, to be inevitable.

The Anthropological Divide

A recent work by a Catholic scholar introduces the terms *anthropology* and *Christian anthropology* as follows:

FAITH AND CITIZENSHIP

Anthropology seeks to describe the essential characteristics of human beings and how those characteristics shape culture, beliefs, and practices.... [It] thus responds to questions like "What is the nature of [a] human being" "What constitutes human life?" "Who are we as human beings in relationship to the world around us?" and "How do human beings shape their world and the world of others in relationship to their beliefs?"[21]

Christian anthropology centers on the core belief that human beings and human life reflect the image of God ... to be the *imago Dei*.[22]

It should come as no surprise that the Vatican is concerned with certain developments in the field of anthropology. In particular, it notes that the classical view of being human has been challenged. The Church says that the

paradigmatic change in anthropology ... is opposed to classical anthropology. It is characterised, for example, by an extreme individualism, seen especially in a concept of conscience that elevates the individual conscience to the level of an absolute, thus raising the subjective criterion above all objective factors and having no point of reference beyond itself.[23]

The issue over homosexuality raised in the Hall litigation and the four human rights disputes point to a fundamental difference between the secular and sacred (Catholic) anthropological interpretation of what human sexuality means with regard to sexual orientation. If one takes the secular viewpoint, then it is clear that the actions and words of Catholic entities are contrary to the values of respect for the Other and fairness, and are ipso facto contrary to the common good of Canadian society as well as being contrary to the democratic will of Canadians as expressed in law. Indeed, those who would characterize the Catholic entities as acting contrary to those values could well be thinking that the Catholic Church's interpretation of anthropology with respect to sexual orientation results in a breaking of the connection between recognition and identity. According to Charles Taylor, the relevant thesis is as follows:

our identity is partly shaped by the recognition or its absence, often by the *mis*recognition of others, and so a person or group of people can suffer real damage, real distortion, if the people or society around them mirror to them a confining or demeaning or contemptible picture of themselves. Nonrecognition or misrecognition can inflict harm, can be a form of oppression, imprisoning someone in a false, distorted, and reduced mode of being.[24]

Given the above, it does seem that the Catholic position is at best misguided and at worst disingenuous and hypocritical in claiming that it supports the four values. Is this in fact the case?

Anthropologically, the Catholic Church takes the position that homosexuality is a disorder; hence, the Church has great difficulty in accepting the secular position that to discriminate against someone due to her or his sexual orientation in word or deed is to fail to show respect for the Other, or to be fair, and hence this position cannot be said to be contrary to the common good within the Catholic faith or, based upon the Church's assumptions, contrary to the common good in the wider society.[25] By its own definitions the Catholic Church's position is respectful to the Other, fair as it is believed to be true, coherent with the common good as it espouses the truth of being human, and not contrary to the democratic ideal, as the Catholic Church is itself not bound by majoritarianism in its fundamental beliefs. I turn now to an explanation of the Catholic Church's position on this matter.

The Catholic Church and Sexual Orientation

What follows is the Catholic Church's view of homosexuality and the Church's reasons for taking a public position contrary to many in society on the topic of same-sex marriage and on sexual orientation—which was important in the Hall case and human rights disputes. It is clear that these views of the Catholic Church would be controversial in Catholic schools, as they are contested by some within the Catholic community and potentially by governments seeking to add anti-discriminatory elements to a province's school curriculum.[26]

The Catholic Church's position regarding homosexuality is made very clear through many official Church documents[27] and public statements.[28] The Catholic **Catechism** states,

> Homosexuality refers to relations between men or between women who experience an exclusive or predominant sexual attraction toward persons of the same sex.... Basing itself on Sacred Scripture, which presents homosexual acts as acts of grave depravity ... tradition has always declared that "homosexual acts are intrinsically disordered." ... They are contrary to the natural law.... Under no circumstances can they be approved.[29]

The Church's position on same-sex marriage is also clear: "There are absolutely no grounds for considering homosexual unions to be in any way similar or even remotely analogous to God's plan for marriage and family. Marriage is holy, while homosexual acts go against the natural moral law."[30]

Members of the Catholic Church, who are in conformity with the **Magisterium**, cannot, therefore, countenance homosexual acts,[31] but its members and institutions are advised in the Catechism that "[Homosexuals] must be accepted with respect, compassion, and sensitivity. Every sign of unjust discrimination in their regard should be avoided. These persons are called to fulfill God's will in their lives and, if they are Christians, to unite to the sacrifice of the Lord's Cross the difficulties they may encounter from their condition."[32]

It is significant that the Catholic Catechism distinguishes between just and unjust discrimination in the treatment of its members. In today's world there does not seem to be any such distinction, in that all discrimination is labelled a negative action. In a country where it is certainly of great benefit to teach against discrimination on the basis of sexual orientation in all schools, this is potentially problematic for Catholic schools.

The Catholic Church states that there are four categories of objection that bind it to oppose same-sex marriage: "the origin of right reason," "the biological and anthropological order," "the social order," and "the legal order."[33]

First, the institutionalization in law of the homosexual relationship would, according to the Church, "result in changes to the entire organization of society, contrary to the common good," as it would arguably "obscure certain basic moral values and cause a devaluation of the institution of marriage." Second, biologically and anthropologically, the Church says that same-sex marriage is not acceptable, because "[s]uch unions are not able to contribute in a proper way to the procreation and survival of the human race ... [and are] totally lacking in the conjugal dimension."[34] Third, "Society owes its continued survival to the family, founded on marriage."[35] Finally, "Homosexual unions, on the other hand, do not need specific attention from the legal standpoint since they do not exercise this function for the common good."[36] The Church recognizes that there is a persuasive secular argument that respect for the Other, fairness, and recognition of the common good due to both these principles leads to justice and the right to be free from discrimination; for non-heterosexual persons, this requires legal recognition of same-sex unions. However, it says in response:

> The principles of respect and non-discrimination cannot be invoked to support legal recognition of homosexual unions. Differentiating between persons or refusing social recognition or benefits is unacceptable only when it is contrary to justice. The denial of the social and legal status of marriage to

forms of cohabitation that are not and cannot be marital is not opposed to justice; on the contrary, justice requires it.[37]

In sum, it appears that if one accepts the teachings of the Magisterium of the Catholic Church on this issue, one must be in favour of the Catholic entities' positions mentioned in the Hall case and in the human rights disputes mentioned in this chapter. Moreover, it is clear that, anthropologically, Catholics can reasonably argue that they too support the values of respect for the Other, fairness, and the common good, notwithstanding that there will be acts of discrimination—which flow, in part, from the anthropological position of the Catholic Church. As such a position presumes a deity—whose will is expressly interpreted through divine inspiration by the Catholic Church—it is necessarily distinctly different from the anthropology espoused by secular society. So must Catholic schools promulgate the Christian (and in this case specifically Catholic) anthropology? The answer is yes. One leading Catholic scholar, Thomas Groome, suggests five theological and three cardinal characteristics of being Catholic, one of which is a "positive anthropology."[38] Moreover, a cleric intimately involved with Catholic education, Archbishop J. Michael Miller, suggests that one of the "Five Essential Marks of Catholic Schools" is that they must be "founded upon a Christian anthropology."[39]

Simply put, the raison d'être of Catholic schools, its nature, purpose, and mission, require that the truth as understood by the Catholic Church be taught in its schools, and thus from the perspective of a Christian (Catholic) anthropology.[40]

The Political Divide

Although democracy is a value for the Catholic Church, it is not one that defines it.[41] Democracy is a positive value for the governance of society but not for the Catholic Church, since, according to Catholic belief, unlike other institutions it was not created by human beings. It is an institution created by a deity, with prescribed beliefs and the means of interpreting fundamental truth—which rests upon the trinity of Holy Scripture (the Bible), tradition, and the Magisterium. Therefore no human being can legitimately change its foundation or dogma, nor can it dictate to the Magisterium what should be believed or allowed, arguing that such is the will of the majority of the members of the Church.[42] To those who say that certain changes would be the will of the majority of the Faithful, one could say in response that the faithful includes those who have died and who now comprise the Commu-

FAITH AND CITIZENSHIP

nion of Saints who participate in and are part of the Church, even though they have left this world. As Sollier says, "The communion of saints is the spiritual solidarity which binds together the faithful on earth, the souls in purgatory, and the saints in heaven in the organic unity of the same mystical body under Christ its head, and in a constant interchange of supernatural offices."[43]

Given the above, it is relatively easy to see how the Catholic Church's position on those issues is politically unpopular, and some in secular society might say unfathomable to those making legal decisions in matters involving various Catholic actors. Supporting the democratic ideal to the wider society yet eschewing it internally has perhaps led some to call the Catholic Church hypocritical, as it acts contrary to its espoused belief in the value of democracy. This was certainly the case in the Hall case, when Mr. Justice MacKinnon seemed swayed in part by the argument that many within the Catholic community failed to agree with the local Catholic bishop's opinion of the significance of a Catholic school board appearing to support a particular sexual orientation. This legal decision provides a useful transition into a discussion of the way in which the four values discussed in this chapter are viewed in law.

The Legal Divide

The Canadian Charter of Rights and Freedoms begins with the words, "Whereas Canada is founded upon principles that recognize the supremacy of God and the rule of law...." One would think that a fair reading of that phrase would entail an understanding that there are moral and ethical benchmarks in Canadian law that are based upon the belief in a deity. However, that assumption is not correct. The Chief Justice of the Supreme Court of Canada, Beverley McLachlin, implicitly stated in a 2005 speech that a belief in a deity is not the basis for the Canadian legal system.[44] In her opinion, the values that have emerged from Canadian history and that have been expressed in the legal system constitute the source of the values that are in turn reflected in Canadian law. The influence of Ronald Dworkin's writings is therefore clearly expressed in her opinion.[45] While such an opinion may be more satisfactory to members of the Catholic Church than the legal positivism of Hart, or Fuller's attempt at addressing morality and law through his eight desiderata, it remains a far cry from Blackstone's, Aquinas's, and Finnis's views of natural law.[46]

Indeed, if the law is, as Hart suggests, just a system of rules—with judicial discretion in cases where the rules do not apply, as in penumbral cases, separate from morality and known by pedigree to the system's rules of recognition—then moral issues do not define the conceptual process of defining the concept of law.[47] Alternatively, if the law is an interpretive process with law as integrity, seeking the right answer to legal conundrums based upon the principles inherent within the system and its history, then we seem to be moving closer to the natural-law theory espoused by Aquinas.[48] In fact, the Catholic Church's official view of law is based, as Aquinas says, on natural law, which is "nothing else than the rational creature's participation in the eternal law."[49] The Catholic view of law is clearly based upon the concept of a belief in God that shapes the meaning, significance, and, indeed, the legitimacy of the law.

The current Canadian secular view of law appears to be positivist or historically/culturally based. Paradoxically, colloquially, and hence politically in some cases, there seems to be the view that if one does not agree with an aspect of the law, then one is acting immorally, unethically, unjustly, unfairly, or undemocratically. In this respect, when Catholic entities seek to employ exceptions to certain rights, as in legally discriminating for bona fide reasons, as alleged in Hall and the human rights disputes discussed in this chapter, the entities are seen as acting unethically, as the law in its educative sense tells the public what is right and wrong, good and bad. It is not difficult to understand how one could wrongly conflate morality and law by saying that if one is acting illegally one is also acting immorally. From the Catholic point of view, there is also the claim to law as natural law from a Thomistic position, which allows one to refuse to follow unjust laws, as in the case of Martin Luther King.[50] In such cases, it would be unethical and immoral to follow such laws. Indeed, given section 2(a) of the Canadian Charter of Rights and Freedoms, which specifically protects freedom of conscience, one could legally argue in favour of the interpretation of the four values from the Catholic Church's perspective, and, further—at least from an internal view—that to hold such interpretations is both ethical and moral.

The legal divide between the secular and the Catholic view is that laws that are promulgated through human rights legislation but that do not conform to Catholic anthropology and philosophy ought not to be followed by Catholic schools, as they are not valid laws—as far as the concept of natural law is understood by the Catholic Church. The latter seems to be at the heart of the debate between many Catholic entities and some in Canadian society who, for what they sincerely believe to be good, moral, and compelling reasons, seek to compel Catholic institutions and some individuals to comply with a secular view of the four values stated in this chapter.

In sum, despite the difference between the secular view of law held by Canadian courts and the sacred view of law held the Catholic Church, Catholic entities will of course follow the law, except where to do so would compromise the raison d'être of Catholic education. If the latter were the case, however, it is possible that many Catholics would stand against the particular law and suffer the legal consequences, saying, as Martin Luther is alleged to have said to his Catholic interrogators, "Here I stand; I cannot do otherwise, … so help me God."

Commentary

This chapter has suggested that the values of respect for the Other, fairness, seeking the common good, and democracy are interpreted and applied differently depending upon whether one has a secular or Catholic view of philosophy, anthropology, politics, and the law. This situation may produce an apparent paradox for teachers in Catholic schools, as the Catholic Church's interpretation and application of those values differ from what is provided for in law and commonly held as secular beliefs. Has that sense of paradox and resulting intellectual uncertainty manifested itself within the institution of Catholic education, or is this just paranoia? The answer is that the difficulties that the secular views can cause in Catholic schools are very real. The possibility that Catholic schools might have to teach their Catholic students the secular interpretation of those values, even though such an interpretation goes against the teachings of the Catholic faith, was evident in the Ontario government's recent Equity and Inclusive Education Strategy, and may be present again through its successor initiative for teaching inclusiveness in Ontario's schools.[51] Certainly some in Catholic schools in Ontario have expressed this very concern, although a clear public understanding of the issues—as articulated in this chapter—does not seem to be present in the public square.[52] Given the ambiguity and uncertainly surrounding the secular and religious interpretations of the four values, the relevance of the Hall case and the human rights disputes mentioned in this chapter to the teaching of the four values in Catholic schools according to the Catholic faith is clear.

Conclusion

It can be argued that necessity, culture, and language are no longer persuasive arguments in favour of the existence of publicly funded Catholic schools, due to the secularization and multicultural nature of Canadian society. Further, it seems clear that some secular institutions are wary of expressing the influence on them of religious institutions, and the courts are concerned with regard to that influence as well. Those facts produce, in civil litigation and disputes in human rights commissions and boards, teachable moments for society and students in Catholic schools.

The importance of Catholics understanding their Church's positions on key issues such as sexual orientation is evident. Catholic schools must teach the values of respect for the Other, fairness, the common good, and democracy, and it must be made clear to those involved that to do so within the Catholic tradition is to act sincerely, honourably, rationally, and faithfully within an institution that has as its raison d'être the beliefs of the Catholic faith. To the wider society within which many may see such beliefs as irrational, the words of Supreme Court of Canada Chief Justice Dixon of the Supreme Court in *R. v. Big M. Drug Mart Ltd.* ring loudly:

> A truly free society is one which can accommodate a wide variety of beliefs, diversity of tastes and pursuits, customs and codes of conduct. ... The essence of the concept of freedom of religion is the right to entertain such religious beliefs as a person chooses, the right to declare religious beliefs openly and without fear of hindrance or reprisal, and the right to manifest religious belief by worship and practice or by teaching and dissemination. But the concept means more than that.... Freedom can primarily be characterized by the absence of coercion or constraint. If a person is compelled by the state or the will of another to a course of action or inaction which he would not otherwise have chosen, he is not acting of his own volition and he cannot be said to be truly free.... Freedom in a broad sense embraces both the absence of coercion and constraint, and the right to manifest beliefs and practices. Freedom means that, subject to such limitations as are necessary to protect public safety, order, health, or morals or the fundamental rights and freedoms of others, no one is to be forced to act in a way contrary to his beliefs or his conscience.[53]

Notes

1 For the purposes of this chapter, the term "fairness" refers to the principle simpliciter that all persons—regardless of any distinctions amongst them—are treated the same with regard to any matter.

2 The term "common good" is seen today as a debate between the liberal and communitarian interpretations of that concept (J. Kent Donlevy, "Catholic Schools and Freedom of Conscience in the Canadian Charter of Rights and Freedoms," *Journal of Catholic Legal Studies* 47, no. 1 [2008]: 69–96). This chapter takes the position that the secular version of the common good is lib-

eral in nature and the Catholic version is communitarian in nature. The liberal vision offers the common good as various shades of individual autonomy, universal freedoms and rights (see Dworkin, *A Matter of Principle*), and value self-determination (see Nozick, *Anarchy, State, and Utopia*), with its focus upon the means to freedom rather than the ends of freedom (see Rawls, *A Theory of Justice*). The communitarian vision of the common good is conceived of as a substantive conception of the good life that defines the community's "way of life" (Will Kymlicka, *Contemporary Political Philosophy*, 2nd ed. [New York: Oxford University Press, 2001], 220).

3 For the purposes of this chapter the term "democracy" is used to refer to the principle that a majority of those eligible to vote carry the day on the salient issue in the community.

4 Beverley McLachlin, "Freedom of Religion and the Rule of Law: A Canadian Perspective," in *Recognizing Religion in a Secular Society: Essays in Pluralism, Religion, and Public Policy*, ed. Douglas Farrow (Kingston: McGill-Queen's University Press, 2005), 21.

5 *Hall (Litigation Guardian of) v. Powers* (2002), 213 D.L.R. (4th) 308 (Ont. scj), http://www.canlii.org/en/on/onsc/doc/2002/2002canlii49475/2002canlii49475 .html

6 J. Kent Donlevy, "Re-Visiting Denominational Cause and Denominational Breach in Canada's Constitutionally Protected Catholic Schools," *Journal of Education and Law* 15, no. 3 (2005): 85–112.

7 Smith and Chymyshyn v. Knights of Columbus and others, 2005 BCHRT 544 November 29, 2005, File Number 1258. Reasons for Decision. http://www .bchrt.bc.ca/decisions/2005/pdf/Smith_and_Chymyshyn_v_Knights_of_ Columbus_and_others_2005_BCHRT_544.pdf

8 Catholic Insight, "Catholic Insight under 'Human Rights' Attack," 2008, http:// catholicinsight.com/online/features/ article_772.shtml

9 Catholic Insight, "Catholic Insight under 'Human Rights' Attack."

10 Patrick B. Craine, "Homosexual Ex-Altar Server Demands Bishop Apologize, Publicly Chastise Parishioners in Human Rights Complaint," July 13, 2009. http://www.lifesitenews.com/news/archive/ldn/2009/jul/09071309. See also http://www.canlii.org/en/on/onhrt/doc/2009/2009hrto1600/2009hrto1600 .html

11 Bishop Frederick Henry, "On Same-Sex Marriage," Pastoral Letter, 2005, http:// www.rcdiocese-calgary.ab.ca/bishop/bishop_articles/ bishop_2005_01_same_ sex_marriage.htm. For this case, see also CTV News, "Calgary Bishop Defiant about Gay Marriage Views," 31 March 31 2005, http://www.ctv.ca/servlet /ArticleNews/story/CTVNews/1112231085323_10; jhw, "Gay Human Rights

Complaint against Calgary Bishop Dropped—Was All about Getting Media Attention," 26 Aug. 2005, http://www.lifesitenews.com/ldn/2005/aug/05082601 .html; Bishop Frederick Henry, "Human Rights Act Foils Reasoned Debate— [Alberta Premier] Stelmach Should Amend Act so That Justice Will Reign: A Shepherd Speaks," *Western Catholic Reporter*, 23 June 2008, http://www.wcr .ab.ca/bishops/henry/2008/henry062308.shtml

12 Congregation for Doctrine of Faith, *Letter to the Bishops of the Catholic Church on the Pastoral Care of Homosexual Persons* (Homosexualitatis problema *Epistula de pastorali personarum homosexualium cura*), 1 Oct. 1986, http: www.vatican.va/ roman_curia/congregations/cfaith/documents/rc_con_cfaith _doc_19861001_homosexual-persons_en.html

13 Congregation for Catholic Education, *The Religious Dimension of Education in a Catholic School,* 1988, http://www.vatican.va/roman_curia/congregations /ccatheduc/documents/rc_con_ccatheduc_doc_19880407_catholic-school _en.html

14 Terence H. McLaughlin, "The Distinctiveness of Catholic Education," in *The Contemporary Catholic School: Context, Identity, and Diversity*, ed. Terence H. McLaughlin, Joseph M. O'Keefe, and Bernadette O'Keefe (London: Falmer Press, 1996), 143.

15 Donlevy, "Catholic Schools and Freedom of Conscience."

16 Catholic Church, *Code of Canon Law*, 1983, http://www.vatican.va/archive/ ENG1104/_INDEX.HTM, §803, 805, 806

17 Michael Himes, "The Mission of the Church and Educational Leadership," *Momentum* 19, no. 1 (1988): 48.

18 Congregation for Catholic Education, *The Catholic School.* http://www.vatican.va /roman_curia/congregations/ccatheduc/documents/rc_con_ccatheduc _doc_19770319_catholic-school_en.html

19 Congregation for Catholic Education, *The Catholic School*, no. 49.

20 Congregation for Catholic Education, *The Religious Dimension of Education in a Catholic School.*

21 David B. Perrin, *Studying Christian Spirituality* (New York: Routledge, 2007), 120.

22 Perrin, *Studying Christian Spirituality*, 122.

23 Congregation of Divine Worship and the Discipline of the Sacraments, *Statement of Conclusions for Meeting of Australian Bishops and the Prefects and Secretaries of Six Dicasteries of the Roman Curia*, http://www.vatican.va /roman_curia/congregations/ccdds/documents/rc_con_ccdds_doc _20000630_dichiarazione-vescovi-australiani_lt.html, 11, 6

24 Charles Taylor, "The Politics of Recognition," in *Multiculturalism and "The Politics of Recognition": An Essay by Charles Taylor with Commentary by Amy Gutmann*, ed. Steven C. Rockefeller, Michael Walzer, and Susan Wolf (Princeton, NJ: Princeton University Press, 1992), 25.

25 Catholic Church, *Catechism of the Catholic Church*, http://www.vatican.va/archive/eng0015/_index.htm

26 See, for example, the Ontario Equity and Inclusive Education Strategy (see http://www.edu.gov.on.ca/eng/policyfunding/EquityQuickFacts.pdf and http://www.edu.gov.on.ca/eng/policyfunding/equity.html), wherein Catholic schools would be unable to accept certain aspects of the policy as it would appear contrary to that policy to state religious beliefs regarding homosexual orientation as a disorder in Catholic schools.

27 See, for example, the following documents: *Catechism of the Catholic Church*, § 2357, 2358, 2359; Congregation for Doctrine of Faith, "Letter to the Bishops of the Catholic Church on the Pastoral Care of Homosexual Persons"; ... "Some Considerations concerning the Response to Legislative Proposals on Non-discrimination of Homosexual Persons"; "Considerations regarding Proposals to Give Legal Recognition to Unions between Homosexual Persons"; ... "Instruction concerning the Criteria for the Discernment of Vocations with Regard to Persons with Homosexual Tendencies in View of Their Admission to the Seminary and to Holy Orders"; ... "Family, Marriage and 'De Facto' unions."

28 John-Henry Westen, "Interview: The Vatican on just vs. unjust discrimination based on sexual orientation: Ban on adoption, marriage, even military are not unjust discrimination," http://www.lifesitenews.com/news/archive/ldn/1991/21/9121512, 15 Dec. 2009.

29 Catholic Church, *Catechism of the Catholic Church*, §2357.

30 Congregation for Doctrine of Faith, *Considerations Regarding Proposals*, §4.

31 There have been—and of course still are—Catholic dissenters to the Church's position. See John J. McNeill, *The Church and the Homosexual* (Kansas City: Sheed Andrews and McMeel, 1976).

32 Catholic Church, *Catechism of the Catholic Church*, §2358.

33 Congregation for Doctrine of Faith, *Considerations Regarding Proposals*, §6.

34 Congregation for Doctrine of Faith, *Considerations Regarding Proposals*, §7.

35 Congregation for Doctrine of Faith, *Considerations Regarding Proposals*, §8.

36 Congregation for Doctrine of Faith, *Considerations Regarding Proposals*, §9.

37 Congregation for Doctrine of Faith, *Considerations Regarding Proposals*, §8.

38 Thomas Groome, "What Makes a School Catholic," in *The Contemporary Catholic School: Context, Identity, and Diversity*, ed. Terence H. McLaughlin, Joseph M. O'Keefe, and Bernadette O'Keeffe (London: Falmer Press, 1996), 108–9.

39 J. Michael Miller, *The Holy See's Teaching on Catholic Schools* (Manchester, NH: Sophia Institute Press, 2006), 22–27.

40 It should be noted, however, that although the Catholic anthropology is Christian, there are other Christian anthropological beliefs that do not comport with the Catholic beliefs.

41 Pontifical Council for Justice and Peace, *Compendium of the Social Doctrine of the Church. Chapter VIII the Political Community IV The Democratic System*, 2004. http://www.vatican.va/roman_curia/pontifical_councils/justpeace/docu ments/rc_pc_justpeace_doc_20060526_compendio-dott-soc_en.html

42 Joseph Ratzinger and Vittorio Messori, *The Ratzinger Report: An Exclusive Interview on the State of the Church* (San Francisco: Ignatius Press, 1985).

43 Joseph Sollier, "The Communion of Saints," in *The Catholic Encyclopedia* (New York: Robert Appleton, 1908), http://www.newadvent.org/cathen/04171a.htm

44 Beverley McLachlin, "Unwritten Constitutional Principles: What Is Going On?" Lord Cooke Lecture, Victoria University of Wellington, New Zealand, 1 Dec. 2005, http://www.scc-csc.gc.ca/court-cour/ju/spe-dis/bm05-12-01-eng.asp

45 Ronald M. Dworkin, *Taking Rights Seriously: New Impression with a Reply to Critics* (Cambridge, MA: Harvard University Press, 1978).

46 Herbert Lionel Adolphus Hart, *The Concept of Law* (Oxford: Clarendon Press, 1961); Lon L. Fuller, *The Morality of Law*, rev. ed. (New Haven, CT: Yale University Press, 1969), 33–94; William Blackstone, *Commentaries on the Laws of England* (1765–69; University of Chicago Press, 1979); Thomas Aquinas, *Summa theologica*, complete English ed. in 5 vols., vol. 1 and 2 trans. Fathers of the English Dominican Province (1274; Allen, TX: Christian Classics, 1948); John Finnis, *Natural Law and Natural Rights* (Oxford: Clarendon Press, 1981).

47 Hart, *The Concept of Law*.

48 Dworkin, *Taking Rights Seriously*; Aquinas, *Summa theologica*.

49 Aquinas, *Summa theologica*.

50 Martin Luther King, Jr., "Letter from Birmingham Jail," 16 April 1963, http://mlk-kpp01.stanford.edu/index.php/encyclopedia/documentsentry/annotated _letter_from_birmingham/

51 "Greater Equity Means Greater Student Success," http://www.edu.gov.on.ca/eng/policyfunding/equity.html

52 Patrick B. Craine, "Ontario Gvmt Won't Say Whether Catholic Schools Can Teach Beliefs on Homosexuality," http://www.lifesitenews.com/ldn/2010/jan/10010807.html

53 *R. v. Big M Drug Mart Ltd.* [1985] 1 S.C.R. 295, http://www.canlii.org/en/ca/scc/doc/1985/1985canlii69/1985canlii69.html

Bibliography

Aquinas, Thomas. *Summa theologica*. 1274. Complete English edition in 5 vols. Vols. 1 and 2 translated by Fathers of the English Dominican Province. Allen, TX: Christian Classics—A Division of Thomas More Publishing, 1948.

Blackstone, William. *Commentaries on the Laws of England*. 1765–69. Chicago: University of Chicago Press, 1979. http://books.google.ca/

Canada. Charter of Rights and Freedoms. Part I of the *Constitution Act, 1982*. http://laws.justice.gc.ca/en/charter/

Catholic Church. *Catechism of the Catholic Church*, 1992. http://www.vatican.va/archive/eng0015/_index.htm

———. *The Code of Canon Law*. 1983. http://www.vatican.va/archive/ENG1104/_INDEX.HTM

Catholic Insight. "Catholic Insight under 'Human Rights' Attack." 2008. http://catholicinsight.com/online/features/article_772.shtml

Congregation for Catholic Education. *Instruction concerning the Criteria for the Discernment of Vocations with Regard to Persons with Homosexual Tendencies in View of their Admission to the Seminary and to Holy Orders*. 2005. http://www.vatican.va/roman_curia/congregations/ccatheduc/documents/rc_con_ccatheduc_doc_20051104_istruzione_en.html

———. *The Religious Dimension of Education in a Catholic School*. 1988. http://www.vatican.va/roman_curia/congregations/ccatheduc/documents/rc_con_ccatheduc_doc_19880407_catholic-school_en.html

———. *The Catholic School*. 1977. http://www.vatican.va/roman_curia/congregations/ccatheduc/documents/rc_con_ccatheduc_doc_19770319_catholic-school_en.html

Congregation for Divine Worship and the Discipline of the Sacraments. *Statement of Conclusions for Meeting of Australian Bishops and the Prefects and Secretaries of Six Dicasteries of the Roman Curia*. 1998. http://www.vatican.va/roman_curia/congregations/ccdds/documents/rc_con_ccdds_doc_20000630_dichiarazione-vescovi-australiani%20_lt.html

Congregation for the Doctrine of the Faith. *Considerations Regarding Proposals to Give Legal Recognition to Unions between Homosexual Persons*. 2003. http://www.vatican.va/ roman_curia/congregations/ cfaith/documents/rc_con_cfaith_doc_20030731_homosexual-unions_en.html

———. *Some Considerations concerning the Response to Legislative Proposals on Non-discrimination of Homosexual Persons*. 1992 [revised]. http://www.ewtn.com/library/curia/cdfhomol.htm

———. *Letter to the Bishops of the Catholic Church on the Pastoral Care of Homosexual Persons*. 1 Oct. 1986. http://www.vatican.va/ roman_curia/congregations/

CANADIAN CATHOLIC SCHOOLS | DONLEVY

cfaith/documents/rc_con_cfaith_doc_19861001_homosexual-persons_en.html

——. *Persona Humana* (Declaration on certain questions concerning sexual ethics). 1975. http://www.vatican.va/roman_curia/congregations/cfaith/documents/rc_con_cfaith_doc_19751229_persona-humana_en.html

Corcoran v. Roman Catholic Episcopal Corporation of the Diocese of Peterborough, 2009. Human Rights Tribunal of Ontario 1600.

Craine, Patrick B. "Homosexual Ex-Altar Server Demands Bishop Apologize, Publicly Chastise Parishioners in Human Rights Complaint." 13 July 2009. http://www.lifesitenews.com/ldn/2009/jul/ 09071309.html

——. "Ontario Gvmt Won't Say Whether Catholic Schools Can Teach Beliefs on Homosexuality." 8 Jan. 2010. http://www.lifesitenews.com/ldn/2010/jan/10010807.html

CTV News. "Calgary Bishop Defiant about Gay Marriage Views." 31 March 2005. http://www.ctv.ca/servlet/ArticleNews/story/CTVNews/1112231085323_10

Donlevy, J. Kent. "Catholic Schools and Freedom of Conscience in the Canadian Charter of Rights and Freedoms." *Journal of Catholic Legal Studies* 47, no. 1 (2008): 69–96.

——. "Re-Visiting Denominational Cause and Denominational Breach in Canada's Constitutionally Protected Catholic schools." *Journal of Education and Law* 15, no. 3 (2005): 85–112.

Dworkin, Ronald M. *A Matter of Principle.* Cambridge, MA: Harvard University Press, 1985.

——. *Taking Rights Seriously: New Impression with a Reply to Critics.* London: Gerald Duckworth & Co., 2005.

Finnis, John. *Natural Law and Natural Rights.* Oxford: Clarendon Press, 1980.

Fuller, Lon L. *The Morality of Law.* Revised edition. New Haven, CT: Yale University Press, 1969.

Groome, Thomas H. "What Makes a School Catholic." In *The Contemporary Catholic School: Context, Identity, and Diversity*, edited by Terence H. McLaughlin, Joseph M. O'Keefe, and Bernadette O'Keeffe, 107–125. London: Falmer Press, 1996.

Hall (Litigation Guardian of) v. Powers (2002). 213 D.L.R. (4th) 308 (Ont. SCJ). http://www.canlii.org/en/on/onsc/doc/2002/2002canlii49475/2002canlii49475.html

Hart, Herbert Lionel Adolphus. *The Concept of Law.* Oxford: Clarendon Press, 1961.

Henry, Bishop Frederick. "Human Rights Act Foils Reasoned Debate—[Alberta Premier] Stelmach Should Amend Act so That Justice Will Reign: A Shepherd Speaks." *Western Catholic Reporter.* 23 June 2008. http://wcr.ab.ca/old-site/bishops/henry/2008/henry062308.shtml

———. "On Same-Sex Marriage." Pastoral Letter, 2005. http://www.calgarydiocese
.ca/messages-from-the-bishop/644-same-sex-marriage.html

Himes, Michael. "The Mission of the Church and Educational Leadership." *Momentum* 19, no. 1 (1988): 47–49.

King, Martin L., Jr. "Letter from Birmingham Jail." 16 April 1963. http://mlk-kpp01
.stanford.edu/index.php/encyclopedia/documentsentry/annotated
_letter_from_birmingham/

Kymlicka, Will. *Contemporary Political Philosophy*, 2nd ed. New York: Oxford University Press, 2001.

LifeSiteNews.com. "Gay Human Rights Complaint against Calgary Bishop Dropped—Was All about Getting Media Attention." 26 Aug. 2005. http://www.lifesitenews.com/ldn/2005/aug/05082601.html

McLachlin, Beverley. "Freedom of Religion and the Rule of Law: A Canadian Perspective." In *Recognizing Religion in a Secular Society: Essays in Pluralism, Religion, and Public Policy*, edited by Douglas Farrow, 12–34. Kingston: McGill-Queen's University Press, 2005.

———. "Unwritten Constitutional Principles: What Is Going On?" Lord Cooke Lecture, Victoria University of Wellington, New Zealand, 1 Dec. 2005. http://www.scc-csc.gc.ca/court-cour/ju/spe-dis/bm05-12-01-eng.asp

McLaughlin, Terence H. "The Distinctiveness of Catholic Education." In *The Contemporary Catholic School: Context, Identity, and Diversity*, edited by Terence H. McLaughlin, Joseph M. O'Keefe, and Bernadette O'Keefe, 136–54. London: Falmer Press, 1996.

McNeill, John J. *The Church and the Homosexual*. Kansas City: Sheed Andrews and McMeel, 1976.

Miller, J. Michael. *The Holy See's Teaching on Catholic Schools*. Manchester, NH: Sophia Institute Press, 2006.

Nozick, Robert. *Anarchy, State, and Utopia*. New York: Basic Books, 1974.

Ontario Equity and Inclusive Education Strategy. http://www.edu.gov.on.ca/eng/policyfunding/EquityQuickFacts.pdf (see also: http://www.edu.gov.on.ca/eng/policyfunding/equity.html)

Perrin, David B. *Studying Christian Spirituality*. New York: Routledge, 2007.

Pontifical Council for the Family. *Family, Marriage and "De Facto" Unions*. 26 July 2000. http://www.vatican.va/roman_curia/pontifical_councils/family/documents/rc_pc_family_doc_20001109_de-facto-unions_en.html

Pontifical Council for Justice and Peace. *Compendium of the Social Doctrine of the Church*. Chapter VIII: The Political Community, Part IV: The Democratic System. 2004. http://www.vatican.va/roman_curia/pontifical_councils/justpeace/documents/rc_pc_justpeace_doc_20060526_compendio-dott-soc_en
· .html

Rawls, John. *A Theory of Justice*. London: Oxford University Press, 1971.

R. v. Big M Drug Mart [1985] 1 S.C.R. 295. http://www.canlii.org/en/ca/scc/doc/1985/1985canlii69/1985canlii69.html

Ratzinger, Joseph, and Vittorio Messori. *The Ratzinger Report: An Exclusive Interview on the State of the Church*. San Francisco: Ignatius Press, 1985.

Smith and Chymyshyn v. Knights of Columbus and others, 2005 BCHRT 544 November 29, 2005, File Number 1258. Reasons for Decision. http://www.bchrt.bc.ca/decisions/2005/pdf/Smith_and_Chymyshyn_v_Knights_of_Columbus_and_others_2005_BCHRT_544.pdf

Sollier, Joseph. "The Communion of Saints." In *The Catholic Encyclopedia*. New York: Robert Appleton Company, 1908. http://www.newadvent.org/cathen/04171a.htm

Taylor, Charles. "The Politics of Recognition." In *Multiculturalism and "The Politics of Recognition": An Essay by Charles Taylor with commentary by Amy Gutmann*, edited by Steven C. Rockefeller, Michael Walzer, and Susan Wolf. Princeton, NJ: Princeton University Press, 1992.

Westen, John-Henry. "Interview: The Vatican on just vs. unjust discrimination based on sexual orientation: Ban on adoption, marriage, even military are not unjust discrimination." 15 Dec. 2009. http://www.lifesitenews.com/news/archive/ldn/1991/21/9121512

CHAPTER SIX

LONDON ISLAMIC SCHOOL: MILLSTONE OR MILESTONE?

Asma Ahmed

"My father came to London because of London Islamic School. I knew how you looked like before the first day of school, we went on the website and I saw your picture," said Zach to his teacher one October morning. Zach's father is the breadwinner for his family. When I was beginning to research the London Islamic School in November 2009, Zach's father had been unemployed since he came to London in August. He had been willing to risk unemployment to ensure that his children could go to the Islamic school of his choice. Zach has an older and a younger sibling. His older brother began associating with disreputable friends and, to the distress of his parents, eventually left home. He had only a superficial knowledge of Islam, and his confidence in the faith had withered. Zach's father vowed that his other children would not struggle like his older son. He researched the cities in southwestern Ontario to find a friendly, academically strong, religiously moderate, and professional school for his children. He chose the London Islamic School (LIS), in London, Ontario.

There are many stories like Zach's. Muslim youth who lose confidence in their faith and are not rerouted or assisted by their family or members of the community often find themselves lost and engulfed by peer groups that have no affiliation to their faith, especially in the modern West. I encountered Zach in my fourth year at LIS. I was working there and enjoying the experience while I was doing my master's, working with like-minded individuals to help educate and raise the next generation. I had begun reading

145

FAITH AND CITIZENSHIP

Tariq Ramadan, and his books on integration and the challenges of youth in the West helped me to better understand their identity crisis. LIS was growing, and it was attracting the children of young first- and second-generation Muslim Canadians. Given my privileged position as a participant observer at LIS, my experiences and those of my family as immigrants to Canada, and my interest in how people acquire their identities, I decided to focus my research on LIS, its activities, and the experiences and expectations of those who attend the school. I selected Tariq Ramadan's work to guide discussion in this chapter due to his extensive work on integration and the plight of Muslims in the West. His books, articles, and lectures revolve around integration and post-integration issues and stress the necessity of Muslim contributions to Western society.[1]

Ramadan asks, "who will restore to them [these and other youth] the elements and sense of their identity? Who will reconstruct it or, at least, give them some milestones which should permit them to find, consciously and freely, their own way?"[2] He argues that central questions such as the following need to be addressed and satisfactorily answered:

> Are Muslims truly capable of living in secularized societies? Are their values compatible with those of democracy? Can they live side by side and mingle with their non-Muslim neighbours? Can they combat the shocking behaviour exhibited in their name, in the form of terrorism, domestic violence, forced marriage, and the like? Can they free themselves from their social ghettos, those breeding grounds of unemployment, insecurity, and marginality?[3]

I sought to explore such questions in the context of the purposes and educational activities of an independent Islamic school. I was interested in considering what Islamic schools are and why they exist. The main focus of my inquiry was the LIS and its purposes. More specifically, I sought to explore Muslim youth integration and the development of a robust Canadian Muslim identity, employing LIS as a case study. I utilized three research tools in my inquiry: key informant interviews, literature and document analysis, and, to a lesser extent, participant observation. I recruited 27 key informants, composed of five parents, ten students (including five graduates), six staff members (including the principal), four Board members, and two non-Muslims.

146

Public Apprehension of Islamic Schools

I could not ignore public suspicion over possible ominous purposes of Islamic schools, which was akin to the proverbial "elephant in the room" throughout my inquiry. In the conceptual frame borrowed from Ramadan, Islamic schools in the West that operate with the single-minded doctrinal focus of the stereotypical *madrassa* would be millstones for young Muslims, rather than milestones along a path to multiple identity, critical loyal citizenship, and "post-integration."[4] (This idea will be further elaborated in the next section.) Indeed, media and public concerns over possible hidden purposes of Islamic schools are potential millstones themselves.

In August 2007, John Tory, then leader of Ontario's opposition Progressive Conservatives, announced that his party would support public funding for faith-based schools in the impending general election, provided they taught the Ontario curriculum, participated in provincial testing, and employed qualified teachers, much as Bernard Shapiro had recommended in *The Report of the Commission on Private Schools in Ontario*.[5] Although representatives of Jewish, Muslim, Hindu, and Sikh faith groups expressed support for Tory's proposal, the idea was rejected by the governing Liberal party on the grounds that it would divert scarce tax monies from the public schools and weaken social cohesion. In their newspaper article in September 2007, Sheikh, Simard, and Awan explained that ill-founded "assumptions and fears come into play ... ranging from equating Islamic schools with the stereotyped 'madrassa' to presuming that these schools will trample over women's rights."[6] They pointed out that there was no evidence that the many Islamic schools operating in Canada, publicly funded or not, were operating in accord with these derogatory stereotypes, or that they constituted a threat to social cohesion.

John Tory's Progressive Conservatives did not succeed in unseating the governing Liberals in the 2007 Ontario election, and it seems clear that public opposition to his proposal to fund faith-based schools contributed to the result; a survey commissioned by *The Globe and Mail* found 71 per cent of voters opposed to it.[7] It is doubtful whether fears of *madrassa*-like indoctrination in Islamic schools figured prominently in the voters' rejection of the policy, as those surveyed seemed to base their opposition more generally on a disapproval in principle of publicly funding any religious schools, including the constitutionally guaranteed Roman Catholic separate schools. But it would also be unrealistic to assume that public suspicions about the purposes of Islamic schools, the content of their curriculum, and the form

FAITH AND CITIZENSHIP

of their pedagogy did not have some effect, or that such concerns have dissipated entirely.

The Plight of Muslims in the Modern West

In modern times the presence of Muslims in North America has been associated with various forms of debate and conflict. The wave of recent Muslim immigrants to North America was driven by dire economic conditions in places such as North Africa, Turkey, India, and Pakistan. The possibility of creating a European or North American Islam would have been a farfetched concept given the economic instability of these immigrants and their struggles for basic needs and settlement.[8] Their children and grandchildren live in different times and changed circumstances, in which international and local events have created various tensions. As eloquently described by Ramadan, these range from the "Rushdie affair to the excesses of the Taliban, from the violence and killings in the Middle East to the daily horrors in Algeria." Such events have, as he explains, "engendered a climate of fear."[9] Indeed, in a 1997 report the Runnymede Trust in Britain referred to this as "Islamophobia."[10]

Mosque leaders and Islamic organizations have recognized that this climate of fear poses a difficult and inescapable problem for contemporary Muslims, especially Muslim youth. Adults have "found themselves obliged to adapt to the situation of their young people, speak their language, reshape the format of religious education and redefine their structures of social and cultural activity. On the other hand, the renewed fashion for religious observance among a minority of young people has led to the creation of a large number of Islamic associations."[11] Many Muslim youth now see themselves as "having a right to be in Europe [or North America] and they expect recognition of their civil rights."[12]

In the 1990s, *ulama* (Muslim religious scholars) from the Muslim world and Muslim leaders and intellectuals in the West recommended principles for Muslims who live in the West. These entailed that a Muslim, whether resident or citizen, should see himself or herself as involved in a contract, both moral and social, with the country in which he lives, and should respect that country's laws; also, since Western legislation (which is secular in nature) allows Muslims to practise the basics of their religion, there is nothing to prevent Muslims, or any other citizens, from making choices that accord with their religion.[13] However, in discussing the challenges faced by a Muslim living in a modern Western society, Ramadan observes that unfortunately most Muslims have reduced Islam to sets of rules and

148

regulations that separate the lawful (*halal*) from the unlawful (*haram*), and that they tend to believe that *fiqh* (Islamic Jurisprudence) has the answer to all the problems Muslims face.[14] Such an understanding of Islam, he argues, makes it "impossible to give birth to an affirmative, confident and constructive perception of Muslim identity which develops real abilities to inscribe itself in the European landscape."[15]

In *What I Believe*, Ramadan identifies three stages of immigrant integration: settlement, integration, and post-integration. He argues that all Muslim immigrants and their descendents should pass through the stages, including those practising Muslims who are hesitant to integrate because they fear they will lose their identity or religion in the process of moving from one stage to another. At the first stage, immigrant youth settle into their new environment and get acquainted with their new surroundings. Their immediate goals will be to meet basic needs such as food, water, shelter, and employment. To some families an immediate need is also "protecting themselves ... [and] the survival of their religious identity."[16] Some may develop an "us versus them" mentality or perhaps may become "reticent to express their Muslimness openly and to facilitate integration they [may have] engaged in 'survival strategies' such as the Anglicization of names."[17]

Ramadan describes the second stage, integration, or adopting the attitude that one is a full-fledged citizen, as being characterized by struggles to adapt or reform, during which immigrants strive for equal treatment as well as for laws and policies to protect minority rights.[18] Ramadan argues that it is at this stage that Muslim youth can achieve a psychological and intellectual sense of belonging—a feeling of being home.[19] In essence, the dynamics of integration usually shift from feelings of not belonging to trying to belong. But some Muslim communities and individuals go beyond such concerns to what Ramadan calls a post-integrative stage. At this stage, immigrant youth such as Zach have mastered the language and the legal framework of the host country,[20] and attitudes of participation and contribution are fostered.[21] Ramadan also refers to this stage as "creative transformational reform."[22] He argues that the process of integration and post-integration requires continuous reconciliation, including reconciling "individuals with the different dimensions of their being, their origins, and their hopes" so as to empower them to let go of defensive, passionate, and anxious reactions when dealing or interacting with others.

Ramadan's discussions are relevant to our discussion of Islamic schools because the students at LIS come from a variety of backgrounds, which might predispose them to be located at any one of Ramadan's three stages,

FAITH AND CITIZENSHIP

or even at intermediary positions between the stages. How is such variety to be accommodated within an Islamic school or single classroom? It is important to understand what schools should ultimately work toward with students. Is the school—its teachers, officials, curriculum, and culture—to accept family expectations in this regard, or should Islamic schools in Ontario and elsewhere in the West encourage progress toward higher stages of Ramadan's model? How might this be done? What types of school environment, curriculum, and pedagogy would foster progress toward the post-integrative stage while remaining sensitive to each student's unique background?

If the family is located at one of the lower stages in Ramadan's model, the children or the youth of that family might be at or close to moving to another stage. In this respect, Ramadan's "genuine applied, critical pedagogy" can foster movement through the stages by reconciling individuals' different dimensions of being in ways that can "enable them to overcome anxious, reactive and passionate reactions."[23] This kind of shift in thinking requires day-to-day, real-life encounters for individuals to feel a sense of comfort and confidence in who they are and who they are dealing with. This would seem particularly important when the learners are children. Such a pedagogy requires a support system, a community that recognizes the challenges faced by the young and has an understanding of the goals and purposes of integration and post-integration—in short, the kind of support system that can be provided by a school and supporting community that are sensitive to the distinctive situations and learning needs of immigrant children. Regular public schools may be able to provide some such environments, but providing complete support can be particularly difficult if the immigrant children concerned are part of one distinct minority among many others.

Ramadan's work includes many ideas on the dimensions of post-integration and how it can be achieved. I have generated a checklist of integration and post-integration features from Ramadan's writings, which I used to help inform and assess the situation in the London Islamic School during my interviews with key informants. Table 6.1 shows an abridged form of this checklist.[24] It contains both the elements of the journey toward his Stage 3 and the end goals for achieving post-integration.

Table 6.1

Stage 3: Integration and Post-Integration Checklist[a]

"Individuals, families, and schools shall ..."

1.	recognize that one can have multiple identities and multiple loyalties. (pp. 36, 38)
2.	never extend a blind support to any of their identities. One shall remain faithful to justice, dignity, and equality, and criticize and demonstrate against government [when justified]. (p. 38)
3.	be confident, through education, to develop better knowledge of oneself and one's history, to shape a conscience and intelligence that is confident and serene: that is both sure of itself and humble toward others. Ultimately, self-confidence shall be allied to confidence in others. (p. 87)
4.	have a reformist approach: to take Qur'anic verses and recognize the various interpretations and suggest understandings and implementations that take into account context in which one lives. (p. 63)
5.	control passion and emotion: have a balanced, critical, and self-critical intervention. (p. 14)
6.	recognize the commonality with Judaism and Christianity and values advocated by humanist, atheists, and agnostics (p. 13). Shall recognize values and hopes are more essential and numerous that differences (pp. 14, 20)
7.	accept Muslim faith and Western culture, to be faithful to fundamental religious principles and have ownership of Western culture. (pp. 42, 44)
8.	become gifts and questions to our fellow citizens, Muslims must remain "questions": with their faith, their practices, their behaviour, and their day-to-day civic commitment, they must positively challenge their fellow citizens. (p. 116)
9.	set up local initiatives where women and men of different religions, cultures, and sensitivities create spaces for mutual knowledge and shared commitment: spaces for trust. (p. 94)
10.	have shared projects, day-to-day mingling with fellow citizens, and personal involvement to awaken the minds, bring awareness, and spur the desire to go further, to understand better, and to carry out a dialogue. One must really live and work *together* on *shared* projects. (p. 115)

11.	develop trust of their fellow citizens. (p. 130)
12.	understand that secular does not mean wiping of religion; it ensures equality; it means separation of church and state. (p. 31)
13.	contribute to a reformulation of the political questions of the day. (p. 126)

ᵃ Adapted from Ramadan, *What I Believe*. The page references from this book that correspond to items in the list are included here in parentheses.

Millstones

The term "millstone" in the title of this chapter is intended in Ramadan's work to serve as a contrast to his usage of "milestone" required for individuals to find their way, consciously and freely, to a strong and confident Muslim and Canadian identity. A millstone is literally "a large round stone used for grinding grain," but Ramadan uses the term figuratively, as I do in my title, to refer to "something that hinders or handicaps." Table 6.2 illustrates the essence of the figurative millstone that Ramadan discusses in his work on Muslim integration, by drawing contrasts with what Ramadan advocates through his use of milestones.

Ramadan's discussion of the negative consequences of having a discriminated minority mindset in the settlement stage mentioned above illustrates how that can act as a millstone. Having a victimized mindset with true loyalty to a specific country, race or denomination, an us-versus-them mentality, all demonstrate a millstone that is handicapping Muslim youth from attaining, or moving along the continuum toward, full-fledged citizenship and post-integration to the Canadian identity. Another kind of millstone for a Muslim youth can be assimilating—as in the case of Zach's older brother, who lost his Muslim cultural identity, perhaps because he did not have opportunities to come to terms with either his Canadian or his Muslim identity.

Integration and milestones can be facilitated with a clear understanding that the core principles of Islam are not contrary to the core values of the West. Given the universality of the message of Islam, *shumuliyat al Islam*, Muslims are truly capable of living and succeeding in a secularized society. Their values and principles are fully compatible with democracy. They can live and work side by side with their non-Muslim fellow citizens and have the "confidence, consistency, contribution, creativity, communication, contestation and compassion"[25] to enable them to make valued contributions to the broader society.

LONDON ISLAMIC SCHOOL: MILLSTONE OR MILESTONE? | AHMED

Table 6.2

Conceptual Contrasts between Ramadan's Milestones and Millstones[a]

Millstones	Milestones
Having a mindset of a discriminated against minority; victimized mindset	Thinking of oneself as among the majority—as a citizen with the same and equal rights
Abode of war	Abode of witness or testimony
Mistrust of fellow citizens	Revolution of trust (p. 124); to become gifts and questions to fellow citizens (p. 115)
True loyalty citizenship	Critical loyalty citizenship
One identity	Multiple identities
Literalist/cultural	Reformist (p. 3)
Defensive/ apologetic approach (p. 62)	Deconstructing and reconstructing without disconnecting (p. 126); reconciliation (pp. 38, 129)

[a] Adapted from Ramadan, *What I Believe.* Page numbers indicate Ramadan's own wording; other entries in the table are paraphrased.

Teaching and Learning at LIS

LIS was established in 1996 as a properly registered, private, fee-charging K–8 day school that is in full compliance with Ontario's Ministry of Education curriculum guidelines.[26] In 2009–10, the school had an enrolment of 189 students and employed 23 staff members (including teachers). It is located adjacent to the London Muslim Mosque and operates under the mosque's jurisdiction. LIS is one of 46 Islamic schools operating in Ontario as part of the 869 registered independent schools as of 2006.[27]

There are a few distinct features of this school that one does not find in the public system, mainly because it adheres to the Islamic faith. First, the school has three extra classes that are directly related to Islam: Qur'an, Islamic Studies, and Arabic Studies. Second, all staff are Muslims. Third, all female staff and all female students above and including those in grade 4 wear the *hijab* (the veil). Fourth, school uniform is mandatory. The school uniform for girls is a blue, long, loose-fitting skirt or pants, while boys wear pants and a shirt that are also loose fitting. Fifth, students in grade 4 and beyond participate in prayers for 20 minutes every afternoon, in congregation, in the gym. On Fridays, staff and students participate in the Friday congregation with the Muslim community at large. The intent is for the students to live and learn "how to be and remain Muslim," which is by definition what *shariah* entails, as mentioned by Ramadan.[28]

In terms of special events, the school is part of many contests with the wider community such as the Jump Rope for Heart, MS Readathon, London District Science and Technology Fair, London-Middlesex Health Unit Contests, All Science Challenge, and the Gauss Math Challenge. Several items in the post-integration checklist (see Table 6.1) encourage such day-to-day interaction with other fellow citizens (items 8–10 in particular). The events above are venues for meaningful interaction between LIS and other surrounding schools, including the secular public schools, Catholic schools, and other independent schools. This is a supervised attempt to encourage respectful interaction with the wider community and therefore develop trust and respect of their fellow citizens.

The non-religious program of studies at LIS is based on the Ontario curriculum, which mainly includes English, math, science, social studies, French, physical education, and art. All classes are co-educational, except for grade 6 and 7/8 Physical Education. Religious instruction, which mainly entails Qur'an, Arabic, and Islamic Studies, amounts to an average of 11.5 classes of 40 minutes per week. The religious curriculum includes exegesis of small chapters of the Qur'an, *hadith* (sayings of the Prophet), *fiqh* (Islamic Jurisprudence), and *aqida* (essential beliefs). The Arabic curriculum comes from the IQRA Foundation in Chicago and is designed to teach Arabic as a second language. From my interviews there was a feeling that LIS provides a compartmentalized Islamic education—as one parent called it, an "add-on"—as opposed to a more interwoven, holistic Islamic education. This view is eloquently captured by a parent in the quotation offered below, but there were five similar responses from parents and teachers.[29] "Okay, I think for the purposes of LIS, as it currently exists and as I have currently experienced it, [it] gives kids is the straightforward curriculum and to add on to it Qur'an, Arabic and Islamic studies. That's how I see it, straightforward like give them the Ontario curriculum and add on to it Arabic and the Qur'an."

Also, with respect to religious instruction, the curriculum is felt to be not as interactive as the core subjects. It does not encourage critical thinking about, or a deep understanding of, the religious instruction presented in class, as noted by one of the teachers: "There is yet to be a religious curriculum which is appealing to the kids (e.g. colorful, animated), cohesive in terms of building vocabulary and grammatical structures, and which encourages conversation through interactive exercises which pertain to a child's everyday life (e.g. a scene in the park, in the grocery store, buying a pet, in the airport, etc)."

With religious schools their goals and commitments are likely to be different, and more demanding in some respects than in public schools or other independent schools. As Ramadan points out, "Commitments may be broken down in turn into two components: commitment to the implementation of the broad values of society and commitment to the performance of a specific type of role within the structure of society."[30] Both components are pertinent to discussions of Islamic schools in Ontario, as their focus on knowledge about and commitment to Islam does not overrule the necessity to abide by the values of the broader society.

The Challenges of Muslim Youth

Zach's story, which I described at the beginning of the chapter, inspired my inquiry into the challenges of Muslim youth from the perspective of the key informants. Having an understanding of the challenges, one can assess if the resources currently in place help or hinder the struggles of the Muslim youth. The themes emerging from the analysis of responses to a questionnaire about challenges facing Muslims (see Appendix A) were the following: (1) a plethora of distractions, (2) gender relations, (3) identity crisis and double personalities, (4) myths and stereotypes, and (5) environment not conducive to maintaining an Islamic identity.

Teachers at the LIS are aware of the challenges that exist. One teacher observed,

> I don't want to say "you don't know what the right thing is anymore." Morals and values have become relative in our time, so relative, that people are really confused. And with the youth, it's even more [so] because they lack experience so they are even more confused.... For most Muslim youth now, they are children of new immigrants. So the parents sometimes, who are the prime support system for the youth, are not really there.

Indeed, Muslim youth coming from new immigrant families find their parents struggling with settlement, survival, and integration. They cannot

FAITH AND CITIZENSHIP

look to them for help understanding the Canadian context and reconciling between the culture and values at home and in the broader society.

One student articulated two distractions she faces:

> during that time [i.e., in the years when one is at school], it's a lot about forming your own identity, so you're getting influenced by so many different directions, like your parents want you to do something, there is also the media, which is a really, really big part ... so like what you see on TV shows, like all the smoking and the drinking and the drugs, that's a really big thing that influences you.

In addition to the media influences described above, one of the other main challenges for youth is the discrepancy between the values of Muslims and non-Muslims in terms of cross-gender interactions, as captured by a former LIS student:

> When I came into high school and started mingling and started forming relationships with non-Muslims, I noticed there are a lot of relationships like between boys and girls, and like boyfriends and girlfriends. That was a major ... I don't know how I can say it ... and now you see that girls and boys not only play with each other, but are also going out with each other, and experimenting [with] different things.

Zine calls the phenomenon alluded to above "split personality syndrome," whereby one "develops a double person in their efforts to resolve the cultural contradictions between home and school."[31] A current board member at the LIS described this struggle as a pressure to "integrate [with] the current materialistic culture of this society, because they [the youth] start to see a divide between their values and their beliefs." Furthermore, he said:

> They have to participate in things that go against their value system ... a double whammy for the Muslim youth [because] in addition to what other youths are experiencing, the Muslim youth has other internal problems. The extreme is that the kids feel that they have to live different lives. That is a huge pressure on somebody to establish a personality ... where they put a different face, when they step out of the home. The outside is a direct contradiction to their heritage, and before they act they stand out as different from the rest of the community [at large].

Muslim youth are faced with some difficulties in their day-to-day life simply because they follow a specific religion. As one graduate student commented: "Terrorism and the stereotypes that surround us from the news and facing people at school is tough, and then trying to confront people who ask questions and they [the Muslims] don't necessarily know how to answer if they don't have enough knowledge. So when people don't have enough knowledge of our religion to answer then this becomes a struggle of being in a public school."

Purposes of LIS

The themes that emerged from the study concerning the purposes of LIS were the following: (1) high academic standards, (2) a community-based facility, (3) provision of a safe, protected and nurturing place to be a Muslim, and (4) provision of an Islamic environment and Islamic education. School and student success has become a major goal of the school. The interview analysis indicates that there is a clear connection between the challenges faced by Muslim youth and the purposes of Islamic schooling. For instance, the challenge of "living in an environment not conducive to maintaining an Islamic identity" corresponds to the purpose "providing an Islamic environment."

One of the comments made with respect to the current purposes of the school by a teacher was the following: "to educate our youth about Islam and let them have the experience to be in an Islamic environment. To feel what Islam means, not just to memorize it, but to feel it, to live it in their heart and their everyday activities."

With respect to the fourth purpose, it is imperative to shed light on the objectives of Islamic education. Ramadan delineates three objectives: (a) the education of the heart, which is to be conscious of God (*taqwa*) and *hayaa*: to recognize our responsibilities toward "ourselves, our bodies, our relatives, our communities, and the human family at large," (b) the education of the mind, which is to have an understanding of the primary sources of Islam (Qur'an and *sunnah*) and to have an awareness of one's surroundings, and (c) joining the education of the heart and the mind to allow for personal growth.[32] Ramadan emphasizes the study of environment and people to help with integration rather than creating isolation.

In terms of Ramadan's second objective, the education of the mind, LIS exceeds its academic expectations in comparison to other schools in London: the students graduating from LIS score high marks in their secondary schools, according to studies conducted by the LIS Board. Moreover,

LIS has incorporated the education of the heart or character education in staff, modelling good Islamic behaviour and integrating Islamic terms in their communication and instructions; however, the school did not have a systematic, school-wide, and overarching system for character education to join the education of the mind and the heart until 2009–10. A school-wide initiative was adopted in 2008–09 to remind students of Islamic values and hone their inner moral compass. One of the teachers suggested that we follow a book given to her by her deaf son's therapist, entitled *Building Moral Intelligence* by Michele Borba. There are seven virtues listed in the book (see below), and the school started to celebrate one virtue each month. The staff decided to call the campaign "Character of the Month." This was part of a broader attempt to institute a **tarbiyah** program in the school. *Tarbiyah* is a systematic, comprehensive (i.e., it addresses all aspects of the personality: spiritual, intellectual, moral, social, physical, etc), and continuous program of character development. The teachers endorsed this campaign because they saw it as necessary given the importance of character education in Islam, and because of some reoccurring incidences of profanity and lack of respect amongst students.

Drawing parallels and exploring common ground between Islamic tradition and core western virtues was a central goal of the character-education activities described above. The seven virtues discussed by Borba and used in the LIS character development campaign, namely empathy, conscience, self-control, respect kindness, tolerance and fairness,[33] are all enduring qualities in the Islamic tradition. Thus, while the campaign's main practical goal was to create a school climate and culture conducive to mutual respect and care, it also demonstrated shared values with other non-Muslim Canadians. The character development campaign also served as a reminder that the Canadian population is a multicultural, multi-faceted, and pluralistic community. It is important for the students to know that this kind of education provides common ground for others outside their school property. By sharing the same values and principles, this helps one to build bonds and facilitates cooperation with others.

There appear to be close connections between the challenges facing Muslim youth in the West and the provision of a safe, protected, and nurturing environment to learn and practise Islam. High academic standards promise to provide students with stepping stones that lead to future academic success, which, in turn, should help build their confidence. As discussed by Coleman, a community-based facility generates a rich reserve of social capital on which students (and others) can draw to assist not just with their education but also in building their identity and dispelling the debilitating threats of negative myths and stereotypes.[34] The themes are intertwined. Moreover, the purposes can be readily seen to be rooted in the basal conceptions of Islam.

Broadly speaking, the purposes of LIS, as articulated in the interviews and interpreted above, complement the theoretical discussion of the main purposes of schools in general, especially with regard to the basic common schooling functions of education, socialization, and safety. With respect to education, at the time of my research, although the school was not fully meeting all the expected levels of instructional time in each subject due to the need to schedule time for religious instruction, all core subjects in the Ontario curriculum were being taught, and changes were in place to rectify the time allocation expectations in 2010–11. Moreover, the school's academic record is strong and growing, as illustrated by its strong reputation in the educational community and the strong performance of its students in city-wide academic competitions. Many examples emerged during the interviews of how LIS provides a protected, supportive, and social-capital-rich environment for nurturing Muslim identity, beliefs, and practices.

Through education, socialization, and corrective intervention, LIS helps its students build and develop a sense of identity and pride. The safety provided by the school is what makes the above functions possible. The physical, psychological, and emotional safety of the students on the school premises is a necessary purpose to allow for education. In these and related ways the theoretical purposes of schools discussed above were clearly reflected in the actual expectations of purposes stated by interviewees.

Millstone or Milestone?

As discussed above, my tentative, working hypothesis was that LIS represents a sincere effort at delivering the "necessary knowledge" that Ramadan identifies for young Muslims to find their way and build a strong, solid, and responsible Muslim identity in the modern West. Ramadan's integrative and post-integrative approach was adopted in order to provide a rich conceptual frame for approaching this issue. On the basis of the findings discussed above, I have developed Figure 6.1 in order to tentatively locate LIS with respect to the conceptual contrast between the milestone and millstone concepts developed from Ramadan's stages of settlement, integration, and post-integration.

FAITH AND CITIZENSHIP

Figure 6.1

Locating LIS on Ramadan's Integration and Post-integration Continuum

Millstone One identity Victimized mindset True loyalty				Milestone Multiple identity Majority mindset Critical loyalty							
				LIS							
Settlement Us-vs.-them mentality Struggling to make ends meet				Integration I am a full-fledged citizen mentality Participation and Contribution				Post-Integration Master language and legal framework Creative transforma- tional reform			

The divided segments in each stage shown in Figure 6.1 are intended to illustrate the continuum and allow for some graduated choice within each of the stages, rather than mark precise internal divisions. I have located LIS toward the middle of the integration stage on the basis of my personal observations of the school and my interpretation of the interview findings reported above, using Ramadan's objectives of education.

The analysis of LIS reveals several features that indicate it is within the milestone spectrum, such as the fact that it does not view the West as abode of war, and its understanding that Western secularism does not imply the elimination of religion, but rather hopes to ensure equality by protecting freedom of religion while ensuring separation of Church and state. Features that received little or no support included: control of passion and emotion; having a balanced, critical and self-critical intervention; becoming gifts and questions to our fellow citizens; becoming a place where Muslims remain "questions" with their faith, their practices, their behaviour, and their day-to-day civic commitment, thereby providing vehicles to positively challenge their fellow citizens; and setting up local initiatives where women and men of different religions, cultures, and sensitivities create spaces for mutual knowledge and shared commitment: spaces for trust. On balance, when considering the level of support for the integration and post-integration features, I concluded that considerable room remains in which LIS could grow toward Ramadan's ideal of citizenship, integration and post-integration.

This view was confirmed when I considered Ramadan's discussion of the three objectives of education described above. As discussed earlier, the school educates and provides mechanisms for socialization focused on the heart so as to be conscious of God (*taqwa*), so as to recognize broader values, conceptions of character, and responsibilities toward "ourselves, our bodies, our relatives, our communities, and the human family at large."[35] The one and only systematic example of this of which I became aware at LIS was the Character of the Month program used as a *tarbiyah* initiative. The second of Ramadan's objectives of education emphasizes understanding the primary sources of Islam (Qur'an and *sunnah*), and develop an awareness of one's surroundings to "find the way of faithfulness in everyday life."[36] The religious instruction at LIS does not seem to be as relevant and engaging to the students as could be wished, nor does it entail a reformist and self-critical approach. Furthermore, as noted by a current parent of LIS, the Qur'an, Arabic, and Islamic studies curriculum is fragmented, which will likely hinder development of the more complete and integrated understanding of Islam advocated by Ramadan.

Furthermore, the interviews showed that at least some participants viewed the school and the students as being "segregated" or isolated from the wider London community. But if one agrees with Ramadan, then a "genuine applied, critical pedagogy"[37] can foster movement through his stages by reconciling "individuals with the different dimensions of their being, their origins, and their hopes" in ways that "can enable them to overcome anxious, reactive and passionate reactions when encountering others."[38] The meshing of both these features is the intent of his third educational objective.

Implications

For Practice

I did not undertake this study with the intent of identifying weaknesses in Islamic schools or proposing recommendations for improvement. Yet I decided I had an obligation to suggest broad themes upon which LIS could focus in order to move toward the post-integration stage and to a more robust cultivation of Canadian citizenship. I believe that these themes would be valuable for other Islamic schools in Canada that have similar aims and outlooks to LIS, since they deal with similar populations, face similar threats, and share similar challenges and issues. The suggestions below have been generated from Ramadan's integration and post-integration checklist and from the themes generated with respect to the case study at LIS:

FAITH AND CITIZENSHIP

1. Islamic schools should investigate ways of working together on shared projects with their non-Islamic school peers and explore other ways to increase the day-to-day interactions between members of the Islamic school community and their fellow citizens.

2. Islamic Schools should seek ways to nurture and celebrate its students' multiple identities and multiple loyalties.

3. Islamic Schools should explore ways to inculcate in students acceptance of their obligations to become contributing global citizens, faithful to the ideals of justice, dignity, and equality.

4. Islamic Schools should constantly nurture consciousness of God.

5. Islamic Schools should give priority to developing a systematic *tarbiyah* program that is pervasive in all its daily activities and practices.

6. Islamic Schools should take appropriate steps to ensure that the pedagogy, curriculum, and resources of the classes of Qur'an, Arabic, and Islamic studies are engaging and relevant.

For Theory and Policy

In *The Report of the Commission on Private Schools in Ontario*, Shapiro observed that the more complex and dynamic the society, the greater is the need for clarifying the functions of its schools and the role that they should play in the ongoing attempt to realize a better society.[39] Dr. Dalton J. McGuinty, a teacher, professor, Ottawa Public School Board trustee, and the father of the current premier of Ontario, submitted a pertinent letter to the Shapiro Commission that stated that independent schools exist by virtue of interest, with parents that send their children to these schools paying their school taxes as well as paying fees to the school. Further, he argued that independent schools justify their right to exist in that they "efficiently serve the needs of their pupils and parents, and society, by fulfilling the basic function of the school."[40] For young Muslims growing up in a complex Western society such as Ontario, it is not at all clear that the public schools can provide an entirely adequate learning environment, especially as they do not seem to have any built-in ways to help young people from widely diverse backgrounds to find their cultural and religious ways, and build appropriately diverse and distinct identities. For these and other reasons, McGuinty endorsed independent religious schools as important and relevant components of our society that are "worthy of public support," and, through his recommendations, Shapiro concurred.

But what kinds of school environment, curriculum, and pedagogy would foster progress toward the post-integrative stage while being sensitive to each student's unique background? The recommendations for improved practice at LIS offered above point to one possible way forward. Greater emphasis, for example, could be placed on systematically developing students' sense of self-confidence through enriched history education, participation in more shared projects, and day-to-day mingling with students and citizens not enrolled in the school. The general approach would be aimed at nurturing feelings of mutual trust at a local level while fostering the development of a critical mind that can pave the road toward reconciliation between cultural traditions.[41] In essence, what appears to be required is a support system based on an understanding of Ramadan's integration and post-integration model. In a school such as LIS, an appropriate approach could be one in which the educational and socialization activities provided by the school and supported by the community are sensitive to the cultural and religious challenges faced by the children.

A major policy implication of my findings is that Islamic schools that seek to pursue Ramadan's path to post-integration will provide a service not only to the Muslim population but also to the larger community. Supporting Islamic schools that follow such guidelines, which can be delineated in policy, will enhance the prospects of confident Muslim youth being engaged in their communities and becoming contributing citizens of Canada. In the absence of such schools, there is a risk that parents who cannot afford to enroll their children in independent Islamic (or other religious) schools become locked into unaided struggles with the challenges and may fail to create positive connections to Canada and their fellow Canadians.

Concluding Remarks

With education and socialization Muslims can free themselves from their "social ghettos" and the minority mindsets that can easily become millstones preventing them from finding, "consciously and freely, their own way."[42] Given the universality of the message of Islam, Muslims are surely capable of living and succeeding in a secularized society.

Yet, in the final analysis, my initial hypothesis was neither completely upheld nor falsified. LIS is on its way to becoming a vehicle to effectively and deliberately deliver the "necessary knowledge" to provide milestones for young Muslims to consciously make their way in this Western society. But insofar as it falls short of the full possibilities of post-integration, and as long as it embodies forms and methods of religious instruction that do not encourage critical thinking and deep understanding, which contrasts sharply with those methods that animate the non-religious curriculum in LIS, it runs the risk of becoming a millstone.

FAITH AND CITIZENSHIP

Society would be diminished in the absence of well-operated schools dedicated to educating and socializing the young into their parents' religion, be they publicly funded or not. The ability of fully secular public schools to adequately, respectfully, and humanely meet the full educational needs of all immigrant children is surely limited. There is thus an important place for schools that can provide safe and secure learning environments in which young people can live and learn about their religion, while also mastering the standard curriculum. Therefore, the optimistic future for Islamic schools developed from Ramadan's vision as discussed in this chapter can be extended to other religious schools. All can contribute to the greater good by providing an education that shapes a conscience and intelligence that are confident and serene: an education that is both sure of itself and humble toward others, and that ultimately contributes to what Ramadan calls "a reformulation of the political questions of the day."

Appendix A
Student Interviews
Questions for Current LIS students
Initial Background Questions:

You attended LIS for grades _____
How many brothers and/or sisters do you have? _____   Did they attend LIS (if not, why not?) _____
Do you think LIS follows specific guidelines with regard to gender interaction?

Formal Interview Questions of current LIS Student:

What is Islam?   What does Islam mean to you?
What are the challenges of youth today?
What are the challenges of Muslim youth today?

How do you think LIS is different from other schools?
How do you think LIS is similar to other schools?

Probes:
a) Do you think your experiences at LIS are different from those of children going to other schools? If yes, how so?
b) Are you aware of attitudes or values that are important to you that you are developing at LIS?
c) Do you feel these will be an asset or a handicap after you leave LIS?
– at school?
– at home?
– in your life in general?

In what ways do you think your relationship with the opposite gender similar to, or different from, those of similarly aged students attending other schools? [probe for differences between public, Catholic, Independent schools]

Why do you think you go to LIS?
Why do you think LIS is here?
What would you change at LIS if you could and why?

Is there anything you wish to add? Have I forgotten to ask anything that you feel is important? Do you have any questions for me?

Notes

1 I would like to offer a word of caution that Ramadan does not speak for all Muslims, and his framework of reformulation and reconciliation is controversial even amongst Muslims living in the West. Some Muslims believe that Islam is a separate entity drastically different to the culture and values of the West, and that Ramadan is trying to change Islam to fit the Western context. Others believe that he is portraying the values and fundamentals of Islam in a framework that is not reflective of the true nature of the religion, that he is attempting to deceive the Western audience. Nevertheless, I believe that Ramadan offers a powerful framework for thinking about how Islamic schools may negotiate the difficult task of cultivating an Islamic identity while simultaneously cultivating citizenship in Western countries. Thus, I believe that his approach sheds unique light upon the research I outline in this chapter.

2 Tariq Ramadan, *To Be a European Muslim: A Study of Islamic Sources in European Context* (London: Islamic Foundation, 1999), 2.

3 Tariq Ramadan, *What I Believe* (New York: Oxford University Press, 2010), 125.

4 Ramadan, *To Be a European Muslim*, 67.

FAITH AND CITIZENSHIP

5 Bernard Shapiro, *Shapiro Commission: Public Funding for Independent Alternative Schools* (1986).

6 Muneeza Sheikh, Daniel Simard, and Khurram Awan, "Fear of Islamic Schools Based on False Stereotypes," *Toronto Star*, 20 Sept. 2007, http://www.thestar.com/article/258456, ¶ 2.

7 J. Pard, "Panel Debates Funding for Faith-Based Schools," *Globe and Mail*, 21 Sept. 2007. www.theglobeandmail.com/incoming/panel-debates-funding-for-faith-based-schools/article1082561/?page=all

8 Tariq Ramadan, "Europe's Muslims Find a Place for Themselves," *Le Monde Diplomatique*, April 1998, http://mondediplo.com/1998/04/07islam

9 Ramadan, "Europe's Muslims Find a Place for Themselves," ¶ 3.

10 Commission on British Muslims, 1992, http://www.runnymedetrust.org/projects-and-publications/projects/pastprojects/commissionOnBritishMuslims.html, ¶ 1.

11 Ramadan, "Europe's Muslims Find a Place for Themselves," ¶ 5.

12 Ramadan, "Europe's Muslims Find a Place for Themselves," ¶ 6.

13 Ramadan, "Europe's Muslims Find a Place for Themselves," ¶ 11.

14 Ramadan, *To Be a European Muslim*, 10.

15 Ramadan, *To Be a European Muslim*, 10.

16 Tariq Ramadan, *Western Muslims and the Future of Islam* (New York: Oxford University Press, 2004), 52.

17 S. Nyang, "Islam, American Society and the Challenges," *The Message* (2000), 2.

18 Ramadan, *What I Believe*, 5–6.

19 Ramadan, *Western Muslims and the Future of Islam*, 67.

20 Ramadan, *Western Muslims and the Future of Islam*, 71–72.

21 Ramadan, *What I Believe*, 5–6.

22 Ramadan, *What I Believe*, 48.

23 Ramadan, *What I Believe*, 38.

24 For the full checklist, see Asma Ahmed, "LIS: Millstone or Milestone," M.A. thesis, University of Western Ontario (2010), 43.

25 Ramadan, *What I Believe*, 85–86.

26 London Islamic School, http://www.londonislamicschool.com/

27 Deani Van Pelt, Patricia A. Allison, and Derek J. Allison, "Ontario's Private Schools: Who Chooses Them and Why?" *Studies in Educational Policy* (Vancouver: Fraser Institute, 2007), 9.

28 Ramadan, *What I Believe*, 360.

29 Using the key informant approach to gathering data, I conducted a total of 27 interviews with current students, graduates of LIS, parents of current students, parents of graduates, teachers, administrators and board members. Interview participants were given a code to maintain their anonymity.

30 Ramadan, *What I Believe*, 81.

31 Jasmin Zine, *Canadian Islamic Schools: Unravelling the Politics of Faith, Gender, Knowledge, and Identity* (Toronto: University of Toronto Press, 2008), 4.

32 Ramadan, *Western Muslims and the Future of Islam*, 129.

33 Michele Borba, *Building Moral Intelligence: The Seven Essential Virtues That Teach Kids to Do the Right Thing* (New York: Jossey-Bass, 2001).

34 James Coleman, "Social Capital in the Creation of Human Capital," *American Journal of Sociology* 94 (1988): S95–S120.

35 Ramadan, *Western Muslims and the Future of Islam*, 129.

36 Ramadan, *Western Muslims and the Future of Islam*, 129.

37 Ramadan, *What I Believe*, 38.

38 Ramadan, *What I Believe*, 38.

39 Shapiro, *Shapiro Commission*, 38.

40 McGuinty, "Why the Government Should Fund Faith-Based and Independent Schools," 1984, http://www.equalfunding.org/articles/Dr.DaltonJ.McGuinty .pdf, 2.

41 Ramadan, *What I Believe*, 132.

42 Ramadan, *To Be a European Muslim*, 2.

Bibliography

Ahmed, Asma. "LIS: Millstone or Milestone." Master's thesis. University of Western Ontario, 2010.

Borba, Michele. *Building Moral Intelligence: The Seven Essential Virtues That Teach Kids to Do the Right Thing*. New York: Jossey-Bass, 2001.

Coleman, James S. "Social Capital in the Creation of Human Capital." *American Journal of Sociology* 94 (1988): S95–S120.

Commission on British Muslims. 1992. http://www.runnymedetrust.org/projects -and-publications/projects/pastprojects/commissionOnBritishMuslims .html

London Islamic School. http://www.londonislamicschool.com/

McGuinty, Dalton J. "Why the Government Should Fund Faith-Based and Independent Schools." 1984. http://www.equalfunding.org/articles/Dr.Dalton J.McGuinty.pdf

Nyang, S. "Islam, American Society and the Challenges." *The Message*, 2000. www .icna.com/tm/feb00

Ontario Ministry of Education. *Report of the Commission on Private Schools in Ontario*. Toronto: Queen's Printer, 1986.

———. *Ontario Curriculum, Grades 1–6: Social Studies*. Toronto: Queen's Printer for Ontario, 2004.

Pard, J. "Panel Debates Funding for Faith-Based Schools." *Globe and Mail*. 21 Sept. 2007. http://www.theglobeandmail.com/incoming/panel-debates-funding-for-faith-based-schools/article1082561/?page=all

Ramadan, Tariq. "Europe's Muslims Find a Place for Themselves." *Le Monde Diplomatique*. April 1998. http://mondediplo.com/1998/04/07islam

———. *To Be a European Muslim: A Study of Islamic Sources in European Context*. London: Islamic Foundation, 1999.

———. *Western Muslims and the Future of Islam*. New York: Oxford University Press, 2004.

———. *What I Believe*. New York: Oxford University Press, 2010.

Shapiro, Bernard. *Shapiro Commission: Public Funding for Independent Alternative Schools*. Toronto: OSSTF, 1986.

Sheikh, Muneeza, Daniel Simard, and Khurram Awan. "Fear of Islamic Schools Based on False Stereotypes." *Toronto Star*. 10 Sept. 2007. http://www.thestar.com/article/258456

Van Pelt, Deani, Patricia A. Allison, and Derek. J. Allison. "Ontario's Private Schools: Who Chooses Them and Why?" *Studies in Educational Policy*. Vancouver: Fraser Institute, 2007.

Zine, Jasmin. *Canadian Islamic Schools: Unravelling the Politics of Faith, Gender, Knowledge, and Identity*. Toronto: University of Toronto Press, 2008.

PART C

DISSENT *and* CRITICAL THINKING

CHAPTER SEVEN

THE CHANGED CONTEXT FOR JEWISH DAY-SCHOOL EDUCATION

Alex Pomson and Randal F. Schnoor

Since the mid-nineteenth century, North American Jews have employed two primary frameworks for providing children with formal Jewish education: religious supplementary schools, operating at evenings and weekends; and all-day parochial schools, offering a dual curriculum of Jewish and general studies within a single institution. Until quite recently, the great majority of Jewish children in Canada and the United States were educated according to the first model. They were instructed in the particulars of Judaism in denominationally sponsored supplementary schools while they received the remainder of their education in government-funded public schools.[1] As Sarna has suggested, this arrangement provided a satisfactory solution to "the most fundamental question of Jewish life: how to live in two worlds at once, how to be both [North American] and Jewish, part of the larger society and apart from it."[2]

Over the last quarter-century, the "supplementary" approach to Jewish education has fallen increasingly out of favour, suggesting a changed assessment of the best means by which to negotiate one's way as a Jew in North America. A number of studies indicate a similar reassessment in other Western countries, as the number of children educated in Jewish all-day schools has risen to unprecedented levels.[3]

While much of day-school growth over the last fifty years—in North America as well as Europe—can be attributed to natural population growth among ultra-Orthodox Jews (still the great majority of those enrolled in

DISSENT AND CRITICAL THINKING

the schools), the increased numbers of religiously liberal day schools and the enrolment of an unprecedented number of students in such schools has been remarkable. The so-called abandonment of public education by sectors of the Jewish community that were once some of the most vocal advocates of public schooling's civic benefits has attracted both popular and scholarly comment.[4] The first religiously non-Orthodox day school in North America opened in 1951, some fifty years after the first Orthodox day school. Today, there are approximately 165 North American day schools either affiliated with **Reform** or **Conservative** denominations or organized as pluralistic or non-denominational institutions, with an enrolment estimated to be just under one-fifth of the total day-school population.[5]

With day-school growth has come a diversification in the profile of day-school families. In most parts of the world until as recently as the 1980s, parents whose children attended Jewish day schools were, typically, residents of Jewish neighbourhoods and were synagogue members who had themselves received a relatively intensive Jewish education.[6] With few exceptions, these parents were Jewish from birth, Orthodox in denominational orientation, and married to other Jews; they were people for whom paying for all-day Jewish schooling constituted the fullest expression of an already intensely engaged Jewish identity. Today, in many countries, Jewish day schools have successfully recruited a greater numbers of families with both diverse Jewish religious and communal commitments.[7] Many of these newer families lack an intensive Jewish education of their own and depend on the schools to teach them Jewish practices and concepts; some come to school with previously acquired Jewish social and cultural capital but are unfamiliar with the norms and expectations of parochial Jewish schools; others are conflicted about educating their children outside the public system and never seem fully reconciled with their educational choices (see, for example a special 2009 issue of the RAVSAK journal *HeYidiyon* that explores how schools must best work with such families).

Through a case study of one school, in this chapter we explore the interactions between these "non-traditional" day-school families and their children's school. We see these interactions as paradigmatic of the challenges for religious institutions more generally, and for parochial educational institutions more particularly, as they seek to build community both from and with increasingly diverse populations—populations who, though identifying with a particular religious or ethnic minority, are more committed to exercising individual choice than conforming with communal norms,[8] and who seem more interested in "personalizing" religion according to

172

their own preferences than in observing traditional communal practices.[9] This case study, of a school committed both to building community and to affirming diversity, provides an opportunity to weigh the prospects for building what Furman, as well as Shields and Seltzer, call "communities of difference": interpersonal webs of relationships founded on diversity rather than sameness.[10]

The Narrower Context for a Case Study

There are few communities where the shift to parochial, all-day Jewish education has been more dramatic than in Toronto, home to Canada's largest Jewish community. In 1970, only 2,600 (or 24 per cent) of Toronto children receiving any Jewish schooling attended parochial day schools, while 50 per cent (or 5,300) were enrolled in supplementary schools.[11] By 1983 some 7,200 children (55 per cent of all Jewish school enrolment) attended elementary day schools, and approximately 6,000 were enrolled in supplementary schools.[12] In 2001, nearly 11,000 (approximately 34 per cent of all Jewish children) were enrolled in day school, while the numbers in supplementary school remained stable at approximately 6,000.[13]

The organization, ethos, and enrolment of Jewish day schools in Toronto mirror sociological patterns in other large Jewish communities where there are also sufficient numbers of Jewish children to populate a variety of institutional options. In Toronto, a community of approximately 200,000 Jews, there are almost 40 all-day Jewish schools, affiliated with a full range of Jewish denominations (**Hasidic**, Yeshivah/ultra-Orthodox, modern Orthodox, Conservative, Reform) and/or aligned with a variety of educational philosophies (arts-based, Montessori, college preparatory). Within this mix there are a small number of schools conceived as "community" or "pluralistic" institutions, meaning that they (a) aim to serve all Jews regardless of religious affiliation and commitment (or lack thereof), (b) are not affiliated with any specific Jewish denomination, or (c) have not been incorporated by a particular religious body. These "community" schools constitute the fastest growing non-Orthodox day school sector; a recent census counted almost 100 such institutions across North America.[14]

One of these community schools was the site for a four-year research project in which the two of us set out to make sense of the relationships between parents and their children's school, and the influence of school and home on each other. At the time of the study, the school, the Downtown Jewish Day School (DJDS), was small, with just under 110 students between kindergarten and grade 6; today, it has almost 150 students on its roll and

DISSENT AND CRITICAL THINKING

extends to grade 8. It is located on the first floor of a building that is home to a long-established Jewish community centre. Situated in a downtown city neighbourhood that was once home to a major concentration of Jews, the school is at some distance from what today are the centres of Jewish residence in the city's suburbs.

As much because of its location as because of its pluralistic religious mission and progressive educational philosophy, the DJDS parent body differs in a number of respects from that of a conventional suburban Jewish day school. For private-school parents, this group seems relatively lacking in materialism; their decision to raise a family in downtown Toronto rather than moving to the suburbs expresses a rejection, in their view, of the large-home, multi-car, and materially excessive life of suburbanites. As one teacher put it, "For these parents, what is important is more the kinds of kids they have than the things their kids have." In terms of their religious behaviour, DJDS parents tend to be non-conformists who are certainly not inclined to do things because they or their own parents have always done them that way. Within our randomly selected research sample, half of the twenty-five couples we interviewed (some more than once) were either intermarried or conversionary, meaning that one parent either was not Jewish at the time of the research or had not been born Jewish but had converted to Judaism. (In turn, these significant life changes may have informed parents' evolving educational choices for their children.)

This is a highly educated—one might say intellectual—group, many of whom have been attracted to the downtown area because of its proximity to cultural institutions and to a major North American university. For most, living downtown is also an expression of their intent to disengage from organized and denominational Jewish life (and its schools). Only about half of the parents belong to Jewish institutions other than the downtown Jewish community centre where the school itself is located. Conventionally, social scientists view synagogue membership as a primary indicator of Jewish communal connection. Yet, while some 85 per cent of day-school parents in Toronto (and 95 per cent in the United States) currently maintain synagogue membership, only 50 per cent do so at DJDS, and a quarter of these are members of what Wertheimer would call a "progressive niche synagogue," a local fellowship where Jews band together periodically for prayer and other activities.[15] Those parents who do attend services at synagogues tend to prefer the style at a local "traditional egalitarian" service that is an idiosyncratic mix of progressivism and tradition rather than at any of the denominational congregations in the city's midtown neighbourhoods.

Others prefer to develop their own rituals either within their own immediate families or with close friends. They "believe without belonging," to use Davie's oft-quoted phrase.[16]

As we have indicated elsewhere,[17] vivid expression of what this mix of commitments means was provided by a DJDS mother who explained during an interview how her family invented its own high-holyday traditions:

> We still feel connected to our Judaism but not necessarily in the traditional way; a little more secular. Neither of us like synagogue, we haven't really found a place that we like to go as a family and our kids completely hate it and we don't want to make them go.... So we sometimes do go to Shaarei Chesed [a Conservative synagogue] ... to be with J's father in respect to him.... Otherwise on Rosh Hashanah we like to apple orchard, and to have our own family ceremonies as well. We sit in the orchard and talk about what our new year's resolutions are and we will go around and say what we want to do.... Or on Yom Kippur we go to a ravine and we ask for forgiveness from one another. We do things that are personally meaningful.... Generally, it is the six of us doing it together.... Our neighbour wanted to come with us this year, she is like a surrogate aunt. She is not Jewish but she is a surrogate aunt; so she came with us.

Accounting for Instability

The limited but steadily accumulating literature concerned with community/pluralistic Jewish day schools emphasizes the "complexity," "difficulty," and "instability" involved in this endeavour. As Shevitz and Wasserfall put it, adapting Beck's work, pluralist schools call people to cooperate with each other and find harmonious ways to deal with difference,[18] a process that is almost always challenging in schools, because, as Huberman observed some time ago, even in the best of circumstances schools tend to be emotional hothouses where difference readily evolves into dispute and even conflict.[19]

For the most part, researchers have attributed the instability of pluralist Jewish education to philosophical or conceptual causes, and in particular to the difficulty of determining what is meant by pluralism in relation to Jewish all-day schooling. Historically, parochial Jewish schools have been decidedly non-pluralistic; they have been founded to preserve or advance particular expressions of Jewish life and belief. Pluralistic day schools have been created to do something different, but it is not clear, as Conyer indicates, whether pluralism is a descriptive, phenomenological term whose purpose is to acknowledge the existence of demographic, ideological and/

DISSENT AND CRITICAL THINKING

or religious diversity, or whether it is a value-laden term that requires a nurturing and embracing of that diversity.[20] If the latter is indeed the central task of pluralist schools, few available models of Jewish schooling exist to indicate how to translate such concepts into educational practice (a task whose uncertainty is explored, for example, by both Seligman and Glaser).[21]

In this chapter, we propose an alternative explanation for the instability frequently found in religiously pluralist Jewish schools, attributing it to sociological rather than philosophical causes. Instead, therefore, of attributing the instability of pluralist Jewish schools to the lack of readily available conceptual or educational models or the ambiguity of their educational missions, we look instead to the social foundations of the schools as certain unstable kinds of self-chosen communities. Put simply, we argue that it is difficult to build community when people's values, commitments, and expectations are so diverse, and when this diversity, in turn, challenges a school's leadership, which, while deeply committed to maintaining a community and pluralistic framework, still feels obligated to adhere to normative standards of Jewish life, so as not to exclude any potential members. These normative standards relate to certain tenets of religious observance or values that encompass Jewish dietary laws, observance of Jewish holy days, a reverence for God and Israel, and the like. As will be seen below, it is these central pillars of Jewish life that become the flashpoints at DJDS that animate tension between the key stakeholders.

Points of Collision

To provide a sense of the challenges in building community in this setting we present some brief vignettes that demonstrate the ways in which constituents collide, negotiate, challenge, and dispute with one another around almost every aspect of school life as it relates to Jewish culture and religion.

Such collisions were especially acute, it seems, during the school's formative years. At that time, the form and purpose of the Judaic curriculum were matters for intense discussion in all kinds of school forums, but then so was almost every aspect of school practice, including dress code, dietary policy, the weekly schedule, student admissions, daily prayer, and affiliation with the organized Jewish community. In a school whose mission (in contrast to most other Jewish day schools) articulates a commitment to "respect the divergent modes of Jewish belief and practice, and welcome children from a broad spectrum of Jewish backgrounds," it was often difficult to devise policies that were both inclusive and unambiguous in their Jewish stance.

The school's dietary policy nicely captures the delicate balance that was needed in resolving these debates. Traditional Jewish dietary law forbids the mixing of meat and milk products or the consumption of a wide variety of meats. The challenge for the school's leadership was to devise a policy that would avoid religious coercion and yet establish a framework that would allow families who keep **kosher** to feel comfortable in the school (no matter how few they were). After much debate it was agreed that the school should allow only dairy or *parve* (neither meat nor dairy) on to the premises so as to prevent the mixing of meat and milk. Food from home could also not be shared. This meant that families were mildly inconvenienced by being limited in what they could give their children for lunch (deli meats were off the menu, for example), but at the same time parents and children were neither required by the school to keep kosher nor were they required to bring specifically kosher products into school. As one parent approvingly put it, this policy indicates how the school "operates within a halachic [Jewish legal] framework, without making it a gold standard."

Debates, even conflicts, about such matters were not confined to the school's founding years; in many ways they have become an integral part of day-to-day life. Take the school calendar, for example. The broad contours of the school's calendar were set in its early years, but almost ten years on, during the time when we were engaged in our research, there were a number of months when Erica Caplin, head of school, had to devote a great part of her time to calendar-related matters. In one instance, she was faced by a heated dispute between parents and teachers over the fact that the school was closed not only for Jewish holidays but also on the eve of a number of holidays, something that is common practice in North American Jewish day schools. In the fall months, DJDS (like most other Jewish schools) is closed for a total of seven days—for the festivals of **Rosh Hashanah, Yom Kippur, Succot,** and **Simchat Torah**—and for a further two days on the eve of some of these festivals. While the great majority of DJDS families might mark some of these holydays in their own homes or in synagogues, only a minority of parents refrain from going to work on all of them, and never on a holyday eve. A time-crunch and child-supervision challenge results.

We observed how the calendar question was opened (actually, reopened) by a highly vocal single mother with no previous experience of Jewish school life and who struggled with child-care arrangements when school was closed. Once the issue was reopened, it drew disputants from both faculty and parents. The problem for teachers, as one of them explained, was

DISSENT AND CRITICAL THINKING

that "you have a parent-body who have chosen to go to day school but want a public school calendar." For certain parents, as one mother explained, the problem was that their children "are at school for a full month less than those in public schools and are expected to cover a double curriculum [of Judaic studies and general studies].... They're not doing a double curriculum and they're not doing academic excellence.... It's not possible in that time."

The tendency for certain issues to erupt despite having been peacefully resolved a few years previously is symptomatic of an environment where newcomers are not well socialized into institutional norms; in other words, either newcomers are unfamiliar with how things are generally done in Jewish schools, or they are ignorant specifically of what might have shaped earlier decisions at this school. Additionally, and more problematically, these newcomers may also assume that the school's inclusive ethos entitles them to demand repeatedly renewed consideration of established school policies.

This mix of factors is what lay behind a number of debates that peppered the school year. These included controversies over whether—in line with traditional Jewish practice—boys had to cover their heads at all times in school or at least during Judaic studies classes, and whether girls should too, in accordance with the school's egalitarian principles; over how often during the week students were expected to pray during school time; over how much time to devote to the study of Hebrew as opposed to French; and more generally about how to reconcile the school's commitment to inclusion with an aspiration for academic excellence. In effect, as is indicated here, there was a ceaseless (actually, exhausting) ferment where discussions and decisions related to the school's Jewish culture were never finally closed.

A different and much less public dynamic related not to the revisiting of established school policy but to the encounter between new "generations" of parents and the content of the curriculum. In one vivid instance, a parent described how she felt compelled to challenge the school over what she thought her son was being taught:

> Early on, it was around Yom Kippur, and B. came home talking about how he was feeling guilty about something. He was worried that God was going to see what he was doing and how he was going to get punished, and God was writing down in a book whether you live or die. He had sort of got things misconstrued. I got really nervous and I wrote this letter asking how [the school was] dealing with this, how [they were] talking about God.... I don't want my kid

to see God as this something out there watching and making sure what you do. ... I wanted him to internalize right and wrong with his own kind of moral compass. I wanted that to be part of who he is, not because he was afraid that he's going to get punished. ... So I wrote this letter to the school ... and then I went in and we [talked] about how they deal with discussions around what God was and how B. may have misinterpreted something that [the kindergarten teacher] said. ... [In the end,] I felt confident that the school was not being really rigid about how they talked about these things ... but I remember when I was at **Talmud Torah** and my Hebrew teacher told me, too, it was around the same thing, which is funny, that when you are walking to shul you should look behind you and if your shadow has no head you were going to die in the next year ... and I was terrified.

At first glance it is surprising that a parent might take so seriously the theological language of a five-year-old and not just dismiss it as childish talk. In fact, we found that quite a few parents complained to the principal for similar reasons: for example, that their children talked "too much" about God, or wanted to recite blessings "all the time," or simply that their children talked about theological matters that made them feel uncomfortable. Most memorably, a parent told us how disturbed she had been when her son returned from school asking, "If God is everywhere, so God is in the air, and I'm swallowing the air, so does that mean that God is in me and I'm God?"

In these instances, parents felt personally challenged, confused or occasionally offended by what their children were learning. These challenges might occasionally have resulted from misunderstanding, as in the God-talk example above, but frequently they derived from a larger philosophical or ideological divide between parents and the school. Further evidence of this divide was provided at parent orientation sessions, where it was not unusual to hear expression of the following kinds of concern: "If we don't believe in God, can we still send our child to the school? If we are not staunch Zionists or supporters of Israel, will we still be comfortable at the school?" We observed that parents expressed genuine concern about whether their non-normative values could be absorbed or embraced within the school plurality.

We suspect, also, that parents' sensitivity to these kinds of experience is tied to the strong educational convictions that inspired them to choose the school in the first place and that continued to animate their relationship with it. Additionally, it is likely that when the schooling that children expe-

DISSENT AND CRITICAL THINKING

rience is so different from that of their parents (most of whom had received a minimalist Jewish education in the hours after public school), there are bound to be surprises, misunderstandings or simply differences of opinion about what school—and Jewish school in particular—ought to look like.

In a setting that brings together an unusually diverse population, day-to-day events that occur without a ripple of controversy in other schools have the potential to become quickly divisive. Elsewhere, we have written about how one such incident became a full-blown crisis that demanded calling an "emergency" meeting of the school's Religious and Educational Policy Committee.[22] This crisis was provoked by scheduling a pre-**Chanukah** event to be led by a local rabbi whose opinions (as far as could be determined from his institutional affiliations) were viewed as "blatantly intolerant of and hostile to" minority groups within the school, as expressed by the author of an email sent to many of the parents. Writing as a gay member of the school community, this parent asked others "to entertain the anguish that many feel in being asked to honour the 'rights' of others who actively seek to diminish or erase our own rights."

Few other incidents we observed ever approached the intensity of this particular crisis, but there was also no shortage of occasions where the deep sense of difference felt by so many in the parent community resulted in intense sensitivity to oversights and errors on the part of others, especially faculty, or to "controversial" decisions taken at school, especially by the administration. As we have written elsewhere, most parents selected the school not because it satisfied a generic set of criteria that might easily be found in other schools, but because they saw DJDS as an educational institution with a particular identity that fit well with the kinds of downtown values to which they themselves were committed.[23] It was because of their commitment to these values that they paid careful attention to what happened in their child's classroom. They wanted to be sure that the school did indeed cultivate the diversity, religious pluralism, commitment to social action, intellectual inquiry, and arts-based education they sought and expected.

Inevitably, against this backdrop, those whose actions are most closely scrutinized are the classroom teachers. On numerous occasions parents told us that while they perceived the core faculty at DJDS as highly competent (even excellent) educators, they perceived the cultural world of the teachers to differ from that of most of the families. Parents had a strong sense of themselves as "downtown" people and of the downtown area as offering a range of resources and opportunities that might enrich their child's education. They felt that because almost all of the teachers came from uptown (and, as one parent complained, didn't even know their way around on public transit), the parents had "to work on the teachers" so as to ensure that their children would receive the kind of "progressive" education they desired. Such interest is not in and of itself problematic—it can actually constitute an important resource for the school—but what made the situation so volatile was that the values that parents expected to find in the school often competed or conflicted with one another, or were not universally shared by all members of the school community, including faculty and other parents. Thus, some parents' desire for an arts-based education clashed with the pursuit of academic excellence sought by others, or the cultivation of strong Hebrew language skills desired by some was presumed incompatible with a more child-centred Jewish-values education preferred by a different minority.

Inevitably, in an environment where there is so much turbulence, there are some who get injured. Leadership in this context calls for immense reserves of patience, generosity of spirit, and clarity. Unfortunately, these are emotional and intellectual assets that are rarely present in the same person. During its first ten years, DJDS was led by three different heads of school and three assistant heads, the turnover a symptom of the challenges they faced. In the classroom, too, it takes rare skill to affirm and include a wide range of views, particularly when those who hold those views (and their parents) assume that they are expressing conventional, even normative, ideas. Not surprisingly, many teachers found such demands overwhelming and moved on to less challenging workplaces.

A Theoretical Frame

In trying to make sense of the eruptions, disputes, and tensions we observed in classrooms, committee rooms, and corridors, it is tempting to see evidence of what some call the "commodification" of schooling:[24] pushy, private-school parents seeking value for money when they pay more than $10,000 a year. No doubt, there is some element of consumerism at play here among parents who came to the school after a carefully calibrated process of choice. There is also probably some reflection of contemporary parenting norms in the intensity of parent involvement, with hyper-involved "helicopter" parents less prepared to let go of their children than their own parents once were.[25] We also see in these episodes, however, evidence of something more integral to the project of nurturing community in the midst of diversity; and this interpretation needs some elaboration.

DISSENT AND CRITICAL THINKING

In theoretical terms, one of the most resilient accounts of the formation of community has been that of Ferdinand Tönnies. One of the founders of modern sociology in the nineteenth century, Tönnies proposed a model that explicated the shift from a hunter-gatherer society to an agricultural society and thereafter to an industrial society.[26] In this model, community—what Tönnies called *Gemeinschaft*—is conceived as being constituted by three elements: shared place (a bounded geographic location), shared kinship (membership in the same ethnic group), and shared mind (shared culture, values, and religion). For Tönnies, these constituent elements, once the bedrock of community, are invariably absent from modern industrial societies.

In conventional, denominational Jewish day schools, at least two of the three components of *Gemeinschaft* are usually present—by definition. Affiliated with particular religious denominations (Orthodox, Conservative, Reform, etc.), schools exhibit shared mind, at least as far as they are formally incorporated. Even more commonly, they exhibit shared kinship, admitting only students defined as Jewish according to some normative formulation. At DJDS, by contrast (and, we suggest, at many other community day schools), all three of the constituent elements of community are weak. Since there are deep differences of opinion over which students really are Jewish, "shared kinship" is present only in the most artificial fashion through the creative notion of admitting "children *raised as* Jews," a construct that is certainly not normative but that reflects the presence in the school of children from so many intermarried families. "Shared mind" is also lacking because of the wide differences in the values and beliefs of enrolled families. Their lifestyles and religious and political commitments are so diverse that if this community is said to share one core value, it is their commitment to respecting their differences. Finally, although DJDS, as a "downtown" school, is founded on a notion of shared place, "downtownness," a concept embraced by the school's founders, is less indicative of Jewish geographic concentration than of a shared cosmopolitan lifestyle that might as readily support a non-Jewish school as a Jewish one.

In classic sociological terms, then, Jewishness and Judaism are only small parts of the components that bind those who come together at DJDS. At most, members of the community are held together by their commitment to Jewish pluralism and to religious heterodoxy. For this reason, in its Jewishness the school more closely resembles Furman's concept of the "postmodern community of difference," one founded not on sameness or on what people share, as in Tönnies's model, but on "processes that

182

promote ... the feelings of belonging, trust of others, and safety" among those who exhibit diversity.[27]

These feelings of belonging, trust, and safety were conveyed to us in many ways by those we interviewed at DJDS. One parent told us that the great attraction of the school was that "people [by which she meant both parents and children] don't have to fit a mould." Or, as another put it, "the school is so accepting of everything, you know, whether it's a mixed marriage, whether it's a gay couple, whether it's poor, whether it's wealthy. You know, artsy, intellectual. Like it really doesn't matter. You want to send your kids for a Jewish education, you want to be part of this community, then, welcome." In these terms, a sense of belonging comes, paradoxically, from knowing that one can be different from others.

As Furman recognizes, this concept of community is an idealistic notion that is hard both to create and sustain over time. As she notes, this notion introduces a deeply subjective quality into the fabric of community. Community, thus understood, is in the eye of the beholder. It is a cognitive or emotional reality more than it is a sociological one. This, we sense, is the tension at the heart of life at DJDS: it is a tension between the subjective postmodern community of difference and community as an objective sociological reality. When the subjective and the objective align, there is almost a sense of magic; the school becomes what some conceive of as a haven, a place that is palpably different from an alienating world beyond its walls. For much of the time, however, in the midst of disputes, disagreements, and general instability, such an outcome seems a long way off (even if community need not mean that all must agree with one another). Those who gather in this shared place continually search for a way forward toward some semblance of institutional peace, but in the meantime they must make do with finding meaning in the journey, through the experience of cooperation, acceptance, and respect. In the postmodern community of difference, the journey is more important than the point of arrival.

Notes

1 Gerald Tulchinsky, *Branching Out: The Transformation of the Canadian Jewish Community*. Toronto: Stoddart, 1998.

2 Jonathan Sarna, "American Jewish Education in Historical Perspective," *Journal of Jewish Education* 64, no. 1–2 (1998): 9.

3 Helena Miller, "Meeting the Challenge: The Jewish Schooling Phenomenon in the UK," *Oxford Review of Education* 27, no.4 (2001): 501–13; Marvin Schick, *A Census of Jewish Day Schools in the United States, 2003–2004* (New York: AVI

CHAI Foundation, 2005); Erik H. Cohen, *Heureux comme Juifs en France? Etude sociologique* (Jerusalem and Paris: Akadem, 2007).

4　Peter Beinart, "The Rise of the Jewish School," *Atlantic Monthly* 284, no. 4 (1999): 21–23; Jack Wertheimer, "Who's Afraid of Jewish Day Schools?" *Commentary*, Dec. 1999: 49–54; Caryle Murphy, "Longing to Deepen Identity, More Families Turn to Jewish Day School," *Washington Post*, 7 April 2001, B1.

5　Marvin Schick, *A Census of Jewish Day Schools in the United States, 2008–2009.* New York: AVI CHAI Foundation, 2009.

6　Walter Ackerman, "Strangers to Tradition: Idea and Constraint in American Jewish Education," in *Jewish Education Worldwide: Cross-cultural Perspectives*, ed. H.S. Himelfarb and S. Della Pergola (Lanham, MD: University Press of America, 1989), 71–116.

7　Marc N. Kramer, "Teaching in a Jewish Community School," in *The Ultimate Jewish Teacher's Handbook*, ed. N.S. Moskowitz (New York: Behrman House, 2003), 66–73; Susan L. Shevitz and Rahel Wasserfall, "Building Community in a Pluralist High School," in *Jewish Schools, Jewish Community: A Reconsideration*, ed. A. Pomson and H. Deitcher (Oxford: Littman Library of Jewish Civilization, 2009), 376–95.

8　Lynn Davidman, "The New Voluntarism and the Case of Unsynagogued Jews," in *Everyday Religion: Observing Modern Religious Lives*, ed. N. Ammerman (Oxford: Oxford University Press, 2007), 51–67.

9　Thomas Luckman, "Transformations of Religion and Morality in Modern Europe," *Social Compass* 50, no. 3 (2003): 275–85.

10　Gail Furman, "Postmodernism and Community in Schools: Unraveling the Paradox," in *School as Community: From Promise to Practice*, ed. G. Furman (Albany: SUNY Press, 2002), 51–75; Carolyn M. Shields and Patricia Ann Seltzer, "Complexities and Paradoxes of Community: Toward a More Useful Conceptualization of Community," *Educational Administration Quarterly* 33, no. 4 (1997): 413–39.

11　J. Klinghofer, "Education: Canada," *Encyclopedia Judaica* 6 (1972): 452–55.

12　Jerome Kutnik, "Jewish Education in Canada," In *Jewish Education Worldwide: Cross-cultural Perspectives*, ed. H.S. Himelfarb and S. Della Pergola (Lanham, MD: University Press of America, 1989), 135–69.

13　Shay Aba, "Forecasting the Demand for Enrolment in Toronto Jewish Day Schools," UJA Federation of Greater Toronto, Board of Jewish Education, 2002; B. Shoub and J. Levine, *2002–2003 Population Survey* (Toronto: UJA Federation of Greater Toronto Board of Jewish Education, 2002).

14　Schick, *Summary of Key Findings.*

15 Jack Wertheimer, "The American Synagogue: Recent Trends and Issues," *American Jewish Year Book* (New York: American Jewish Committee, 2005), 105: 3–83.

16 Grace Davie, *Religion in Britain since 1945: Believing without Belonging* (Oxford: Blackwell, 1994).

17 Alex Pomson and Randal F. Schnoor, *Back to School: Jewish Day School in the Lives of Adult Jews* (Detroit: Wayne State University Press, 2008), 25.

18 Shevitz and Wasserfall, "Building Community," 392; Lynn G. Beck, "The Complexity and Coherence of Educational Communities: An Analysis of Images that Reflect and Influence Scholarship and Practice," in *School as Community: From Promise to Practice*, ed. G. Furman (Albany: SUNY Press, 2002), 23–49.

19 Michael Huberman, "The Model of the Independent Artisan in Teachers' Professional Relations," in *Teachers' Work: Individuals, Colleagues and Contexts*, ed. J.W. Little and M.W. McLaughlin (New York: Teachers College Press, 1993), 11–50.

20 Bryan Conyer, "Pluralism and Its Purposeful Introduction to Jewish Day School," *Religious Education* 104, no. 5 (2009): 463–78.

21 Adam Seligman, "Tolerance: For a Minimalist Definition of Pluralism," *HaYidion* (Winter 2009): 16–17; Jennifer Glaser, "Rival Versions of Pluralistic Jewish Education," *HaYidion* (Winter 2009): 20–21.

22 Alex Pomson, "Day School Parents and Their Children's Schools," *Contemporary Jewry* 24, no. 1 (2003): 104–23.

23 Pomson and Schnoor, *Back to School*.

24 Stephen J. Ball, "Education for Sale! The Commodification of Everything," Annual Education Lecture, King's College, London, 17 June 2004; Michael Apple, "Audit Cultures, Commodification, and Class and Race Strategies in Education," *Policy Futures in Education* 3, no. 4 (2005): 378–99.

25 Carol Keyes, "Parent–Teacher Partnerships, Challenging but Essential," *Teachers College Record*, 16 May 2005, http://www.tcrecord.org

26 Ferdinand Tönnies, *Community and Society* (East Lansing: Michigan State University Press, 1957).

27 Furman, "Postmodernism and Community," 61.

Bibliography

Aba, Shay. "Forecasting the Demand for Enrolment in Toronto Jewish Day Schools." UJA Federation of Greater Toronto, Board of Jewish Education, 2002.

Ackerman, Walter. "Strangers to Tradition: Idea and Constraint in American Jewish Education." In *Jewish Education Worldwide: Cross-Cultural Perspectives*, edited by H.S. Himelfarb and S. Della Pergola, 71–116. Lanham, MD: University Press of America, 1989.

Apple, Michael. "Audit Cultures, Commodification, and Class and Race Strategies in Education." *Policy Futures in Education* 3, no. 4 (2005): 378–99.

Ball, Stephen J. "Education for Sale! The Commodification of Everything." Annual Education Lecture. King's College, London. 17 June 2004.

Beck, Lynn G. "The Complexity and Coherence of Educational Communities: An Analysis of Images that Reflect and Influence Scholarship and Practice." In *School as Community: From Promise to Practice*, edited by G. Furman, 23–49. Albany: SUNY Press, 2002.

Beinart, Peter. "The Rise of the Jewish School." *Atlantic Monthly* 284, no. 4 (1999): 21–23.

Cohen, Erik H. *Heureux comme Juifs en France? Etude sociologique.* Jerusalem and Paris: Akadem, 2007.

Conyer, Bryan. "Pluralism and Its Purposeful Introduction to Jewish Day School." *Religious Education* 104, no. 5 (2009): 463–78.

Davidman, Lynn. "The New Voluntarism and the Case of Unsynagogued Jews." In *Everyday Religion: Observing Modern Religious Lives*, edited by N. Ammerman, 51–67. Oxford: Oxford University Press, 2007.

Davie, Grace. *Religion in Britain since 1945: Believing without Belonging.* Oxford: Blackwell, 1994.

Furman, Gail. "Postmodernism and Community in Schools: Unraveling the Paradox." In *School as Community: From Promise to Practice*, edited by G. Furman, 51–75. Albany: SUNY Press, 2002.

Glaser, Jennifer. "Rival Versions of Pluralistic Jewish Education." *HaYidion* (Winter 2009): 20–21.

HeYidiyon. Special issue: Parents. New York: RAVSAK—The Jewish Community Day School Network, 2009 (winter).

Huberman, Michael. "The Model of the Independent Artisan in Teachers' Professional Relations." In *Teachers' Work: Individuals, Colleagues and Contexts*, edited by J.W. Little and M.W. McLaughlin, 11–50. New York: Teachers College Press, 1993.

Keyes, Carol. "Parent–Teacher Partnerships, Challenging but Essential." *Teachers College Record.* 16 May 2005. http://www.tcrecord.org

Klinghofer, J. "Education: Canada." *Encyclopedia Judaica* 6 (1972): 452–55.

Kramer, Marc N. "Teaching in a Jewish Community School." In *The Ultimate Jewish Teacher's Handbook*, edited by N.S. Moskowitz, 66–73. New York: Behrman House, 2003.

Kutnik, Jerome. "Jewish Education in Canada." In *Jewish Education Worldwide: Cross-cultural Perspectives*, edited by H.S. Himelfarb and S. Della Pergola, 135–69. Lanham, MD: University Press of America, 1989.

Luckman, Thomas. "Transformations of Religion and Morality in Modern Europe." *Social Compass* 50, no. 3 (2003): 275–85.

Miller, Helena. "Meeting the Challenge: The Jewish Schooling Phenomenon in the UK." *Oxford Review of Education* 27, no. 4 (2001): 501–13.

Murphy, Caryle. "Longing to Deepen Identity, More Families Turn to Jewish Day School." *Washington Post*, 7 April 2001, B1.

Pomson, Alex. "Day School Parents and their Children's Schools." *Contemporary Jewry* 24, no. 1 (2003): 104–23.

Pomson, Alex, and Randal F. Schnoor. *Back to School: Jewish Day School in the Lives of Adult Jews*. Detroit: Wayne State University Press, 2008.

Sarna, Jonathan. "American Jewish Education in Historical Perspective." *Journal of Jewish Education* 64, no. 1–2 (1998): 8–21.

Schick, Marvin. *A Census of Jewish Day schools in the United States, 2008–2009*. New York: AVI CHAI Foundation, 2009.

Seligman, Adam. "Tolerance: For a Minimalist Definition of Pluralism." *HaYidion* (Winter 2009): 16–17.

Shevitz, Susan L., and Rahel Wasserfall. "Building Community in a Pluralist High School." In *Jewish Schools, Jewish Community: A Reconsideration*, edited by A. Pomson and H. Deitcher, 376–95. Oxford: Littman Library of Jewish Civilization, 2009.

Shields, Carolyn M., and Patricia Ann Seltzer. "Complexities and Paradoxes of Community: Toward a More Useful Conceptualization of Community." *Educational Administration Quarterly* 33, no. 4 (1997): 413–39.

Shoub, B., and J. Levine. *2002–2003 Population Survey*. Toronto: UJA Federation of Greater Toronto Board of Jewish Education, 2002.

Tönnies, Ferdinand. *Community and Society*. East Lansing: Michigan State University Press, 1957.

Tulchinsky, Gerald. *Branching Out: The Transformation of the Canadian Jewish Community*. Toronto: Stoddart, 1998.

Wertheimer, Jack. "The American Synagogue: Recent Trends and Issues." *American Jewish Year Book* 105: 3–83. New York: American Jewish Committee, 2005.

———. "Who's Afraid of Jewish Day Schools?" *Commentary*, Dec. 1999: 49–54.

CHAPTER EIGHT

TEACHING SUBJECT MATTER THAT IS CONTROVERSIAL AMONG CATHOLICS: IMPLICATIONS FOR INTELLECTUAL GROWTH IN THE CHURCH

Graham P. McDonough

Introduction

Catholic school curriculum content and experiences are aimed toward ends that extend well beyond simply the transmission of knowledge for its own sake. Similarly, the socialization of students in a Catholic school is also intended to be accomplished for something beyond simply effecting an efficiently operating institution. In the Catholic school these "aims" or "ends" coordinate the two distinct domains of encouraging a student's spiritual life in relationship with the divine,[1] and developing a more uplifting picture of life on Earth according to Catholic ideals of the common good. While Catholic schools have faced many external accusations that they cause social divisiveness, fail to promote student autonomy, unjustly draw on public funds, and indoctrinate students,[2] recent scholarship suggests many things to the contrary. Mark Halstead provides a persuasive defence against the first three criticisms,[3] and the Catholic Church's own "Declaration on religious liberty" (*Dignitatis humanae*, henceforth DH) from the Second Vatican Council presents the institution's most authoritative statement opposing indoctrination and other coercive means of religious education on the grounds that inauthentic faith results.[4] Bryk, Lee, and Holland's extensive study found that Catholic schools are in fact quite effective in promoting and contributing to the common good of secular society,[5] and Walter Feinberg makes a compelling case that Catholic schools (and

189

DISSENT AND CRITICAL THINKING

faith schools in general) contribute well to pluralism in a democratic society.[6] Catholic school advocates can therefore find ample support for claims that Catholic schools aim toward and perform a good service to contemporary society. There is much more to their mission and actions than simply "handing over" knowledge or providing experiences that are relevant only in an insular context.

An interesting problem arises, however, when one asks what *conception* of the common good is present among Catholic school supporters and in the schools themselves. The temptation might be present here to conclude that the common good is understood uniformly within each school and across all schools. The literature on Catholic education, after all, tends to speak of the common markers of Catholic school identity,[7] and most importantly the school's theological foundations rest upon and reflect the Magisterium's singular authority to determine Catholic orthodoxy on spiritual, social, and moral matters. It might therefore be reasonable to postulate that those persons who constitute the school—including students, parents, staff, and community interests, along with the clergy and Magisterial Church—share the same vision of the common good in the Church and society. This vision would therefore permeate the whole school, and so the curricular content and experiences would be aimed at reinforcing a gradual increase in the complexity of student thought and action in this respect. However, if Catholicism's vision of the common good is tied in part to some of its socio-moral teachings that are controversial among Catholic persons, then the question arises as to what function these issues have as curriculum in the school, and what the school's and teachers' corresponding roles are in teaching them.

What is the substance of these intra-ecclesial controversies? For the purposes of this chapter I have chosen to focus on a specific controversial topic, out of many possible, to illustrate a larger issue in pedagogical philosophy. The disagreement and debate surrounding the reception of Pope Paul VI's 1968 **encyclical** *Humanae vitae* (henceforth *HV*)—which proscribes "artificial" contraception and promotes "natural" methods instead—represents a classic controversial issue within post-conciliar (Second Vatican Council, 1962–1965) Catholicism and Catholic schooling.[8] This issue is well known as one of the major departures that Catholic orthodoxy makes from the norms of secular liberal society, but in spite of its status as official, normative teaching, however, a significant number of Canadian Catholics disagree with it.[9] In addition to this sociological description of those it serves, the Catholic school also encounters the facts of a documentary record in recent history that Canadian bishops have permitted Catholics to depart from *HV* should they find good reasons in conscience to do so,[10] and a theological argument that would permit a Catholic person to dissent from its teaching.[11] Recalling that the school is composed of multiple players, and that each player has its own intentions,[12] it follows that in some cases the Catholic school's responsibility to teach the orthodox position on contraception clashes with the experiences, expectations, and desires of many Catholic students and their parents. How might the school respond to the pedagogical challenge of being true to all parties?

This chapter is based on an observation that the inclusion and teaching of controversial Catholic subject matter in school curricula reveals an important unsolved problem in Catholic educational theory. Specifically, it exposes a pedagogical tension that arises when competing visions of Catholic morality and the Catholic common good appear in the school. The school has a responsibility to present and uphold Magisterial teaching, on the one hand, but on the other hand there is also an imperative to teach students to respond well to difference and to make positive contributions to the groups in which they participate, even if in disagreement.[13]

Unpacking the Initial Theoretical Implications

The curricular inclusion of issues featuring intra-Church difference raises questions about what current and future roles students are imagined to have within the Church. Competing conceptions of the common good are implicit in this controversy, and they range from the ethical questions in theology or philosophy concerning what is "right" concerning contraception and how this affects society at large,[14] to the politico-ecclesiological question concerning the epistemic claims that ground the Magisterium's teaching authority, the laity's obligation to obey, and how this Magisterial–lay relationship, as the foundation of Church governance, affects life within the Church.[15] The school depends upon the Magisterial Church to be an authentically Catholic institution;[16] it also depends upon students to populate it. Without students, there is no school. As educational projects are only successful to the extent that they are able to coordinate the intentions of all participants,[17] a one-sided approach to teaching controversial issues is bound to meet resistance in some quarters should it tend too rigidly toward the Magisterial norm, on the one hand, or display excessive partiality with the dissenting views of some lay persons, on the other. How might the school treat issues like this fairly so as not to alienate any side in this controversy and others like it?

DISSENT AND CRITICAL THINKING

Pedagogically, the school's role in treating intra-Church controversies is potentially controversial in itself. This chapter tracks this diversity of pedagogical responses to intra-Catholic controversy through an adaptation of Miller and Seller's threefold classification of the primary purposes inherent in curriculum theory, organization, and teaching methods into (1) transmission, (2) transaction, and (3) transformation.[18] In general terms, the term *transmission* is adapted and defined here as the one-way delivery of information and values in a fashion exclusively partial to the Church, where learners are conceived of as receptive vessels of the content's established truths; *transaction* as engaging with students to solicit their opinions and engage in debate, but ultimately working within a framework that leaves orthodoxy unchallenged publicly outside the classroom; and *transformation* as envisioning students moving away from the role of "receivers of teachings" and toward a public stance as "critically faithful actors in dialogue with teachings and their loyal criticisms." No methods of teaching are necessarily exclusive to any one of these categories, but the purposes behind their use are mutually distinct. Therefore one might have a "discussion" within the transmission approach that is limited by a prior assumption that some truth about the topic discussed is already fixed. Importantly, the transaction and transformation approaches to teaching and learning do not preclude a student's choice to subscribe to and defend the prevailing view, but the transformation approach does prescribe that a dissenting student should receive pedagogical supports on an intellectual par with those who hold the prevailing view receive.[19] In sum, the question arises as to which of these stances the school ought to prefer.

In this chapter I review these three pedagogical approaches to studying controversial issues like contraception, and propose that each has advantages and disadvantages. The evaluation of each stance is made in consideration of what implications it has for controversy in the Church, and for the role of the school as the public place where the disagreeing parties converge. Embedded in this analysis and evaluation is an argument that the transformation approach is preferable because it maintains the greatest reciprocal fidelity to all partners in the educative relationship. It will be shown concurrently that this curricular approach to controversial intra-Catholic issues offers students the most rigorous means of developing their learning because it necessitates a comparatively more comprehensive picture of the Catholic Church that is broader than the Roman Magisterium, without diminishing its importance.

The Canadian Contraception Controversy

The story of controversy in the post-conciliar age surrounding Catholic teaching on the regulation of birth is long and complex, and it permits only a short summary to be presented here for reference. The Church had discussed marriage and the regulation of birth long before the Second Vatican Council, and the most notable contextually recent Magisterial document upon which HV relies is Pope Pius XI's 1930 encyclical letter *Casti connubii*, which follows closely St. Augustine's view that sex acts not aimed at procreation are immoral. The introduction of oral contraceptives in the early 1960s contributed to the revival of this issue's prominence worldwide and in the Church, and in response Pope John XXIII (r.1958–63) created the Pontifical Commission on Birth Control in 1963 to examine the current questions that this new technology implied. In 1964, however, Pope Paul VI (r.1963–78) instructed the Second Vatican Council to discontinue discussion on contraception in favour of reiterating and confirming the teaching in *Casti connubii*.[20] The Papal Commission continued its work despite this instruction to the Council, but ostensibly the Pope "had reserved the question of the birth control pill to himself."[21] Discussions in the Council continued in spite of this instruction, and they eventually produced an agreed upon statement in §47–52 of the *Pastoral Constitution* (*Gaudium et spes*—GS) that "is carefully ambiguous on certain points—enough so for Popes Paul VI and John Paul II to claim, later, that the Council reaffirmed *Casti connubii* and for Bernard Häring and others to claim that it moved some way off that encyclical."[22] Specifically, GS §50 upholds the judgments of married couples "before God" and maintains that they are "ruled by conscience," while §51 explicitly states, "[in] questions of birth regulation, the daughters and sons of the church ... are forbidden to use methods disapproved of by the teaching authority of the church in its interpretation of the divine law."[23]

The Commission's final report was released in 1966, in the aftermath of the Council. Entitled "On Responsible Parenthood," it made a strong majority decision to recommend in favour of Church teaching that permitted artificial contraception. Its original membership had been two priests and four lay persons, but by the time of its conclusion had grown to 65, including 15 cardinals and bishops (nine voting in favour, three abstaining, and three opposing), 19 theologians (15 in favour and four opposed), and 31 lay persons (all in favour). In spite of this recommendation, one year later Paul VI issued HV, which dismissed the Commission's findings because they were not "definitive and absolutely certain," did not emerge from "complete agreement concerning the moral norms to be proposed,"

DISSENT AND CRITICAL THINKING

and finally because "certain approaches and criteria for a solution to this question had emerged which were at variance with the moral doctrine on marriage constantly taught by the magisterium of the Church."[24] Kaufman and Wills argue that Paul VI's priority to uphold *Casti connubii*, maintain consistency with his papal predecessors, and so protect the authority of the Roman Magisterium ultimately overshadowed any concern with reflecting the views of the faithful.[25] Paul VI did not issue another encyclical during his papacy, presumably as a result of his response to the fact that *HV* was not universally welcomed.[26]

The immediate reaction to *HV*, in Europe and North America at least, at best reflected a mixture of favourable and unfavourable reception. Theologian Charles Curran, along with several supporters at the Catholic University of America in Washington, D.C., issued a statement that "[did not] accept the encyclical's specific rejection of artificial contraception, [claiming] that it was based on an inadequate, static view of natural law."[27] Here in Canada, the CCCB's immediate formal response to the encyclical, informally known as the 1968 "Winnipeg Statement," permitted persons to act according to their conscience, should it reveal that agreement with *HV* were not possible. The Canadian bishops open "Winnipeg" with a section that affirms their solidarity with the Pope, but later in the document they also acknowledge that

> It is a fact that a certain number of Catholics, although admittedly subject to the teaching of the encyclical, find it either extremely difficult or even impossible to make their own all elements of this doctrine.... Since they are not denying any point of divine and Catholic faith nor rejecting the teaching authority of the Church, these Catholics should not be considered or consider themselves, shut off from the body of the faithful.[28]

The implications of this passage are that the bishops place the responsibility for action in the hands of the actor who must consult and consider *HV*, but might legitimately act outside its prescriptions. Shortly thereafter, the bishops reaffirm this view: "In accord with the accepted principles of moral theology, if these persons have tried sincerely but without success to pursue a line of conduct in keeping with the given directives, they may be safely assured that, whoever honestly chooses that course which seems right to him does so in good conscience."[29]

This position has been very controversial. Notable among its Canadian critics is Monsignor Vincent Foy, whose article "Tragedy at Winnipeg" represents the view that the "Winnipeg Statement" is erroneous and should be abandoned in favour of strongly re-inscribing *HV*'s normative authority. Most particularly, Foy refers to "Winnipeg's" paragraph 26 as "The Worst" because it is "self contradictory," "embraces the error of proportionalism," refers to Church teachings as "directives" instead of "divine natural law," and "embraces the wrong concept of conscience."[30] If Canadian Catholics who agree with *HV* and reject "Winnipeg" nonetheless find Foy's polemic unattractive, today they might find a more measured support for their views within the CCCB's most recent statement on contraception, which, interestingly, expresses support for *HV* without mentioning "Winnipeg":

> Pope Paul vi's encyclical *Humanae Vitae* and the subsequent "theology of the body" developed by Pope John Paul ii issue an immense challenge to a world that is too often occupied with protecting itself against the extraordinary life potential of sexuality. In the wake of these two prophetic Popes, the Church, "expert in humanity," issues an unexpected message: sexuality is a friend, a gift of God.... We invite the faithful to be the first to experience its liberating potential.[31]

Finally, contemporary sociologists of religion in Canada and the United States have found that a significant number of Catholics disagree with this teaching. The most recent Canadian evidence must be inferred indirectly, however. Sociologist of religion Reginald Bibby has found that 69 per cent of students in Catholic school systems approve of premarital sex if the act is based upon love, a figure that is very close to the 72 per cent of secular public-school students who hold the same view. For all Catholic adolescents nationally, Bibby has found that 61 per cent of Quebec's Catholic adolescents who attend Mass monthly or more share this view of premarital sex with the 59 per cent outside Quebec. For those who attend Mass less than monthly, the rate rises to 92 per cent in Quebec, and 83 per cent outside.[32] Likewise, Andrew Greeley has found that only 9 per cent of all Canadian Catholics maintain that "premarital sex is always wrong."[33] Based on the twin assumptions that these adolescents are approving of activity that they and their peers would participate in, and that they are not interested in conception or using exclusively contraceptive methods that would restrict intercourse to the female partner's infertile days, in accord with *HV*, Bibby's and Greeley's results suggest that Canadian Catholic adolescents do not hold *HV*'s message in high esteem.[34] Correspondingly, Greeley finds that in the United States "a large majority of both [American] priests and laypeo-

DISSENT AND CRITICAL THINKING

ple reject the Church's official teachings on the ordination of women, birth control, premarital sex, in utero and in vitro fertilization, oral sex, and the legality of abortion under some circumstances."[35] Only 25 per cent think that birth control is "always wrong."[36]

Some students therefore arrive at the Catholic school with very serious questions about HV. Currently, anything to do with sexual ethics seems to be a bulwark for proclaiming and reinforcing Catholic identity, so these questions can very easily turn into moments of frustration in students' encounters with the Church and their feelings of identification with it. An example of the classroom controversy could go like this: Student X believes that obedience to the Pope and bishops, as mediators of Christ's truth, is paramount, and from this standpoint supports and defends HV and its arguments as essential to one's Catholicity. Student Y finds HV difficult to accept because it imposes hardships on women and married couples, blocks efforts at disease prevention, and quite simply stands outside the demographic pattern of modern Catholic family size, where more than three to four children would be considered exceptionally large. Student Y's difficulty therefore extends to developing a reasonable and responsible disagreement *in Catholic terms* with Student X's claims. Moreover, the school must serve both students while openly agreeing with the views of Student X and not, officially at least, supporting Student Y's thought, thus placing Student Y in a position where he or she is opposed to both Student X and the institution itself. So where the pedagogical tire hits the ecclesiological pavement, so to speak, is on the question of how the school ought to treat controversial issues within Catholicism.

How Should a Teacher Respond?

The question of what pedagogical response is most appropriate to student dissent on subjects such as HV is important because it requires the school (or educator) to confront directly its assumptions regarding what the student is expected to learn regarding (1) his or her place in the Church and relation to ecclesial authority, and (2) how the educative experiences in the school are designed to promote that ecclesiological model. These two points bring into high relief the fact that in the Catholic school, *intra-Church* controversial issues are unlike *secular–civil* controversial issues. This dissimilarity has a meaning that begins with but immediately exceeds the simple fact that "should (married) couples use contraceptives" has different subject matter than "should the Northern seal hunt be permitted." This difference in subject matter is instructive, however, for revealing a difference in aims.

196

SUBJECT MATTER CONTROVERSIAL AMONG CATHOLICS | MCDONOUGH

Where there is a widely acknowledged agreement within the school that a genuine secular–civil controversy exists, because of the incommensurable epistemic and moral positions that inhere in the topic and that students also bring with them to school (as in the controversy over sealing), a set of philosophical aims and pedagogical methods may prevail that keeps it an open question, encourages ambiguity, and suspends closure. In cases where a major partner in the school, in this case the Magisterial Church, is publicly partial to a singular moral and epistemic view, the aims and methods are ultimately quite different.

In cases like the Northern seal hunt controversy, the school ostensibly has no prior truth claim to uphold in this matter regarding a student's responsible citizenship; hence the issue is genuinely controversial in the school, and the school can present it in terms of how well it serves as fodder for developing students' thinking about an important civil matter. In this case a good citizen is conceived of as a thinking citizen, and so the school assumes little or no obligation to impose any prevailing prior commitment upon students. In the case of HV, by contrast, since the school holds a public and principled commitment to the Magisterium's epistemology, morality, and ecclesial politics, there is, at least in the official epistemology and morality, no controversy in the school. Controversy, if it exists, is acknowledged officially and pedagogically only in the sociological sense that opinions vary among those who come to the epistemically, morally, and politically committed institution.[37] Officially there is no controversy insofar as the school is partial to one point of view, but teachers may still present HV as though it is controversial, knowing that their students do not receive it well. So the difference here is that concerning the Northern seal hunt the school recognizes the controversy in its sociological sense and supports it in the epistemic and moral sense—promoting good information gathering and reasoning about the subject with the aim not to foreclose controversy. Practices may vary from place to place, but with some exceptions the following pattern is usual. On subjects such as HV, the school recognizes controversy as a secondary sociological fact, but in its pedagogical response does not present it with equivalent cognitive and moral supports. Students are given limited classroom time and intellectual space to voice their assenting or dissenting views, but those who dissent do not receive the same intellectual supports or public affirmation as those who assent.[38] The school's partiality toward maintaining the prevailing view is paramount here. This partiality ensures the support of the Magisterial Church; it comes at the cost of potentially alienating dissident Catholic students who are frustrated with it.

DISSENT AND CRITICAL THINKING

The contrast between the presentation of controversial civil and Catholic issues in the Catholic school raises questions about the aims of Catholic schooling, especially in relationship with the official, institutional Church. These aims are abstract philosophical statements that inform the corresponding curricular approach. With the intent of enumerating and evaluating the possibilities in teaching controversial issues in Catholic schools, I present three theoretical approaches to curriculum as distinct choices that a religious educator would have available and might choose when responding to a dissenting point of view on *HV*, or any other controversial issue.

The first approach, "transmission," is based on an orientation to curriculum wherein the epistemic and moral suppositions are that knowledge and values are fixed, and a corresponding political imperative that it is the role of the school to implant these into students, who ideally are receptive.[39] The Catholic school's role in presenting *HV* would therefore correspond to its perceived instrumental capability in authoritatively presenting the Magisterial message, and the student's responsibility would be to receive and (hence, it is assumed) to learn it. At first blush this pedagogical approach might imply behaviourism and indoctrination to some, although DH influences Catholic transmission pedagogy to such a degree that it must depart from the behaviourist psychology that is part of that orientation in its classic secular sense.[40] The aim of indoctrinating persons *qua* initiating them into a particular belief may thus be discarded as a legitimate charge against the Catholic school.

In this sense the question returns of the fundamental role of the school. Within this transmission approach it could be simply stated that the obligation is to disseminate knowledge and values from the thinking, teaching Magisterium (*ecclesia docens*) to a receptive, obedient laity (*ecclesia discens*), whose thinking is based upon fidelity to their spiritual superiors. This approach is consistent with the current rhetoric regarding the Catholic school's evangelizing mission,[41] and it also seems to tend toward the side of "proclaiming" the Church's salvific truth to others as opposed to finding it in dialogue with them.[42]

If the transmission orientation accurately matches the aims the Catholic school espouses with respect to teaching *HV*, then the pedagogical question arises as to whether it is even fruitful to bother with discussion of it or any controversial issue. It may be granted that discussion might be a critical and beneficial technique for better understanding the Church's position on a topic with which there is more universal agreement, like the uncontroversial acceptance today of the teaching on the Triune God. However, on a topic that is controversial, a transmission aim is bound to meet resistance, as the student's intent for achieving "better understanding" is not directed toward assenting to what the Church proclaims as truth.[43] On controversial topics the discussion method inevitably implies something more than privileging one point of view with the intent that it will ultimately be learned and adopted in preference to others. If the purpose of the discussion method is given greater scope than this limited view allows, then the issue arises as to whether discussion is, at worst, merely instrumental in allowing students the illusion of believing that their opinions matter, or, slightly better, an intellectual practice for generic "good thinking skills" that is based on content divorced from the scope of possibility in the real world. The presentation of HV is not impossible under the transmission orientation, but its legitimacy in being treated as a genuinely controversial issue within the school is suspect. Within this orientation, discussion of HV is poorly advised and bound to lead to student frustration.

Alternatively, a "transactional" approach would suggest that the role of the school is to present knowledge about the Church to students so that they can use it to respond to current problems in conscience. In this scenario, the student's learning intentions and other psychological needs are given more prominence than in the first. The teacher and student retain respect for Church teachings and the Magisterium, and Church teaching-as-curriculum remains a model upon which students who wish to believe stringently may adhere, but it is not viewed as an object that students are invited to internalize to the diminution of others. Since the teacher in this scenario emphasizes student self-esteem, opinion, and choice,[44] the curriculum content becomes more like a set of data that students evaluate for its potential to inform and guide them in solving moral problems. As Feinberg notes, both these scenarios share a similar goal of students being able to understand the Church, but the first scenario emphasizes acceptance of Church teaching, while the second emphasizes "engagement, dialogue, and reflection."[45] However well student voices are accommodated in this perspective, the intellectual grounds for their disagreement rests on their own subjective authority, and there is little to no mention of available resources that would aid in their study of alternative *Catholic* positions. The tension between pedagogical promotion of critical thought and the ecclesiological mandate to hand over sacred truths emerges here in high relief. If transmission is in fact the desired ecclesiological outcome of discussing HV, it remains only silently or very softly stated. The implication for discussing a controversial subject like HV thus follows. In this scenario a student would be allowed to disagree and would likely have his or her point of view appropriately tested by his or her peers and the teacher during class discussion. However, since the justification for his or her disagreement is given little intellectual resources other than impromptu informal logic and personal fiat upon which to stand, and since this point of view likely receives not nearly the same support in Catholicism's official public life outside the classroom than it does within, the evaluation of this stance's wisdom is mixed. From the teacher's and school's perspective this stance achieves a good balance between devoting significant time to the official Magisterial voice and the views of students, so where students in the first scenario might object to being overexposed to a message without an opportunity to respond individually, this scenario achieves some greater degree of balance between the school's partners. However, its entertainment of student disagreement ultimately leaves them on potentially thin intellectual and ecclesiological ice, especially since the warrant for their disagreement stands outside what the Church regards as objective truth. The disagreeing student is offered no rigorous means of understanding how he or she can disagree and remain a faithful Catholic. The apparent choice is stark: adhere fully to HV and be Catholic, do not and be not, or settle for some potentially soggy rapprochement by continuing with the Church but in some variety of silent, intellectually unsupported, isolated, and private disagreement.

Finally, there is an approach that would draw upon what Miller and Seller term a "transformational" orientation to curriculum,[46] or what Feinberg names a "postmodern" approach to Catholic education. In this perspective, curricular content and experiences are selected according to their potential to "foster students' awareness of cultural and economic forces that influence their lives" and their "commitment to working for positive social change" on "pressing social concerns."[47] While this position has many things in common with the more traditional, transmissionalist view of Catholic education, it also departs from that view, according to Feinberg, to the extent that it "also holds a critical light up to the practices of the Church and will criticize government or church when it finds either one supporting oppressive policies."[48] It must be noted that several possibilities are evident within "transformational" pedagogy as Miller and Seller describe it, generally including among them those variants that might even reject organized religions like Catholicism for perpetuating repressive patriarchal structures or existentially unsatisfactory spiritual conformity. Ideological variants that fit within a Catholic perspective are those congruent with what Feinberg observes are based on Catholic feminist and liberation theology.

SUBJECT MATTER CONTROVERSIAL AMONG CATHOLICS | MCDONOUGH

For the purposes of this discussion, I suggest that two general kinds of Catholic attitude are available within the transformational orientation when one looks to serve students who disagree on doctrinal controversies like HV. The first would take HV itself as the object of transformation and so offer disagreeing students the radical approach of completely rejecting and replacing it with a new grassroots manifesto. A second, more moderate approach would not aim to alter or directly challenge the teaching, but instead would look to modify learners' view of their relationship to it, and the meaning of this relationship to their agency and relationship to authority throughout the whole Church,[49] through an examination of comparative views from *within* the faith.

Among all "transformational" perspectives that would promote student disagreement,[50] the perspective that would likely receive the greatest acceptance across all partners in the school would be the moderate view. Officially, there is nothing within the prevailing Catholic views on education that would state explicitly that the school cannot or should not entertain this kind of approach to curriculum. Moreover, there is nothing at all *wrong* with a person knowing that dissent exists in the Church. What does emerge as the main point of resistance, though, are several claims that, if they do not attempt to preclude student disagreement, at least would slow or stop any immediate leap to the Catholic school enabling student dissent based on arguments that it is for their pedagogical benefit. These views, which follow for illustration, are not exclusive to the Magisterium and clergy but are also held to varying degrees by individuals in the school and its community.

For instance, there is a common view that students need to know the teaching on HV before they can criticize it. This view would not require that the discussion of controversial issues should be eliminated from the curriculum; however, it would be congruent with aiming that discussion at exercising the student's intellect at least upon a complete picture of HV that is uncorrupted by the secular mass media and other secular influences. The prevailing Catholic perspective is thus to be given priority in the school, and it might even be inferred that an internal critique of Catholic orthodoxy is incompatible with this status. Granted, students should be taught that straw-person criticisms are fallacious, but if this rationale is overextended to justify limiting the curriculum to presenting and imparting the prevailing view, the question of aims resurfaces regarding the school's attitude toward the faithful dissenting student. The pedagogical consequence that remains from this stance, though, is well summarized by the question of what next step logically follows for the student who sufficiently knows

201

DISSENT AND CRITICAL THINKING

the teaching and its rationale but still disagrees.[51] A similar criticism emerges from the view that students are too immature to appreciate the complexities of faithful dissent from the Magisterium—a view that overlooks the fact that if disagreement persists as a de facto student interest, any subordination or even denial of that interest with the aim of promoting and repeating the views with which the student already disagrees appears unlikely to ameliorate any prior alienation that the student might feel from the Church and so be bringing to the school.

Finally, there is a trio of concerns about the practicality of making any meaningful commitment to the discussions of dissenting views on HV. The first of these is the view that there is no time for the topic of dissent in the curriculum. However, since discussion of HV requires students to learn the teaching and respond to it, if the school closes the possibility of developing any meaningful disagreement in the direction of faithful dissent that would apply to the real lives of students outside the school, then responsibility for meeting this question inevitably passes to parents. While parents have an important place in the Catholic education of their children and as a partner in Catholic schools, it would seem strange for the pedagogical professionals in the school to hand over their imperative to provide a value-added critical thinking experience to non-professionals.[52] This criticism is hence disingenuous and a non-starter. Second, it might be stated that the classroom is an appropriate venue for students to raise objections that are natural at their stage of life, but that ultimately these objections can only be entertained to humour students and that they will remain irrelevant outside school life. This stance unfortunately trivializes schooling and education, reducing it to an activity for its own sake. Finally, there is the possible objection that religion teachers themselves are too ill-prepared theologically to tackle such a demanding subject. This objection unfortunately reduces the desired role of the exemplary teacher to theological expert, and so ignores and even de-professionalizes the requisite knowledge of teaching methods, curricular organization and planning, student psychology, leadership, and so forth that the person in that station must possess. Moreover, it begs the question philosophically, for if teachers are incompetent with the dissenting views, then how might they be presumed competent as presenters, defenders, models, or teachers of the theology in the prevailing view?

Conclusion

The question of how to treat controversial Catholic issues in a Catholic school is itself a controversial topic. The pedagogical act of discussing controversial intra-Church issues opens a salient ecclesiological issue and its pedagogical implications. To begin, one would assume that the Catholic School's commitments to the common good and the student's good would neither desire nor aim for any learning to have meaning only in the abstract. So if *HV* and other controversial issues like it are assumed to have implications in the world beyond the school, one is led to wonder what role the *discussion method* specifically has in contributing to the learning desired from the study of this topic. More specifically, in the world outside the school, the questions of who in the Church discusses it, in what contexts and for what purposes it is discussed, and what the consequences are of adopting the various outcomes that would arise in that discussion map onto and reflect the aims of presenting this subject. Students are well aware of when they are participating in genuine discussions and when their opinions matter and are of consequence in its aftermath. They are also inevitably able to detect when they are participating in pretend conversations that are instrumental only to learning outcomes that have little real-world application or, worse, merely give them the illusion that their views count. It is also of special interest to students if they are required to assent fully to obey *HV*'s teaching in order to remain Catholic, if their dissent or disobedience would require them to leave the Church, or if disagreement or partial agreement would require them to remain Catholic in poor conscience or standing. The implication from this array of concerns is that Catholic schools should be prepared to fully expose to all persons—and especially parents and students—to the pedagogical aims and possible ecclesiological consequences of discussing controversial issues like *HV* in religion class.

The fact that there is difficulty in treating controversial intra-Church issues in Catholic schools points to two problems in Catholic educational theory. First, it reveals an ambiguity regarding the stated aims of the school regarding student belief. Is it to produce students who know the data of Catholicism, believe it, or believe it in a certain way that is pleasing to those in charge of the school?[53] Second, there is the matter of the pedagogical aims in discussing controversial issues, specifically the following: for what purpose are controversial issues introduced and discussed with students, and can issues such as *HV* be recognized as truly controversial within the school setting even if they are not controversial within the Magisterium? Catholic schools accomplish much toward the promotion and improve-

DISSENT AND CRITICAL THINKING

ment of the common good, but unfortunately the fact that there is little latitude for students to meaningfully encounter controversial teachings that are integral to the socio-moral foundations of Catholicism's outlook remains a blind spot within Catholic school pedagogical theory.

The implications for the whole Church of ignoring or dealing poorly with student dissent on issues like this one are several. First, it reinforces a popular misconception that the Church never changes, and in doing so overlooks the opportunity for a historical view of how the institution has become its present self.[54] Second, it constructs agency in the Church by way of reducing "Church" to the Magisterium and reducing the laity to mere receptors of its teaching.[55] When students sense this ecclesiology within classroom discussions of controversial issues, it signals to them that the discussion is merely a trivial exercise; furthermore, it alienates students who disagree and subsequently discover that their disagreement will apparently carry no meaningful effect in the real world of the Church. In fact there are meaningful effects, although their meaning as such is probably more pronounced in negative than in positive terms. When lay persons who disagree with the Magisterium on some controversial issues are alienated, the whole Church is denied the potentially learned contributions of its members. Doctrinal unity on moral and social issues thus comes at the expense of wrenching intellectual (and in this case youthful) diversity from the Body of Christ. Alienation on a controversial issue like *HV* also especially tightens the reduction of Catholic Church identity to its official views on sexual ethics, hence overlooking the possibility of agreement in other places such as Church teachings on social justice, Christology, and the sacraments. This situation reveals the need for further new pedagogical theory regarding whether and how it might be appropriate to admit, encourage, and teach students how to improve the scholarly and ecclesiological value of their dissent.[56]

Notes

1 For Catholic students this ostensibly refers to the Triune conception of God. For non-Catholic students the aim is modified so that they might achieve greater spiritual depth within their own traditions: See Saskatoon Catholic Schools, *Celebrating the Gift of Catholic Education in Saskatchewan: 1905–2005* (Saskatoon, 2005), 1.

2 See J. Mark Halstead, "In Defense of Faith Schools," in *Faith in Education: A Tribute to Terence McLaughlin*, ed. Graham Haydon (London: Institute of Edu-

cation, 2009), 46–67, for an enumeration of these criticisms. See Antony G.N. Flew, "'What Is Indoctrination': Comments on Moore and Wilson," *Studies in Philosophy and Education* 5, no. 2 (1967): 273–83, for a well-known version of the criticism that Catholic schools indoctrinate students.

3 Halstead, "In Defense of Faith Schools." See also Harry Brighouse, "Faith Schools, Personal Autonomy, and Democratic Competence," in *Faith in Education: A Tribute to Terence McLaughlin*, ed. Graham Haydon (London: Institute of Education, 2009), 78–93. While Brighouse prefers the ideal common school to a faith school, he concludes that faith schools currently exceed de facto expressions of secular common schools in measures of promoting autonomy and democratic citizenship, given that materialism and social pressure for peer conformity pervade the latter institutions.

4 Vatican Council II, *Dignitatis humanae* / Declaration on religious liberty, in *Vatican Council II: The Basic Sixteen Documents*, ed. A. Flannery (Northport, NY: Costello Publishing, 1996), 551–68, §10. Note that while this is the official theoretical view, that fact does not preclude some practices from being *perceived as* or even plainly *being* indoctrinatory in practice.

5 Anthony S. Bryk, Valerie E. Lee, and Peter B. Holland, *Catholic Schools and the Common Good* (Cambridge, MA: Harvard University Press, 1993).

6 Walter Feinberg, *For Goodness Sake: Religious Schools and Education for Democratic Citizenry* (New York: Routledge, 2006).

7 J. Michael Miller, "Challenges Facing Catholic Schools: A View from Rome," in *International Handbook of Catholic Education: Challenges for School Systems in the 21st Century*, ed. Gerald Grace and Joseph O'Keefe (Dordrecht, The Netherlands: Springer, 2007), 459–63.

8 Contraception is an issue that arguably more Catholics face or experience directly than they do abortion, same-sex marriage, or female ordination, which are examples of other salient contemporary controversial issues.

9 Discussed in detail below under "The Canadian Contraception Controversy"; cf. notes 33 and 34.

10 Canadian Conference of Catholic Bishops (hereafter CCCB), Statement on the Encyclical *Humanae vitae* ["Winnipeg Statement"], in *Love Kindness: The Social Teaching of the Canadian Catholic Bishops (1958–1989)—A Second Collection*, ed. E.F. Sheridan (Sherbrooke, QC: Editions Paulines, 1991). The discussion below under "The Canadian Contraception Controversy" reveals the relevant details and responses to this document.

11 Charles E. Curran and Robert Hunt, *Dissent in and for the Church: Theologians and Humanae vitae* (New York: Sheed and Ward, 1969), 5–8.

DISSENT AND CRITICAL THINKING

12 David R. Olson, *Psychological Theory and Educational Reform: How School Remakes Mind and Society* (New York: Cambridge University Press, 2003), 22, 209, and 224–25.

13 Karol Cardinal Wojtyla (later Pope John Paul II) states as much in his conceptual treatments of "solidarity" and "opposition." He writes: "The one who voices his opposition to the general or particular rules or regulations of the community does not thereby reject his membership; he does not withdraw his readiness to act and to work for the common good. Different interpretations of opposition that an individual may adopt with respect to society are of course possible, but here we adopt one that sees it as essentially an attitude of solidarity; far from rejecting the common good or the need of participation, it consists on the contrary in their confirmation" (*The Acting Person*, trans. A. Potocki [Boston: D. Reidel, 1979], 286).

14 *HV* lists several negative social consequences that would result from the use of artificial contraceptives, among them "marital infidelity and a general lowering of moral standards" and causing attitudes within men such that they would "forget the reverence due to a woman, [thereby reducing] her to being a mere instrument for the satisfaction of his own desires." Finally, it makes several warnings about power over the regulation of birth "passing into the hands of … public authorities." If the state is motivated in ways contrary to the natural law, it "may even impose their use on everyone" should it determine such action to be necessary (§17).

15 The treatment of this subject is only secondarily germane to this chapter. Its detailed treatment is the topic of my "What Is Assumed about Catholic Students' Ecclesial Agency, and Why It Matters to Catholic Schooling in Canada," *Catholic Education: A Journal of Inquiry and Practice* 14, no. 3 (2011): 272–91.

16 Vatican Council II, "*Apostolicam actuositatem / Decree on the Apostolate of the Laity*," *Vatican Council II: The Basic Sixteen Documents*, ed. A. Flannery (Northport, NY: Costello Publishing, 1996), 403–42, §24; Catholic Church, *The Code of Canon Law* (Ottawa: Canadian Council of Catholic Bishops, 1983), §300 and 312.

17 In *Psychological Theory and Educational Reform*, Olson observes: "High level institutional reforms fail because they ignore local conditions and human diversity, imposing rather one norm, rule, goal or standard on everyone. On the other hand, pedagogical reforms fail because they pay insufficient attention to the special nature of the school as an institution" (20).

18 John P. Miller and Wayne Seller, *Curriculum: Perspectives and Practices*, (Toronto: Copp Clark Pitman, 1990), 178–79.

19 See Graham P. McDonough, "The Moral and Pedagogical Importance of Dissent to Catholic Education," Ph.D. dissertation, University of Toronto (2007), for an extended treatment of this claim. Miller and Seller's framework does not appear in that work, but it nonetheless strongly claims that students who disagree with the prevailing Catholic view ought to receive the pedagogical supports that would justify a faithful dissent, and that these supports should be equal to those that a student who agrees with the prevailing view would receive (426–28).

20 John Horgan, ed., *"Humanae vitae" and the Bishops: The Encyclical and the Statements of the National Hierarchies* (Shannon, Ireland: Irish University Press, 1972), 238; Philip S. Kaufman, *Why You Can Disagree and Remain a Faithful Catholic* (New York: Crossroad Publishing, 1995), 45.

21 Kaufman, *Why You Can Disagree*, 8; *Council Daybook*, Vatican II, Session 3, 203ff. (Washington, DC: National Catholic Welfare Conference, 1965).

22 Garry Wills, *Papal Sin: Structures of Deceit* (Toronto: Doubleday, 2000), 85; B. Häring, "Fostering the Nobility of Marriage and Family," in *Commentary on the Documents on Vatican II*, ed. Herbert Vormlinger (New York: Herder and Herder, 1969), 225.

23 Vatican Council II, "*Gaudium et Spes* / Pastoral Constitution on the Church in the Modern World," in *Vatican Council II: The Basic Sixteen Documents*, ed. A. Flannery (Northport, NY: Costello Publishing, 1996), 163–282, §50–51. The instruction in §51 directly cites *Casti Connubii*.

24 *HV*, §6

25 Kaufman, *Why You Can Disagree*, 102; Wills, *Papal Sin*, 74.

26 Andrew M. Greeley, *The Catholic Revolution: New Wine, Old Wineskins, and the Second Vatican Council* (Los Angeles: University of California Press, 2004), 34–35.

27 Robert B. Kaiser, *The Politics of Sex and Religion: A Case History in the Development of Doctrine* (Kansas City: Leaven Press, 1985), 197–98, cited in Kaufman, *Why You Can Disagree*, 9.

28 CCCB, "Winnipeg Statement," §17.

29 CCCB, "Winnipeg Statement," §26.

30 Vincent Foy, "Tragedy at Winnipeg," LifeSiteNews.com, 1988, http://www.life sitenews.com/ldn/2004_docs/tragedyatwinnipeg.pdf, 7–8.

31 CCCB, "Liberating potential," 2008, http://www.cccb.ca/site/images/stories/ pdf/humanae_vitae_en.pdf §19

32 Reginald W. Bibby, Sarah Russell, and Ronald Rolheiser, *The Emerging Millennials: How Canada's Newest Generation Is Responding to Change and Choice* (Lethbridge, AB: Project Canada Books, 2009), 56–57.

DISSENT AND CRITICAL THINKING

33 Greeley, *The Catholic Revolution*, 92. The figure is 20 per cent for the United States.

34 Although current data is lacking on Canadian Catholic adolescents' and adults' responses to the direct question "Do you approve of contraception?" the data that show an approval of premarital sexual intercourse in itself reflects opinions that stand firmly in contradiction to HV's general norms, which are based upon reserving sexual intercourse to married heterosexual couples. HV makes its first mention of the sexual couple in this context (§8).

35 Greeley, *The Catholic Revolution*, 58.

36 Greeley, *The Catholic Revolution*, 124.

37 Observe that in this construction "the school" and its partiality are assumed to be prior to those whom it serves, instead of being partly constituted by them.

38 McDonough, "The Moral and Pedagogical Importance," 309, 322, 348, and 365–66.

39 Miller and Seller, *Curriculum*, chapters 2 and 3; Congregation for Catholic Education, *The Catholic School*, 1977, http://www.vatican.va/roman_curia/ congregations/ccatheduc/documents/rc_con_ccatheduc_doc_19770319 _catholic-school_en.html, §49. Recall that the Catholic school also serves non-Catholics, who would see this issue differently.

40 Miller and Seller, *Curriculum*, chapter 2. Recall that DH forbids indoctrinatory intentions and practices, since truth has its own binding power (§1), and therefore "everyone should be immune from coercion" and must not "be restrained from acting in accordance with their convictions in religious matters in private or in public" (§2).

41 Miller, "Challenges Facing Catholic Schools," 453.

42 Gregory Baum, *Amazing Church: A Catholic Theologian Remembers a Half-century of Change* (Toronto: Novalis, 2005), 118. Baum notices that even within the Roman Curia it is not certain which of "proclamation" or "dialogue" should be emphasized, or if and how they are complementary.

43 I argue elsewhere that dissident students who achieve better understandings of the teachings with which they disagree are left with their pedagogical needs underserved at this point. "Can There Be 'Faithful Dissent' within Catholic Religious Education in Schools?" *International Studies in Catholic Education* 1, no. 2 (2009): 197–98.

44 Feinberg's observations (*For Goodness Sake*, 49) regarding this particular kind of thinking and method fall within Miller and Seller's (chapter 4) articulation of the "transaction" position.

45 Feinberg, *For Goodness Sake*, 50.

46 Miller and Seller, *Curriculum*, chapter 6.

47 Miller and Seller, *Curriculum*, 187.

48 Feinberg, *For Goodness Sake*, 50.

49 In "What Is Assumed," I argue that "a lack of explicit and clearly stated intentions regarding the development Catholic students' ecclesial agency through their schooling leads to potential problems as they experience and imagine themselves as lay persons in the Church."

50 The transformation perspective is not exclusive in scope to those who would disagree with Church teachings. Educators whose view of social justice is based on Catholic teachings quite easily fit within this perspective, including Paulo Freire's *Pedagogy of the Oppressed*, regardless of their opinion on HV. As well, some Catholic transformation teachers would propose that society ought to be adjusted to HV in the service of the common good. The difference here is that the orthodox teacher takes the norms and structures of *secular society* as objects of transformation to a Catholic perspective, and the dissident, by contrast, would likely aim to transform controversial *teachings* or one's *ecclesial attitude* toward them. This orthodox approach counts as a third general Catholic category within the transformation orientation, in addition to the radical and moderate modes articulated above.

51 McDonough, "Can There Be 'Faithful Dissent'?" 198–99.

52 Graham P. McDonough, "The Problem of Catholic School Teachers Deferring to the Home on Controversial Religious Issues," *Catholic Education: A Journal of Inquiry and Practice* 13, no. 3 (2010): 300–302.

53 This threefold framework is adapted from Scheffler's distinction between teaching the fact of religion, to be religious, and how to be religious. Israel Scheffler, *The Language of Education* (Springfield, IL: Charles C. Thomas, 1960), 100–101.

54 See Baum, *Amazing Church*, and Kaufman, *Why You Can Disagree*, for enumerations of several Catholic teachings that have changed, and the resulting implications for the People of God.

55 The question of how the laity is positioned next to the Magisterium and clergy is itself unsettled in post-conciliar Catholic ecclesial theory. Pope John Paul II's apostolic exhortation "*Christifideles laici*" specifically articulates the laity's dependence on the Magisterium and clergy (§22 to 24), while theologian John Nilson ("The Laity," in *The Gift of the Church: A Textbook on Ecclesiology*, ed. Peter C. Phan [Collegeville, MN: Liturgical Press, 2000], 395–413) articulates a critique that this arrangement excludes competent laity from the governance of their own Church simply by the fact of ordination and consecration.

56 My *The Moral and Pedagogical Importance* articulates this initiative in detail.

Bibliography

Baum, Gregory. *Amazing Church: A Catholic Theologian Remembers a Half-century of Change*. Toronto: Novalis, 2005.

Bibby, Reginald W., Sarah Russell, and Ronald Rolheiser. *The Emerging Millennials: How Canada's Newest Generation Is Responding to Change and Choice*. Lethbridge, AB: Project Canada Books, 2009.

Brighouse, Harry. "Faith Schools, Personal Autonomy, and Democratic Competence." In *Faith in Education: A Tribute to Terence McLaughlin*, edited by Graham Haydon, 78–93. London: Institute of Education, 2009.

Bryk, Anthony S., Valerie E. Lee, and Peter B. Holland. *Catholic Schools and the Common Good*. Cambridge, MA: Harvard University Press, 1993.

Canadian Conference of Catholic Bishops. Statement on the Encyclical *Humanae vitae* ["Winnipeg Statement"]. In *Love Kindness: The Social Teaching of the Canadian Catholic Bishops (1958–1989)—A Second Collection*, edited by E.F. Sheridan. Sherbrooke, QC: Editions Paulines, 1991 [original statement published 1968].

———. Liberating potential. 2008. http://www.cccb.ca/site/images/stories/pdf/humanae_vitae_en.pdf

Catholic Church. *The Code of Canon Law*. Ottawa: Canadian Council of Catholic Bishops, 1983.

Congregation for Catholic Education. *The Catholic School*. 1977. http://www.vatican.va/roman_curia/congregations/ccatheduc/documents/rc_con_ccatheduc_doc_19770319_catholic-school_en.html

Council Daybook. Vatican II, Session 3. Washington, DC: National Catholic Welfare Conference, 1965.

Curran, Charles E., and Robert Hunt. *Dissent In and For the Church: Theologians and Humanae vitae*. New York: Sheed and Ward, 1969.

Feinberg, Walter. *For Goodness Sake: Religious Schools and Education for Democratic Citizenry*. New York: Routledge, 2006.

Flew, Antony G.N. "'What Is Indoctrination': Comments on Moore and Wilson." *Studies in Philosophy and Education* 5, no. 2 (1967): 273–83.

Foy, Vincent. "Tragedy at Winnipeg," LifeSiteNews.com. 1988. http://www.lifesitenews.com/ldn/2004_docs/tragedyatwinnipeg.pdf

Freire, Paulo. *Pedagogy of the Oppressed*. Translated by M.B. Ramos. New York: Herder and Herder, 1970.

Greeley, Andrew M. *The Catholic Revolution: New Wine, Old Wineskins, and the Second Vatican Council*. Los Angeles: University of California Press, 2004.

Halstead, J. Mark. "In Defense of Faith Schools." In *Faith in Education: A Tribute to Terence McLaughlin*, edited by Graham Haydon, 46–67. London: Institute of Education, 2009.

Häring, B. "Fostering the Nobility of Marriage and Family." In *Commentary on the Documents on Vatican II*, edited by Herbert Vormlinger. New York: Herder and Herder, 1969.

Horgan, John, ed. *"Humanae vitae" and the Bishops: The Encyclical and the Statements of the National Hierarchies*. Shannon, Ireland: Irish University Press, 1972.

John Paul II, Pope. *The Acting Person*, translated by A. Potocki. Boston: D. Reidel, 1979.

———. "Christifideles laici." 1988. http://www.vatican.va/holy_father/john_paul_ii/apost_exhortations/documents/hf_jp-Ii_exh_30121988_christifideles-laici_en.html

Kaiser, Robert B. *The Politics of Sex and Religion: A Case History in the Development of Doctrine*. Kansas City: Leaven Press, 1985.

Kaufman, Philip S. *Why You Can Disagree and Remain a Faithful Catholic*. New York: Crossroad Publishing, 1995.

McDonough, Graham P. "Can There Be 'Faithful Dissent' within Catholic Religious Education in Schools?" *International Studies in Catholic Education* 1, no. 2 (2009): 187–99.

———. "The Moral and Pedagogical Importance of Dissent to Catholic Education." Ph.D. dissertation, University of Toronto, 2007.

———. "The Problem of Catholic School Teachers Deferring to the Home on Controversial Religious Issues." *Catholic Education: A Journal of Inquiry and Practice* 13, no. 3 (2010): 287–305.

———. "What Is Assumed about a Catholic Student's Ecclesial Agency, and Why It Matters to Catholic Schooling in Canada." *Catholic Education: A Journal of Inquiry and Practice* 14, no. 3 (2011): 272–91.

Miller, J. Michael [Archbishop]. "Challenges Facing Catholic Schools: A View from Rome." In *International Handbook of Catholic Education: Challenges for School Systems in the 21st Century*, edited by Gerald Grace and Joseph O'Keefe, 449–80. Dordrecht, The Netherlands: Springer, 2007.

Miller, John P., and Wayne Seller. *Curriculum: Perspectives and Practice*. Toronto: Copp Clark Pitman, 1990.

Nilson, Jon. "The Laity." In *The Gift of the Church: A Textbook on Ecclesiology*, edited by Peter C. Phan, 395–413. Collegeville, MN: Liturgical Press, 2000.

Olson, David R. *Psychological Theory and Educational Reform: How School Remakes Mind and Society*. New York: Cambridge University Press, 2003.

Paul VI, Pope. "*Humanae vitae* / On Human Life." http://www.vatican.va/holy_father/paul_vi/encyclicals/documents/hf_p-vi_enc_25071968_humanae-vitae_en.html

DISSENT AND CRITICAL THINKING

Pius XI, Pope. "*Casti connubii* / On Chaste Wedlock." http://www.vatican.va/holy
_father/pius_xi/encyclicals/documents/hf_p-xi_enc_31121930_casti
-connubii_en.html.

Saskatoon Catholic Schools. *Celebrating the Gift of Catholic Education in Saskatchewan: 1905–2005.* Saskatoon, 2005.

Scheffler, Israel. *The Language of Education.* Springfield, IL: Charles C. Thomas,
1960.

Vatican Council II. "*Apostolicam actuositatem* / Decree on the Apostolate of the
Laity." In *Vatican Council II: The Basic Sixteen Documents*, edited by A. Flannery, 403–42. Northport, NY: Costello Publishing, 1996 [original work published 1965].

———. "*Dignitatis humanae* / Declaration on religious liberty." In *Vatican Council II: The Basic Sixteen Documents*, edited by A. Flannery, 551–68. Northport,
NY: Costello Publishing, 1996 [original work published 1965].

———. "*Gaudium et spes* / Pastoral constitution on the Church in the modern
world." In *Vatican Council II: The Basic Sixteen Documents*, edited by A. Flannery, 163–282. Northport, NY: Costello Publishing, 1996 [original work published 1965].

Wills, Garry. *Papal Sin: Structures of Deceit.* Toronto: Doubleday, 2000.

CHAPTER NINE

A CANADIAN ISLAMIC SCHOOL IN PERSPECTIVE: A CRITIQUE OF THE "MODERATE" AND "STRONG" CATEGORIES IN FAITH-BASED SCHOOLING

Qaiser Ahmad

I remember being asked an obvious question that I should have expected during my interview to become a teacher at a well-known Islamic school[1] in Toronto in August 1997: "How will you make your classroom feel like an Islamic school classroom?" I was prepared to answer interview questions related to curriculum implementation, instructional strategies, classroom management, assessment and evaluation, learning theories, and all the other aspects related to education that I had learned throughout my post-graduate certificate of education program at the University of London. However, I must admit, I did not think prior to the interview about how my classroom would be set up to present an "Islamic" environment of learning. My answer was so basic that, after the interview, I thought I would not be hired for neglecting to consider such an obviously important question: "I would place a copy of the Qur'an at the front of my desk to make sure students knew the importance of the Qur'an in their daily lives." To my surprise at the time, I did get hired, likely because the school needed to fill urgent staffing needs.

The Islamic school where I taught for six years is co-educational, as are the majority of Islamic schools in Western countries. At the time, the overwhelming majority of the school's teachers were educated in Canada, and all were adherents of the **Sunni** Orthodoxy of Islam. My academic portfolio was a charge to teach all subjects—except for French and Arabic language—including Islamic Studies, an assignment that was of special significance.

DISSENT AND CRITICAL THINKING

In my view, and in the view of my colleagues at the time, teaching Islamic Studies had become the raison d'être for working at the school because of the personal impact it made on the lives of educators teaching it, including myself. Not only did I teach what I knew of the Islamic sciences, but I was also motivated to learn more at a personal level and reflect upon my own experiences to ensure that my students knew how to *live* Islam throughout their daily lives rather than simply memorize content that had little to no connection to what they may experience in life. It was in Islamic Studies that students learned critical-thinking skills, enabling them to understand and challenge the issues they might face when they left the Islamic school. I believe that the task of an educator is to help students to critically analyse the world around them and work to make positive changes in society, as opposed to conditioning students to fit into that society. My concern was that if we did not discuss these issues in school, they might have challenges understanding and addressing them in society.

In 2003, ending my sixth year at the Islamic school, I resigned and enrolled at the University of Toronto to pursue graduate studies in education. One of the topics that interested me during my study was the debates about faith-based schooling in Canada. In my review of literature on this issue, I found that faith-based schooling was—and still is—one of the main educational concerns within a pluralistic, democratic society. Although Catholic schools have existed in many Western countries for centuries, there has been a more recent rise in the number of religious schools of other faiths: Jewish, (non-Catholic) Christian, Islamic, Hindu, Sikh, and others. The increasing popularity of such schools has been the focus of many debates of competing perspectives, on topics such as equal funding of religious schools, constitutional rights of parents, social cohesion, tolerance, and liberal values, to name but a few. What caught my attention was the classification of faith-based schools into two categories, distinguishing "moderate" from "strong" schools.[2] In this chapter, I draw upon my experience teaching at an Islamic school to argue that this distinction is problematic because the schools that might be labelled "strong" offer a place for the type of discussion and debate that is essential to cultivating a critical disposition necessary for citizenship in multicultural Canada, the very aim that is supposed to characterize the education of "moderate" schools.

My account is based on personal experience rather than formal research that one would expect from scholarly work. Given the modest amount of empirical research on Islamic schools, personal accounts and analyses still provide the clearest insight into the contemporary challenges faced by researchers in this field.[3] In order to challenge the "moderate" and "strong" distinction, I shall discuss how I dealt with three controversial issues—living Islam in the West, gender, and sexuality—during my time teaching at the Islamic school as a means to support my argument that some Islamic schools that exhibit the qualities of strong schools may achieve the aims often thought to be those met only by moderate schools. I will begin with a brief review of the two categories before addressing the issues.

Moderate and Strong Schools

Moderate schools are taken to offer each student an initial conception of their faith, cultivate critical reflection, and enable individual autonomy, especially with regard to future decisions about their religious and other beliefs.[4] Many scholars argue, therefore, that moderate schools are acceptable alternatives to secular public schools. They provide an educational environment that promotes student autonomy from which self-determination can proceed, and they have not been shown to result in social divisions or intolerance.[5] Some researchers have found that such schools have helped minorities to assimilate into society even better than secular public schools in fostering the type of citizenship that is based on genuinely productive and mutually respectful cooperation with others outside of their faith and a concern for the common good for all.[6]

In contrast, strong schools aim to foster a stable, pre-determined religious identity. In a few cases, strong schools have been shown to encourage separation from the wider multi-racial society, with little emphasis placed on multicultural policies.[7] Hall warns against such schools because, in his view, an emphasis on national, cultural, and religious identity may lead to the adoption of "closed versions of culture or community [and] the refusal to engage with the difficult problems that arise from trying to live with difference."[8] Burtonwood, too, has noted a greater likelihood that strong schools may not prioritize the promotion or development of social cohesion and individual autonomy of their students.[9]

What I found problematic about this categorization was that the Islamic school I had worked at—and, incidentally, others I was aware of—exhibited some characteristics of both strong and moderate schools. For example, educators at the Islamic school did not merely present Islam to provide an initial conception of the religion. Rather, to a significant extent, we attempted to provide a comprehensive understanding of Islam to make certain that students would continue to practise and believe in Islamic teachings throughout their lives. Almost opposite to what Kevin McDonough states, we believed that providing a comprehensive understanding of Islam served as a starting point for autonomous ethical reflection, enabling children to *revive* their religion and adhere to it, rejecting alternative identities.[10] In this sense the school embodied the characteristics of strong schools. However, similar to the characteristics of moderate schools, we did not do so in order to insulate our students from the wider society, and we actively sought to develop students' capacities for critical thinking. I do not recall any staff member at the Islamic school ever shying away from or feeling uncomfortable about addressing questions or concerns on any topic that students brought up in the classroom. In fact, from an Islamic perspective, Muslims are encouraged to direct questions about their religion to scholars of Islam, as indicated in the **Qur'an**: "Ask the people of remembrance,[11] if you know not" (16:43). We wanted our students to develop religious affiliation and be proud of their identity, without rejecting multiculturalism and the need to integrate into a diverse society. It did not make sense to me that educational researchers could classify a broad spectrum of faith-based schools into two categories, because the faith-based school in which I worked was strong in its stance on religious identity but moderate in its position on multicultural citizenship.

My experience working in this school led me to believe that the categories of strong and moderate schools are not mutually exclusive. One should not be under the impression that moderate schools alone emphasize multicultural citizenship while only strong schools emphasize a comprehensive religious education that would limit religious autonomy. In my opinion, the Islamic school where I worked met most of the criteria of a strong school but also some of the criteria of moderate schools. Through my discussion of the three issues introduced above, I will show that the Islamic school encouraged and facilitated questioning while delivering a comprehensive religious doctrine, simultaneously fostering autonomy and laying the foundation for social cohesion and citizenship by cultivating critical thinking.

Living Islam in the West: Religion vs. Culture

What exactly does it mean to *live* Islam from an educational perspective? Hewer has found that Islamic schools in the United Kingdom tend to integrate Islam throughout the curriculum: "[T]here are no 'secular' subjects within a Muslim world view. Every aspect of study should be permeated by Islamic values and the divinely ordained harmony should be brought out by the educational process."[12] In my experience, the educational program at the Islamic school was structured in such a way that Islamic knowledge permeated its curriculum without detracting from government-mandated guidelines. To share a few examples, the contributions made by Muslim scholars to the fields of the sciences and mathematics were discussed as part of our lessons; Islamic art that did not focus on drawing animate objects was woven into the visual arts program; and language and literature were linked to stories found in the Qur'an and the life of the Prophet Muham-mad, peace be upon him.[14]

For Muslims, there is no tension in distinguishing between sacred and secular knowledge. Burtonwood has argued that a distinction should be made between the two, however, as they may be incompatible. He spe-cifically refers to science, stating that the "rational, secular and empirical approach to science" is rejected by a curriculum based on sacred, faith-based knowledge.[13] Yet from an Islamic perspective, "rationality and rev-elation interact and complement each other and play a part equally in the education of the young."[14] Although Islamic Studies was a course in itself, we did not compartmentalize religion classes into a course that had no con-nection to the knowledge they were learning in other subjects. If we had done so, this would have sent the message to our students that religion does not have a place in the public sphere.[15] I believe that this would be true for most faith-based schools; that is, most religious schooling aims at cultivat-ing students who understand and appreciate the secular world while doing so within the framework of their faith. Indeed, when doing so, students have a focus in life—what Neil Postman refers to as a "narrative" to live by.[16] With respect to Islam and Muslims, the ideal focus of the narrative is to strive toward pleasing God in every aspect of our lives. From an educational perspective, this translates to the need to attain an education that will allow students to have a profession that will contribute positively to the society in which they live because helping and serving humanity are considered to be *'ibadaat* (Arabic for acts of worship) that are rewarded by God. The recog-nition of the unity of sacred and secular knowledge was part of the ethos of our school and something we strived to impart to our students.

I recall religion, more so than cultural identity, being the primary reason why Muslim parents sent their children to Islamic schools. It is therefore appropriate here to discuss the second part of the title for this section: reli-gion vs. culture. Interestingly, many of the authors who employ the strong–moderate distinction use the two terms interchangeably in their writing, which adds confusion to how certain religious schools are categorized. The word "culture" is not a synonym for the word "religion." They are related, however, with respect to how they can be applied. I have found it impor-

DISSENT AND CRITICAL THINKING

tant, for example, to discuss with my students in both the Islamic school and in the public school where I currently work that religious traditions and rites may be part of the culture of a people, but certain cultural practices are not necessarily part of the religion. With regard to Muslims, Halstead mentions that "it is their religion which gives them their distinct identity, and it is their religion rather than other aspects of their cultural heritage which they are most anxious to preserve."[17] He further notes: "The identity of Muslims in the West, for example, is undoubtedly influenced by contact with the surrounding cultures, but may nonetheless remain true to core Islamic values."[18]

Similar views have been expressed by others.[19] In my experience at the Islamic school, rarely was culture brought up except with respect to the validity of cultural practices within the religion. Although customs of a culture may influence how Islamic law adapts to certain practices within a society, the focus is not to preserve the cultural practices of a people. Islamic law is grounded on five permanent and irrevocable universal priorities—religion, life, intellect, family, and wealth—that cannot be set aside or violated in any way.[20] Maintaining and passing on cultural practices are not included as part of the priorities. For the majority of Muslim parents with whom I was in contact at the Islamic school, learning and understanding the religion (and thus preserving it) were of utmost importance.

The staff at the Islamic school where I taught at would not classify our school as strong, since integrating into society was a key concern. We as a staff were actively looking for ways to help Muslim students integrate and contribute to society, which by definition is incompatible with the characteristics of a strong school. One of the questions that I continually thought about during my six years at the Islamic school was how well students would participate in, and contribute to, both the public schools in which they enrolled after graduating from the Islamic school, and the broader society. All of us were aware that our students would eventually leave our school and join the secular public-education system since, in my final year, the school ended at grade 10 (although the school has now expanded to grade 12). Having been educated in the secular public-education system myself, I would share examples of potential challenges they might face when they left our school. The challenges were more social in nature than academic; the only academic issue that I would present to them was related to macro-evolution (that human beings evolved from apes)—the one scientific theory I am aware of that is incompatible with Islam. On this issue, I would explain the Islamic perspective—that God created humankind to inhabit the earth for a period of time—and provide them with other resources to consider reading that challenge the theory of evolution.[21] I did not see a problem with their learning about the theory in the secular public-education system as long as they understood the Islamic perspective. Indeed, in order for them to critique the theory, they would need a good understanding of it.

The main challenges, however, were with respect to social pressures. Substance abuse, gang-related issues, and gender interactions were at the forefront of what I would discuss with my students, relating the issues to personal experiences that I had when I was in secondary school. I would emphasize the need to have a comprehensive understanding of Islam in order to confront these challenges. In my opinion, such an understanding would allow them to make ethical decisions and sound judgments respectfully that would be of benefit to society without imposing their beliefs and practices on others. Sweet found a similar viewpoint expressed during her interview with the principal of an Islamic school in the Netherlands: "Our philosophy ... is if we want to integrate into a multi-faith society, then children should know their own religion and culture. They should come from a position of strength in order to contribute to society. If they have nothing to contribute, then they will be assimilated."[22]

Our goal at the Islamic school was to ensure that our students neither became insular nor lost their faith when they entered society, in whatever capacity that might be. Again, in this respect the Islamic school met some of the criteria of strong schools but also some of the criteria of moderate schools. I found that one of the main reasons for parents sending their students to Islamic schools was to ensure that their children did not compromise their faith in any way, yet still maximized their ability to contribute positively and effectively to the society in which they live. By "compromise" I mean that students would not willfully change Islamic practice, and would respectfully challenge those who believe Islam needs to be reformed to suit the status quo. I do not recall ever having a conversation with a staff member or parent about the need to keep the children away from the society in which they live. I used to tell my students that there are common values shared by all faiths, and it was important to recognize and respect this throughout their life encounters.[23]

Gender Issues

My school sought to impart a strong Islamic position on gender, but it did so with a view to healthy, multicultural integration for the students by enabling and empowering them to practice their religion publicly while being knowledgeable of Canada's rights and freedoms—both to defend

DISSENT AND CRITICAL THINKING

their own religious decisions and to understand and appreciate the decisions of others. At the Islamic school, we tried to ensure that all our students were reading with a critical lens, especially regarding gender-related issues. What was becoming commonplace in the media during my years at the Islamic school was how Muslim women were presented: individuals who were subservient to men, oppressed by their faith, and without a voice for contributing to their families and society. We tried to challenge such views in our classrooms by highlighting contributions made by Muslim women in the past and present, and critiquing misconceptions and biases by having students identifying the author's social position and political affiliations, as well as the events that might have influenced their position. Similar exercises of critiquing viewpoints are presented elsewhere.[24] I believe that the importance of challenging this narrative was to empower our students to ensure they would not inhabit the narrative presented in the media.

Such misconceptions are even more prevalent in Canadian society today and are highlighted and sensationalized in the media when incidents such as domestic violence occur amongst Muslims.[25] Assumptions and claims are made based on hastily drawn conclusions from superficial observations of Muslims in society and their portrayal in the media, without truly analysing why things are the way they are or whether they are based on other societal factors that are prevalent in every society. As Murata notes, "Society in the contemporary Islamic world knows abuses like society anywhere else. But we need to distinguish between abuses that arise from living in accordance with Islamic ideals and those that arise from breaking with those same ideals."[26] Some fail to recognize that the oppression of women is a global phenomenon that is often based on societal and economic factors rather than a reflection of an adherence to any particular faith.[27] As Bouhdiba comments, "only a naïve or dishonest mind could be surprised at the gaps that exist in any society between its ideals and its practices."[28]

Unfortunately, some authors of young adult books have added to the misconceived narrative presented in the media by including Muslim characters in their books. Erroneously, educators may feel they are inclusive or fulfilling multicultural practice by incorporating books in their programs that include characters from diverse cultural and religious backgrounds. The most popular of these books portray Muslim characters—especially Muslim women—in a negative light, reinforcing stereotypes and biases, which is far from being inclusive. Sensoy and Marshall have analysed such books and found that they "reinforce the idea that Muslim women are *inherently* oppressed, they are oppressed in ways that Western women are not, and that this oppression is a function of Islam."[29] One of the main problems that arise when such books make their way into a school's English language program is that some educators in the secular public education system believe it is their duty to "liberate" their female Muslim students, whom they falsely perceive as having been denied an education or oppressed because of their faith. This is highly problematic, especially when a recent Gallup survey found that "Muslim American women are among the most highly educated female religious groups, second only to Jewish American women."[30] As Halstead notes, the "attitude 'why can't Muslims be more like us?' ... has shown to be the sort of attitude which can be very damaging to social integration and harmony in a culturally diverse society."[31]

Of course, my students at the Islamic school would raise concerns about how Muslim women were treated "back home," so to speak, even giving their own examples of how some female elders (and undeniably a few male elders) in their extended family were not able to obtain an education. To deny this would be to deny the reality of the situation. My purpose was not to present every issue we discussed in a positive light and deny what is happening amongst Muslim communities. But I would challenge them to analyse the issues and determine whether these issues were part of the Islamic world view or because of societal factors such as cultural influences, socio-economic status, or lack of access. Anyone who has read resources on Muslims and Islam will know that Islam promotes equality between women and men.[32] In all my years of teaching at the Islamic school, I reinforced the message that men and women are equal and should have equal access to opportunities in any society in which they live. I would emphasize that they need to be aware of the difference between cultural practices and what the religion of Islam says; religious traditions can be part of a culture, but what is practised in a culture is not necessarily part of the religion. It was their responsibility to ensure that they knew the difference and advocated for the correct view in matters related to religion and daily life. Therefore, for example, when my students encountered the misconception that it was Muslim men who ordered women to wear the *hijab*, they could clearly respond that the *hijab* was ordained by God in chapter 24, verse 31 of the Qur'an.[33]

What may seem surprising to many non-Muslims is that many of my female Muslim students had intentionally chosen to wear the *hijab* in accordance with their reading of the Qur'an, and they did not dispute or problematize this choice as sexist, subjugating, or indoctrinatory. A verse from

DISSENT AND CRITICAL THINKING

the Qur'an that many may not be aware of states, "Let there be no compulsion in religion" (2:256). So what of the dress code at the Islamic school? Of course, the dress code did ensure that Muslim girls wore a uniform that included a *hijab*, and this may be viewed as the Islamic school forcing female students to wear it. However, they were not forced to wear the *hijab* outside of the school, and indeed some female students did take it off once they left school property. Was this school policy a contradiction to the verse quoted above? In my opinion, a uniform is a uniform, and parents were aware that the *hijab* was part of the uniform for girls. Parents also had the choice to enroll their children or not. I never questioned this policy because I did not find anything wrong with it. The school provided a safe environment for girls to have first-hand experience of wearing the *hijab* throughout the day. The environment allowed them to wear it, and they were encouraged to do so by their teachers and peers—a training period of sorts. For young female adults, this time is especially important. For some, they need the support of seeing others wearing it and being in an encouraging environment. Wearing the *hijab* is not an easy thing to do, especially when one lives in an environment where the majority do not cover their hair. Some girls may be the only ones in their family who wear it, others may be struggling to wear it because they may not feel they fit in with their friends, and still others may not want the added attention that comes along with wearing it. I told my students that they have the right to dress as they wish, but they should strive to do so in accordance with Islamic principles. This is what was taught, but whether students chose to adopt Islamic attire outside of the school was entirely up to them.

It might seem strange that I would need to explain to students that because they live in a democratic society they have the right to wear Islamic clothing with confidence and not feel that such clothing would hinder their interactions and opportunities. Ironically, a few Western democracies are considering imposing bans on particular types of Islamic clothing that women choose to wear, under the pretence that such clothing undermines the dignity of Muslim women and threatens Western *liberal* values. Belgium was the first European democracy to impose a ban on the *burqa*, a full-length cloak-like dress that includes a *niqab*, a face-covering veil; more recently, France also imposed such a ban.[34] Oddly, in a country known for its successful model of pluralism,[35] the Canadian province of Quebec has proposed legislation to proscribe facial covering in the public-services sector. Most troubling is the latter case, where the province's proposal is to deny public services to those who choose to wear the *niqab*. Siddiqui notes,

222

A CANADIAN ISLAMIC SCHOOL IN PERSPECTIVE | AHMAD

"As the Supreme Court of Canada has ruled, it is not up to the state but rather individuals to interpret their religion."[36] What appears to be emerging is a new form of political correctness that defines one particular way to be open and liberal, equating this with freedom and modernity.[37]

Unfortunately, Islamophobia has become gender specific, and the message we constantly emphasized amongst our students was that it was up to them to learn about Islam to help them educate others in order that such fears might be overcome.[38] In this regard, the Islamic school adopted a mission that was more strong than moderate because of the importance of preserving the religion, as we believed our students required a higher level of understanding of Islam in order to help others in society overcome their fears towards it. However, the preservation of Islam is not meant to override the rights and value systems of others, as is becoming the apparent trend toward Muslim women. In the classroom, my emphasis was to reinforce the understanding that all citizens—including Muslims—are to be treated equally in any society. In essence, I was repeating the vision of democratic citizenry that Halstead describes: "The recognition of all citizens as equal in respect to fundamental rights and freedoms, the rejection of racism, prejudice and discrimination as an affront to individual identity, and the duty of all citizens to support and uphold institutions that embody a shared conception of justice and the rule of law."[39] One of my principal aims, however, was to teach about democratic citizenry in a way that "does not require the annulment of different values and loyalties" of individuals.[40]

Sexuality

With respect to the notion of democratic citizenry, how is sexuality understood within the context of the Islamic school? Any young adult raised in a society as diverse as Canada is exposed to a range of images, beliefs, and discussions about sexuality. Students in Islamic schools are no exception, and part of the teacher's job in an Islamic school includes facilitating critical discussions about the subject. Muslims are among the most vocal about curriculum related to sexuality and health education in secular public schools in the West, prompting recommendations from some Muslim organizations to withdraw Muslim children from sections of health education classes.[41] Several other religious groups share their opposition to some extent, although it appears that most of the media attention has been focused upon Muslims. It should be noted from the outset that many aspects of sexuality and health education have been addressed in detail in Islamic law.[42] It can be accurately stated that Islam does not oppose sex education. So what is the issue? San-

DISSENT AND CRITICAL THINKING

jakdar states it quite clearly: "While many people in the Islamic community would agree that Muslim students need to understand the nature of their developing sexuality, *how* it should be taught and by *whom* is also a source of contention among many Muslim parents and students."[43] Halstead accurately sums up three areas that contravene the Islamic approach to covering this topic in schools: "First, some of the materials used in sex education offend against the Islamic principle of modesty and decency. Secondly, contemporary sex education tends to present certain behaviour as normal or acceptable which Muslims believe is sinful. Thirdly, sex education is perceived as tending to undermine the Islamic concept of family life."[44]

It might be surprising to many that we did not shy away from addressing issues related to sexuality during our health education classes at the Islamic school from grade 7 onward. I began the topic of sexuality by first addressing relationships between men and women. From an Islamic perspective, nothing is wrong with having feelings toward the opposite sex, because God is the one who created such feelings and placed them in the hearts of humankind. Our challenge, as Muslim educators, was to encourage students to subdue such feelings until the time was right to express them. We discussed relationships from the perspectives of emotional stability, academic performance, parental implications, societal impact, modesty, dating, chastity, sexual responsibility, and sexually transmitted diseases. Contraceptives were discussed with regard to marriage and family planning, and I did connect this indirectly to premarital sex by stating that some people in society engage in such relationships. This may sound like more of a moderate approach to religious education than strong, as sex before marriage is strictly prohibited in Islam (and in most other faiths). I did not doubt that a few of my students *would* have sex before marriage; however, the intention behind sharing this was to ensure that the student who might potentially fall into sinful behaviour did not contract or transmit sexually transmitted diseases. One cannot be blind to the possibility of a Muslim student—despite the values the school upheld and the strengths of its teachers—choosing to engage in sexual behaviour prior to (or outside of) marriage.

We also discussed relationships at a professional level. Muslims are not restricted from interacting with both male and female members in society. Having a career anywhere in the world would not be possible for a Muslim if this was the case. Muslims are, however, required to ensure that the parameters of such interactions as defined by Islam are not disregarded. One issue that often came up was physical contact. Islam prohibits any sort of physical contact between opposite genders unless it is between certain family members or for medical reasons.[45] The issue of the non-Muslim custom of greeting one another with a handshake therefore tends to raise some eyebrows. Some observant Muslims do not shake hands with members of the opposite sex, and this may cause confusion to others. I remember when my colleague and I took our classes to a conservation area for a school trip. Our two hosts came to us and one of them extended her hand to me to welcome our classes. I placed my hand on my heart as a symbolic gesture of acknowledgement and said hello. In an annoyed tone she commented, "What, am I inferior to you?" After I explained to her that there is no physical contact between men and women in Islam, my female colleague added, "I don't shake hands with males either, so please don't be offended." Interestingly, our second host later came to me and said that she is aware of such "religious norms" and added that this practice was also common among some First Nations groups she had worked with in northern Ontario. A few students who witnessed this discussion were quite surprised by the reaction of our host; they commented that people should be more open to learning about others to avoid being offended.

Perhaps one of the more contentious issues that arose at the Islamic school was the matter of homosexuality. We debated amongst teachers and with the administrator whether or not this should be addressed in the classroom. The following diverse views on this issue were presented: one group of teachers believed that we did not need to address homosexuality as a faith-based school; another group believed that parents sent their students to the Islamic school to avoid being exposed to homosexuality, and therefore, we should not address this issue at the school; meanwhile, another group believed that the Islamic school should address homosexuality from an Islamic perspective to avoid potential confusion that might arise in the minds of our students. The latter view was adopted by the school.

The Islamic stance based on Sunni Orthodoxy is that homosexuality is prohibited, and this position has very much to do with the prohibition of anal intercourse, be it between two males, between a male and a female, or between two females. Addressing males, the Qur'an states: "Of all the creatures of the world, will you approach males and abandon those whom God created for you as mates?" (26:165). By extension, this verse applies equally to females.[46] As an Islamic school, we did not need to discuss issues related to homosexuality with our students, and I believe this to be the case for any faith-based school.[47] We did, however, have a discussion on this issue in health education classes because we were aware that secular public school

DISSENT AND CRITICAL THINKING

students were learning that homosexuality was considered to be an acceptable lifestyle choice. We wanted to make sure our students understood the Islamic perspective so that they would not get confused by what is presented in the media or from their secular-school colleagues.

Returning to the two categorizations of faith-based schools, it is clear that the Islamic school was "strong" in its attempts to limit students' future choices with respect to sexuality. Reflecting on how this was addressed at the Islamic school, I think it would have been beneficial to have also addressed homosexuality from the perspective of human rights. As Sheikh notes, "While Muslims may condemn acts of homosexuality, the *Shari'ah* [Islamic Law] requires that the basic rights of life and safety of all human beings must be protected. Thus Muslims may not accost or treat proclaimed homosexuals unjustly."[48] The issue at hand is of protecting students and individuals in society from harm and from being oppressed by others because of their beliefs. I do not see a problem with raising awareness about homophobia as I am advocating for a safe learning environment for all students, irrespective of their race, ethnicity, religion, or sexual orientation. However, this does not have to mean that I accept homosexuality as permissible in Islam. At first glance, this approach may appear to be more moderate than strong. However, I believe that even if we had addressed homosexuality in this way, the classification of strong would still be applicable in this case, because of our defence of Islamic views against homosexuality, while at the same time the approach could also be considered moderate because of our attempts to enable meaningful participation in a multicultural society.

Conclusion

This chapter has presented an open and honest perspective of my experiences at the Islamic school. The ways in which I dealt with the three "controversial" issues during my time there should highlight the difficulties I faced when trying to categorize this experience in the framework of a moderate or a strong school, since the school fits most of the criteria of strong schools *and* exhibits characteristics of moderate schools. Even though the information provided in this chapter is based on *one* Islamic school in Canada, this experience should spark some debate on the strong/moderate categorization and where Islamic schools fall along the continuum.

The problem of labelling Islamic schools as either moderate or strong is thus evident. The emphasis on a comprehensive religious understanding is a characteristic of a strong school and not of a moderate school, yet the emphasis on social cohesion and citizenship is a characteristic of a moder-

226

A CANADIAN ISLAMIC SCHOOL IN PERSPECTIVE | AHMAD

ate school and not a strong school. Islam has no problems with people integrating into any society, as long as they are able to uphold their faith, "for Islam has always accepted the coexistence of other faiths."[49] At the Islamic school, we did not attempt to keep our students away from the broader society, nor did we promote a disregard for multiculturalism. What we did promote was a vision of social cohesion and individual autonomy that upheld the Islamic faith. We frequently emphasized integrating and contributing positively and effectively to the society in which students were living as Muslims. The intention of doing so was always connected back to the primary goal of attaining the pleasure of God, over secondary goals of attaining wealth and reputable status. As far as I know, Islamic schools want their students to be able to address questions and differences that arise in any society. I would think that most would agree that one of the main reasons behind acquiring an education is to make a positive contribution to society.

I would not hesitate to say that many other Islamic schools in Western countries may be very similar to the school I have presented in this chapter. However, it is possible that other Islamic schools may not have addressed issues in the same way. I can only speculate on possible reasons for this. First, the ideological perspective of the school has an impact on how issues are addressed. The majority of Islamic schools in North America are based on Sunni Orthodoxy, which comprises of over 85 per cent of the Muslim population worldwide. Whether Islamic schools based on **Shi'a** theology would address the issues I have presented in this chapter in similar ways is possibly something to research. Second, and something that is specific to the Canadian context, due to the shortage of Muslim teachers available to work in Islamic schools, some administrators will hire teachers who do not have a degree from a Canadian institution. The potential problem with this is that teachers who come from another country may not have the same views about societal issues as those who have been educated in Canada. Since they may not have arrived in Canada from a democratic country, they may fail to understand Canadian cultural nuances, their school experience may not reflect the school experience of Canadian students, and so on. Lastly, it is important to realize that Islam is not a monolithic reality; there are diverse viewpoints that are acceptable as long as they fall within parameters defined by Islamic law.[50] Teachers in Islamic schools have diverse schooling experiences, and these experiences influence how issues are addressed in their own classrooms.

If educationalists are to continue categorizing faith-based schools, more research is required on Islamic schools in order to get a better understanding of how these schools function on a day-to-day basis. As a result, the need for additional categorizations will arise, illustrating the complexity and diversity of the broad spectrum of faith-based schools rather than grouping such schools into simplistic categories that do not truly reflect how they operate. The distinction between the two categories of "moderate" and "strong" must be re-evaluated, and it is hoped that the information presented in this chapter will enable researchers to establish more precise criteria when referring to religious schools, since simplistic categorizations may steer the debate, and the perspective of researchers, in limited directions.

Notes

1 I have chosen not to identify the school by using its real name because I do not want the views expressed in this paper to be taken as representative of the school's teachers and administrators. I will simply refer to the school as "the Islamic school" in this chapter.

2 Neil Burtonwood, "Social Cohesion, Autonomy and the Liberal Defence of Faith Schools," *Journal of Philosophy of Education* 37, no. 3 (2003): 415–25; Walter Feinberg, *Common Schools, Uncommon Identities: National Unity and Cultural Difference* (New Haven, CT: Yale University Press, 1998); Kevin McDonough, "Can the Liberal State Support Cultural Identity Schools?" *American Journal of Education* 106, no. 4 (1998): 463–99; Terence McLaughlin, "'Education for All' and Religious Schools," in *Education for a Pluralist Society: Philosophical Perspectives on the Swann Report*, ed. Graham Haydon (London: Institute of Education, University of London, 1987); Elmer J. Thiessen, *In Defence of Religious Schools and Colleges* (Kingston: McGill-Queen's University Press, 2001).

3 Chris Hewer, "Schools for Muslims," *Oxford Review of Education* 27, no. 4 (2001): 515–27.

4 Burtonwood, "Social Cohesion"; McDonough, "Can the Liberal State Support Cultural Identity Schools?"

5 McLaughlin, "'Education for All'"; Thiessen, *In Defence of Religious Schools.*

6 Charles Glenn, "Protecting and Limiting School Distinctiveness: How Much of Each?" in *School Choice: The Moral Debate*, ed. Alan Wolfe (Princeton, NJ: Princeton University Press, 2003), 173–94; Thiessen, *In Defence of Religious Schools.*

7 Burtonwood, "Social Cohesion"; Feinberg, *Common Schools*; McDonough, "Can the Liberal State Support Cultural Identity Schools?"; Geoffrey Short, "Faith-Based Schools: A Threat to Social Cohesion?" *Journal of Philosophy of Education* 36, no. 4 (2002): 559–72; Andrew Wright, "Freedom, Equality, Fra-

ternity? Towards a Liberal Defence of Faith Community Schools," *British Journal of Religious Education* 25, no. 2 (2003): 142–52.

8 J. Mark Halstead, "Voluntary Apartheid? Problems of Schooling for Religious and Other Minorities in Democratic Societies," *Journal of Philosophy of Education* 29, no. 2 (1995): 257–72.

9 Burtonwood, "Social Cohesion," 417.

10 I emphasize the word *revive* because from an Islamic world view, Islam cannot be reformed or altered to "fit" the status quo; rather, it is revived by individuals through practice.

11 According to scholars of Qur'anic exegesis, "the people of remembrance" refers to Muslim scholars who are well versed in the Qur'an and the people of knowledge. See al-Qurtubi, *al-Jami' li ahkam al-Qur'an* (The Compendium of the Rules of the Qur'an).

12 Hewer, "Schools for Muslims," 522.

13 Burtonwood, "Social Cohesion," 421.

14 J.M. Halstead and A. Khan-Cheema, "Muslims and Worship in the Maintained School," *Westminister Studies in Education* 10, no. 1 (1987): 27.

15 Thiessen, *In Defence of Religious Schools,* 178.

16 Neil Postman, *The End of Education: Redefining the Value of School* (Toronto: Random House, 1995).

17 Halstead, "Voluntary Apartheid?" 265.

18 Halstead, "Voluntary Apartheid?" 271.

19 Lois Sweet, *God in the Classroom: The Controversial Issue of Religion in Canada's Schools* (Toronto: McClelland and Stewart, 1997); Jasmin Zine, "Muslim Youth in Canadian Schools: Education and the Politics of Religious Identity," *Anthropology and Education Quarterly* 32, no. 4 (2001): 399–423.

20 Nazim Baksh, *Illuminating Islam: Addressing Misconceptions about Muslims and Their Faith* (Al-Ain: Zayed House for Islamic Culture, 2010), 10.

21 For example: Michael J. Behe, *Darwin's Black Box: The Biochemical Challenge to Evolution,* 10th ed. (New York: Free Press, 2006); Maurice Bucaille, *The Bible, the Qur'an and Science: The Holy Scriptures Examined in the Light of Modern Knowledge,* 4th ed. (Paris: Seghers, 1985); Nuh H. Keller, *Evolution Theory and Islam: A Letter to Suleman Ali* (Cambridge: Muslim Academic Trust, 1999).

22 Sweet, *God in the Classroom,* 134.

23 Graham Haydon also advocates the view that educators should create and maintain an appropriate ethical environment that supports and fosters individual respect for diverse religions and cultures. "Respect for Persons and for Cultures as a Basis for National and Global Citizenship," *Journal of Moral Education* 35, no. 4 (2006): 464.

DISSENT AND CRITICAL THINKING

24 See, for example, Susan Bauer and Jessie Wise, *The Well-Trained Mind: A Guide to Classical Education at Home*, 3rd ed. (New York: W.W. Norton), 2009.

25 Gerald Caplan, "Honour Killings in Canada: Even Worse Than We Believe," *Globe and Mail*, 23 July 2010, http://www.theglobeandmail.com/ news/politics/ honour-killings-in-canada-even-worse-than-we-believe/article1650228

26 Sachiko Murata, *The Tao of Islam: A Sourcebook on Gender Relationships in Islamic Thought* (New York: SUNY Press, 1992), 2.

27 Baksh, *Illuminating Islam*, 105.

28 J. Mark Halstead, "Muslims and Sex Education," *Journal of Moral Education* 26, no. 3 (1997): 323.

29 Özlem Sensoy and Elizabeth Marshall, "'Save the Muslim Girl!' Does Popular Young Adult Fiction about Muslim Girls Build Understanding or Reinforce Stereotypes?" *Rethinking Schools Online* 24, no. 2 (2010), http://www.rethink ingschools.org/archive/24_02/24_02_muslim.shtml; emphasis in original.

30 Haroon Siddiqui, "Banning Veil Undermines Secular Democracy," *Toronto Star*, 18 July 2010, http://www.thestar.com/news/world/article/836961--siddiqui -banning-veil-undermines-secular-democracy

31 J. Mark Halstead, "Teaching about Homosexuality: A Response to John Beck," *Cambridge Journal of Education* 29, no. 1 (1999): 134.

32 Baksh, *Illuminating Islam*; Murata, *The Tao of Islam*; Munir Sheikh, *Teaching about Muslims and Islam in the Public School Classroom*, 3rd ed. (Fountain Valley, CA: Council on Islamic Education, 1995).

33 The Arabic term *khumur*, plural of *khimar*, is used in this verse to denote the type and style of veil to be worn by women, commonly referred to as *hijab*.

34 John Lichfield, "France Wakes Up to a Burka Ban as Sarkozy Unveils a New Era," *The Independent*, 11 April 2011, http://www.independent.co.uk/news/ world/europe/france-wakes-up-to-a-burka-ban-as-sarkozy-unveils-a-new -era-2266054.html; Vanessa Mock and John Lichfield, "Belgium Passes Europe's First Ban on Wearing Burka in Public," *The Independent*, 1 May 2010, http://www.independent.co.uk/news/world/europe/belgium-passes-europes -first-ban-on-wearing-burka-in-public-1959626.html

35 Neil Desai and Charles Burton, "Promoting Pluralism Abroad Must Be a Foreign Policy Pillar," *Globe and Mail*, 13 April 2011, http://www.theglobeand mail.com/news/opinions/opinion/promoting-pluralism-abroad-must-be -a-foreign-policy-pillar/article1982544/; John Stackhouse and Patrick Martin, "Canada: 'A Model for the World,'" *Globe and Mail*, 2 February 2002.

36 Siddiqui, "Banning Veil Undermines Secular Democracy."

37 Tariq Ramadan, "Islam and Homosexuality," 29 May 2009, http://www.tariq ramadan.com/Islam-and-Homosexuality.html

38 Jasmin Zine, "Unveiled Sentiments: Gendered Islamophobia and Experiences of Veiling among Muslim Girls in a Canadian Islamic School," *Equity and Excellence in Education* 39, no. 3 (2006): 239–52.

39 Halstead, "Voluntary Apartheid?" 269.

40 David Hargreaves, "Diversity and Choice in School Education: A Modified Libertarian Approach," *Oxford Review of Education* 22, no. 2 (1996): 140.

41 Halstead, "Muslims and Sex Education."

42 Fida Sanjakdar, "'Teacher Talk': The Problems, Perspectives and Possibilities of Developing a Comprehensive Sexual Health Education Curriculum for Australian Muslim Students," *Sex Education* 9, no. 3 (2009): 264.

43 Sanjakdar, "'Teacher Talk,'" 262; emphasis in original.

44 Halstead, "Muslims and Sex Education," 319.

45 Baksh, *Illuminating Islam*; Sanjakdar, "'Teacher Talk'"; Zine, "Muslim Youth in Canadian Schools."

46 Sheikh, *Teaching about Muslims and Islam in the Public School Classroom.*

47 Halstead, "Teaching about Homosexuality."

48 Sheikh, *Teaching about Muslims and Islam in the Public School Classroom*, 42.

49 Thiessen, *In Defence of Religious Schools,* 28; Roger DuPasquier, *Unveiling Islam,* trans. Timothy J. Winter (Cambridge: Islamic Texts Society, 1992); Seyyed H. Nasr, *Islam: Religion, History, and Civilization* (San Francisco: HarperSanFrancisco, 2003).

50 Nasr, *Islam.*

Bibliography

Ali, Abdullah Y., trans. *The Holy Qur'an: English Translation of the Meanings and Commentary.* Madinah: King Fahd Holy Qur'an Printing Complex, 1985.

al-Qurtubi, Muhammad ibn Ahmad. *al-Jami' li ahkam al*-Qur'an. Edited by Ahmad 'Abd al-'Alim al-Burduni, Bashandi Khalaf Allah, Ibrahim Atfish, and Muhammad Muhammad Hasanayn. 20 vols. Beirut: Dar Ihya' al-Turath al-'Arabi, n.d. Reprint 1967.

Baksh, Nazim. *Illuminating Islam: Addressing Misconceptions about Muslims and Their Faith.* Al-Ain, United Arab Emirates: Zayed House for Islamic Culture, 2010.

Bauer, Susan, and Jessie Wise. *The Well-Trained Mind: A Guide to Classical Education at Home.* 3rd ed. New York: W.W. Norton, 2009.

Behe, Michael J. *Darwin's Black Box: The Biochemical Challenge to Evolution.* 10th ed. New York: Free Press, 2006.

Bucaille, Maurice. *The Bible, the Qur'an and Science: The Holy Scriptures Examined in the Light of Modern Knowledge.* 4th ed. Paris: Seghers, 1985.

DISSENT AND CRITICAL THINKING

Burtonwood, Neil. "Social Cohesion, Autonomy and the Liberal Defence of Faith Schools." *Journal of Philosophy of Education* 37, no. 3 (2003): 415–25.

Caplan, Gerald. "Honour Killings in Canada: Even Worse Than We Believe." *Globe and Mail.* 23 July 2010. http://www.theglobeandmail.com/news/politics/ honour-killings-in-canada-even-worse-than-we-believe/article1650228

Desai, Neil, and Charles Burton. "Promoting Pluralism Abroad Must Be a Foreign Policy Pillar." *Globe and Mail.* 13 April 2011. http://www.theglobeand mail.com/news/opinions/opinion/promoting-pluralism-abroad-must -be-a-foreign-policy-pillar/article1982544/

DuPasquier, Roger. *Unveiling Islam,* translated by Timothy J. Winter. Cambridge: Islamic Texts Society, 1992.

Feinberg, Walter. *Common Schools, Uncommon Identities: National Unity and Cultural Difference.* New Haven, CT: Yale University Press, 1998.

Glenn, Charles. "Protecting and Limiting School Distinctiveness: How Much of Each?" In *School Choice: The Moral Debate,* edited by Alan Wolfe, 173–94. Princeton, NJ: Princeton University Press, 2003.

Halstead, J. Mark. "Muslims and Sex Education." *Journal of Moral Education* 26, no. 3 (1997): 317–30.

———. "Teaching about Homosexuality: A Response to John Beck." *Cambridge Journal of Education* 29, no. 1 (1999): 131–36.

———. "Voluntary Apartheid? Problems of Schooling for Religious and Other Minorities in Democratic Societies." *Journal of Philosophy of Education* 29, no. 2 (1995): 257–72.

Halstead, J.M., and A. Khan-Cheema. "Muslims and Worship in the Maintained School." *Westminister Studies in Education* 10, no. 1 (1987): 21–36.

Hargreaves, David. "Diversity and Choice in School Education: A Modified Libertarian Approach." *Oxford Review of Education* 22, no. 2 (1996): 131–41.

Haydon, Graham. "Respect for Persons and for Cultures as a Basis for National and Global Citizenship." *Journal of Moral Education* 35, no. 4 (2006): 457–71.

Hewer, Chris. "Schools for Muslims." *Oxford Review of Education* 27, no. 4 (2001): 515–27.

Keller, Nuh H. *Evolution Theory and Islam: A Letter to Suleman Ali.* Cambridge: Muslim Academic Trust, 1999.

Lichfield, John. "France Wakes Up to a Burka Ban as Sarkozy Unveils a New Era." *The Independent.* 11 April 2011. http://www.independent.co.uk/news/world/ europe/france-wakes-up-to-a-burka-ban-as-sarkozy-unveils-a-new-era -2266054.html

McDonough, Kevin. "Can the Liberal State Support Cultural Identity Schools?" *American Journal of Education* 106, no. 4 (1998): 463–99.

McLaughlin, Terence. "'Education for All' and Religious Schools." In *Education for a Pluralist Society: Philosophical Perspectives on the Swann Report*, edited by Graham Haydon. London: Institute of Education, University of London, 1987.

Mock, Vanessa, and John Lichfield. "Belgium Passes Europe's First Ban on Wearing Burka in Public." *The Independent*. 1 May 2010. http://www.independent .co.uk/news/world/europe/belgium-passes-europes-first-ban-on-wearing -burka-in-public-1959626.html

Murata, Sachiko. *The Tao of Islam: A Sourcebook on Gender Relationships in Islamic Thought*. New York: SUNY Press, 1992.

Nasr, Seyyed H. *Islam: Religion, History, and Civilization*. San Francisco: HarperSanFrancisco, 2003.

Postman, Neil. *The End of Education: Redefining the Value of School*. Toronto: Random House, 1995.

Ramadan, Tariq. "Islam and Homosexuality." 29 May 2009. http://www.tariqrama dan.com/Islam-and-Homosexuality.html.

Sanjakdar, Fida. "'Teacher Talk': The Problems, Perspectives and Possibilities of Developing a Comprehensive Sexual Health Education Curriculum for Australian Muslim Students." *Sex Education* 9, no. 3 (2009): 261–75.

Sensoy, Özlem, and Elizabeth Marshall. "'Save the Muslim Girl!' Does Popular Young Adult Fiction about Muslim Girls Build Understanding or Reinforce Stereotypes?" *Rethinking Schools Online* 24, no. 2 (2010) http://www.rethink ingschools.org/archive/24_02/24_02_muslim.shtml

Sheikh, Munir. *Teaching about Muslims and Islam in the Public School Classroom*. 3rd ed. Fountain Valley, CA: Council on Islamic Education, 1995.

Short, Geoffrey. "Faith-Based Schools: A Threat to Social Cohesion?" *Journal of Philosophy of Education* 36, no. 4 (2002): 559–72.

Siddiqui, Haroon. "Banning Veil Undermines Secular Democracy." *Toronto Star*. 18 July 2010. http://www.thestar.com/news/world/article/836961--siddiqui -banning-veil-undermines-secular-democracy

Stackhouse, John, and Patrick Martin. "Canada: 'A Model for the World.'" *Globe and Mail*. 2 Feb. 2002.

Sweet, Lois. *God in the Classroom: The Controversial Issue of Religion in Canada's Schools*. Toronto: McClelland and Stewart, 1997.

Thiessen, Elmer J. *In Defence of Religious Schools and Colleges*. Kingston: McGill-Queen's University Press, 2001.

Wright, Andrew. "Freedom, Equality, Fraternity? Towards a Liberal Defence of Faith Community Schools." *British Journal of Religious Education* 25, no. 2 (2003): 142–52.

DISSENT AND CRITICAL THINKING

Zine, Jasmin. "Muslim Youth in Canadian Schools: Education and the Politics of Religious Identity." *Anthropology and Education Quarterly* 32, no. 4 (2001): 399–423.

———. "Unveiled Sentiments: Gendered Islamophobia and Experiences of Veiling among Muslim Girls in a Canadian Islamic School." *Equity and Excellence in Education* 39, no. 3 (2006): 239–52.

CONCLUSION

CHAPTER TEN

DIVERSITY AND DELIBERATION IN FAITH-BASED SCHOOLS: IMPLICATIONS FOR EDUCATING CANADIAN CITIZENS

Avi I. Mintz

"Faith-based schools" are often treated as a single category in Canada. Critics, employing one of their most frequent objections, group faith-based schools together because they share features that allegedly pose a fundamental threat to Canadian unity: rather than bringing students from different religions together so that they may come to understand and respect each other, as secular common schools are designed to do, faith-based schools separate students, entrenching their differences and rendering the possibility of inter-religious collaboration remote. In addition to this common concern that faith-based schools are an obstacle to social cohesion, many critics worry that because of the priority placed upon a faith's historical doctrines and scriptural sources, faith-based schools may teach material that omits or opposes the standard teaching of Canada's secular public schools. Faith-based schools may make curricular decisions that may be harmful to the health of the student (for example, by refusing to teach about contraception) or to the intellect and academic potential of the student (for example, by challenging the scientific consensus about evolution).

These two common objections to faith-based schools—two of many, I might add—are notable in that they tend to treat all such schools similarly. But it is not only critics who group faith-based schools as a single category; their defenders and advocates have done so as well. When political and legal decisions to extend funding to faith-based schools have been in question, leaders from various religions have formed coalitions to organize uni-

CONCLUSION

fied responses. For example, The Ontario Multi-Faith Coalition for Equity in Education (OMFCEE) was formed in the early 1990s to advocate for the importance and value of religious education and was composed of representatives from Christian, Muslim, Sikh, and Hindu communities. In 2002 the Multi-Faith Coalition for Equal Funding of Faith-Based Schools (MFC) developed a proposal for equal funding in Ontario and comprised representatives from Armenian Orthodox schools, Coptic Orthodox schools, Evangelical Christian schools, a Greek Orthodox day school, a Hindu school, Muslim schools, a Sikh (Khalsa) school, Jewish day schools, Seventh Day Adventist schools, and Mennonite schools.[1]

Yet although faith-based schools are often grouped together, one encounters much diversity both among and within them. Indeed, in many of this book's chapters, diversity of various sorts has been a subtle, if not an explicit, theme. In my discussion here, I focus on a theme of diversity that has arisen in many places in this volume, and I discuss its implications for the role of faith-based schools in cultivating Canadian citizens. Graham McDonough, Nadeem Memon, and I highlighted the book's major themes and provided a description of its contents in the introduction. Based on juxtapositions of several of the contributors' central or peripheral claims, I contend in this chapter that the diversity found in Canada's faith-based schools can serve as a dynamic and valuable wellspring of citizenship education. I am interested in the diversity *among* faith-based schools, but more so in the diversity *within* them—the diversity of priorities, interests, beliefs, and expectations among administrators, teachers, parents, students, and community members.

Returning to the idea that faith-based schools have much in common, readers of this volume will recognize that grouping schools together by either their advocates or their defenders is problematic. On the one hand, the OMFCEE is an excellent example of a group that came together around a common goal, bridging differences in faith. Indeed, not only was the coalition composed of members of Christian, Muslim, Sikh, and Hindu communities, but it also intervened in various legal cases, including the 1996 *Adler v. Ontario*, in which the appellants were both Jewish and Christian.[2] Coming together to bring about and support the Adler case to fund Ontario's other religious schools at a level equal to that of the Roman Catholic schools is yet another example of interfaith cooperation and unity. On the other hand, it is important to note that not all religious communities supported the Adler case specifically, or the effort to seek public funding for faith-based schools more generally. Lois Sweet, for example, notes that the

Buddhist community declined an invitation to join the OMCEE. She quotes Michael Kerr, a Buddhist community leader, who argued, "We are on public record as not being in pursuit of our own independent schools because of a fear of division and fragmentation in society. The Buddhist Communities of Greater Toronto, which represents fifty temples, decided to put our efforts behind multi-faith religious education in all schools. We'd rather work to build shared understanding between people."[3]

Further, although the Muslim community was represented in the MFC, the support from within that community was not unanimous. When the debate over extending funds to faith-based schools was escalating in Ontario in 2007 because of John Tory's election-campaign proposal, the Muslim Canadian Congress issued a statement strongly opposing Tory's plan. They claimed that, among other things, separate Islamic schools fail to cultivate Canadian citizens because they isolate students from the wider community and culture. Their statement argued that "every child has the right to learn Canada's culture ... and how we interact with each other formally and socially. Immigrants who have chosen Canada must allow their children to become Canadian."[4]

Jasmin Zine, one of the leading scholars of the Canadian Muslim diaspora, dismisses the Muslim Canadian Congress's position because of its basic ignorance of the reality of Islamic classrooms (in which much learning about Canadian culture takes place and the student body is not composed uniformly of immigrants), and she argues that their position reinforces a false dichotomy of progressive Muslims versus bad Muslims.[5] Zine is right that the Muslim Canadian Congress's position misconstrues the aims, curricula, and methods of many Islamic schools. As Memon shows in chapter two, however, there is a history of Muslim opposition to separate Islamic schooling in Canada. His chapter identifies the presence of three distinct views during the initial conversations about establishing Islamic schools in Ontario in the 1970s. There were community members who did not support establishing Islamic schools because they believed that Islamic schools would fail to provide children with an adequate academic education and fail to integrate them into the broader society. At the other extreme were some who wanted to establish institutions that focused primarily on instilling a traditional Islamic religious education. Between these extremes were parents who favoured the establishment of Islamic day schools that could offer a strong academic curriculum while providing students with a sufficiently strong knowledge of Islamic religion and Muslim culture. The existence of dissenting views presented by the Muslim Canadian Congress and those

CONCLUSION

that were voiced in the 1970s during discussions of establishing Islamic schools in Ontario serves as a valuable reminder that within the Muslim community—just as in communities of other faiths in Canada—uniform support for separate, faith-based education cannot be assumed and often does not exist.

Further, these diverse views about the importance of faith-based schools can play a positive role for a faith community. Discussion and debate about the nature and purposes of separate schooling requires a confrontation with fundamental questions about what it means to be both a good member of the faith and a good Canadian. Some sort of resolution to those questions— even if it is only a tentative one—is necessary for a community, its parents, its teachers, and others to envision an ideal of an educated Muslim Canadian, Jewish Canadian, Sikh Canadian, Christian Canadian, Hindu Canadian, or a Canadian with any other religious affiliation. Once that ideal has been articulated, a community must grapple with the logical entailments of that ideal, especially by exploring what sort of education would be a means to achieving it. The community must decide whether the support for, or the establishment of, secular schooling, separate schooling, after-school religious programs, summer camps, and so on, is in children's best interests. And once a faith community or a sub-group of that community settles on a way to institutionalize its desired educational options, it must then address further complex issues such as what content and methods should be adopted. As I argue later, communal deliberation that results from the conflict of diverse perspectives on educational options can be a powerful source of democratic education, both for the community's children and adolescents and for the community as a whole.

Alex Pomson and Randal Schnoor demonstrate in chapter seven that the Downtown Jewish Day School (DJDS), a faith-based school in Toronto, embraces the diversity of values, commitments, and religious observance of its families. As a result of this diversity, however, various "collisions" have occurred in the school. For example, in a debate over closing the school during Jewish holidays, administrators favoured closing because they were concerned about adhering to Jewish norms, the teachers balked at closing because they felt intense pressure to do justice to the double curriculum in reduced classroom hours, and parents resisted closing because they had to make alternative arrangements for their children's supervision on those days. Though Pomson and Schnoor note that the constant re-examination and reopening of the school's policies could be "exhausting," their research indicates a promising way in which schools can foster deliberation among

DIVERSITY AND DELIBERATION IN FAITH-BASED SCHOOLS | MINTZ

their community members about the means and aims of education. A school may make an institutional commitment to facilitating and encouraging deliberation about these issues by establishing a number of standing committees empowered to raise concerns and address them, just as DJDS's creation of a Religious and Educational Policy Committee provided a venue for discussion of various contentious aspects of Jewish education at the school.

While opening and reopening debate about a school's policies and practices can be destabilizing if it occurs too often, these debates can make a positive contribution to the school's community. The kind of deliberation that can take place in these committees may allow community members to revisit and renew their religious identity and practice[6] and, simultaneously, I would suggest, sends a powerful message to the school's students about the value of communal deliberation and dissent. The creation of forums for communal deliberation, therefore, can be an important aspect of citizenship education.

The curriculum at The Toronto Heschel School that Greg Beiles describes in chapter four suggests another way in which a school's institutional commitment to diversity can be enacted. The kind of positive deliberation that takes place among parents, administrators, and teachers at DJDS is also a cornerstone of the curriculum at Heschel. Beiles shows how Heschel's curriculum is explicitly intended to cultivate the deliberative powers of its students. The curriculum does so by drawing on aspects of the Jewish tradition that lend themselves particularly well to this practice, such as Talmudic debates that highlight the conflicting perspectives of the leading Rabbinical scholars. Since the **Talmud** has legitimized dissent—not only is the prevailing view recorded but the dissenting view is too—students come to appreciate the value of questioning their own positions and those of others, and the benefit of decisions that acknowledge and resolve differences.[7]

The Toronto Heschel School and DJDS are community schools and by their very missions recognize and appreciate the denominational diversity within Judaism. They are both progressive schools that have carefully considered how they might best bridge the sacred–secular divide by designing an educational experience in which the values of Canadian citizenship are broached within a Jewish framework. However, not all Jewish schools bridge this divide. Indeed, Seymour Epstein points out in chapter one that those schools represent only one of the many different types of Jewish school in Canada. As Epstein notes, Canada's *Charedi* schools accept the sacred–secular divide and, though intending that their students will be

CONCLUSION

productive Canadian citizens, render secular studies secondary. One of the frequent concerns of many religious minorities like the *Charedi* community is the influence of secular culture on children. The influence of media and peers sometimes causes children embarrassment or uneasiness about their religious practices, dietary requirements, and dress, among other things (a point that is also raised in both Asma Ahmed's and Qaiser Ahmad's chapters six and nine, respectively).

The *Charedi* community manages to reduce the outside influence because, for example, televisions are not usually brought into their homes. A community with a shared, deep commitment to a particular way of life will manage to avoid many of the conflicts that characterize community schools because there will be less diversity in the community members' interests, expectations, and beliefs. Drawing on Tariq Ramadan's work, Asma Ahmed proposes a framework for understanding various ways in which Islamic schools negotiate citizenship in Western countries. Though many of the elements of her framework refer specifically to Islamic schools, it clearly could be made broader to encompass all faith-based schools. *Charedi* schools that emphasize separatism to a significant extent operate at the "settlement" stage of her framework. Ahmed argues, however, that faith-based schools would better cultivate Canadian citizens if they actively moved away from a separatist identity to one of integration or, even better, post-integration, by recognizing shared commitments with the broader community and seeking joint activities and projects, among other things.

It may be harder for a faith-based school of a particular denomination to move through the stages that Ahmed describes than it may be for a community school like Heschel or DJDS. However, one of the themes that has arisen in the chapters of this book is that, whether or not a school embraces the diversity within it—be it denominational diversity, diversity of practice and belief, or another kind of diversity—diversity nonetheless exists and persists. In addition to the kinds of diversity that are present within a faith-based school community is sometimes a divergent narrative that is brought into a school from outside, as Qaiser Ahmad's chapter reveals. Ahmad shows how a popular narrative of the ills of Islam has an impact on Muslim students, a damaging narrative that enters the classroom by means of the media's influence on students. Ahmad identifies one of the most important aspects of his teaching as bringing this narrative to the forefront so that he could enable students to examine it critically and to counter it, and to be prepared to defend their religion among non-Muslim Canadians.

DIVERSITY AND DELIBERATION IN FAITH-BASED SCHOOLS | MINTZ

A particular challenge facing teachers like Qaiser Ahmad in Islamic schools is that Canada's Islamic schools do not benefit from a central organization that advises on curriculum, methods, and aims. As Mario D'Souza demonstrates in chapter two, Catholic schools, in contrast, do benefit from much guidance; the Catholic Church has outlined fundamental aspects of its aims and its intentions for them. The long-established tradition of Catholic schooling and its central pedagogical documents promotes similarities among Catholic schools both inside and outside Canada. Indeed, D'Souza argues that there exists a universality of Catholic education that extends beyond the local, Canadian contexts of Catholic schools that is fundamental to its mission. D'Souza conveys how Canada's Catholic schools strive to enhance the common good and build genuine fellowship among Canadian citizens of different faiths because those values are central to Catholic faith. The Church's promotion of fellowship presupposes diversity; fellowship is all the more important in a world in which differences can easily lead to social segregation and antagonism. Catholicism itself is an ethnically diverse religion, and Catholic schools are populated by students of many different religions and of various Christian denominations, and so fellowship can be understood to be a key component of Catholic schools' civic education.

As Donlevy demonstrates in chapter five, however, Canada's Catholic schools, and the Catholic Church generally, have had to confront internal and external challenges. The authority of the Church may well provide Catholic schools with a cohesive conception of core values that it seeks to instill in students, but the Catholic Church's values are not without controversy. Donlevy discusses four values—respect for the Other, fairness, the common good, and democracy—and shows that in several legal disputes there have been conflicts between the Church and others over the interpretation of the philosophical, anthropological, political, and legal warrants for these four values. But as the Marc Hall case demonstrates, for example, there are various ways in which Catholic schools have encountered dissent and diverse viewpoints not only from outside but from within. Marc Hall was a student who challenged the Church's disapproval of homosexual relationships. It was not simply a case of a single student versus the Catholic School and Church; there were also divisions among two groups that both have an important stake in Catholic schools. On the one hand, the Catholic school board rejected Hall's request to bring a male companion to the prom. On the other hand, Hall was supported by the Ontario English Catholic Teach-

CONCLUSION

ers Association. Further, not only do diverse opinions over school policy and philosophy exist within the administrative bodies of Canada's Catholic schools, but the Hall case illuminates the fact that students do not always accept or embrace in their entirety the religious doctrines of the faith-based schools they attend.

Students in Catholic schools will undoubtedly be exposed to various secular norms that differ from the Catholic norms on matters such as homosexuality, gender equality, and contraception, to name only some of the most familiar examples. Thus students come into classrooms predisposed to question some of the Church's teachings. To the Church's credit, critical thinking is strongly implied throughout the aims and pedagogy of Catholic schooling, and it is an important means of achieving the aim of freedom that D'Souza describes. Donlevy ultimately contends that Canadian democracy requires that Catholics and Catholic schools must be afforded the freedom of conscience to maintain their interpretations of these values. McDonough, on the other hand, begins chapter eight with the fact that within Catholic schools there exist multiple parties—Church authorities, teachers, administrators, students, and parents—and, among these parties, the Church's teachings will sometimes clash with others' beliefs and expectations. Thus, McDonough argues that Catholic schools are in need of a theory for the teaching of controversial subjects. McDonough's point is that, given the fact that the Church is explicitly concerned with the intellectual growth of its students, it does not currently have an adequate theory to deal with classroom discussions in which students dissent from the Church's teachings. McDonough discusses how, within the theological and pedagogical framework of Canada's Catholic schools, it is difficult, though important, to articulate a theory of students' ecclesial agency such that their growth as autonomous and reflective dissidents can be legitimized.

McDonough is essentially addressing the need to create a space in classrooms for meaningful deliberation about pressing religious questions (in addition to the space for meaningful deliberation that already exists in Catholic schools about non-controversial issues—at least, non-controversial from the Catholic perspective). Likewise, two key elements of the post-integration stage in Ahmed's model are creating dialogue with the broader community and contributing to "reformulating political questions of the day." These elements call for meaningful deliberation (a) within the Muslim community and its schools and (b) among Muslims and the broader community, both among school-age children and adolescents and adults in the public sphere. In addition, when Beiles argues that The Heschel School cul-

244

tivates Canadian citizenship effectively, his argument rests in large part on the kind of deliberation that is a fundamental aspect of its curriculum.

Considering the place of deliberation in Canada's faith-based schools provides a valuable alternative way of thinking about faith-based schools' role in creating a genuinely multicultural Canada. In the Canadian provinces that extend public support to faith-based schools, the schools are typically required to do two things: employ certified teachers and teach the provincial curriculum. These two requirements of faith-based schools were prominently included in John Tory's proposal to extend funding to Ontario's faith-based schools, but they did little to convince the public that such schools warranted public funds. Why did these requirements fail to persuade people in Ontario that the provincially supported schools would adequately cultivate Canadian citizens? I would suggest that these two requirements fail to address the issue of citizenship in a meaningful way. Adhering to the provincial curriculum may eliminate some of the most controversial practices of faith-based schools such as, for example, teaching creationism in place of evolution. But by focusing on the provincial curriculum, the public might believe that it focuses too narrowly on what students should know, at the expense of considering how well prepared they are to understand and respect a diverse array of Canadian citizens. Likewise, provincial certification for teachers may ensure that a faith-based school's teachers have a strong background in the content and teaching methods of their subjects, but does certification do much to ensure that teachers can create citizens who will be a part of a cohesive citizenry?

Ultimately, what seemed most strongly to concern Ontario's voters was that Tory's proposal would have increased the segregation of religious minorities in a province that features tremendous diversity and whose citizens pride themselves on their multiculturalism.[8] Segregated schooling by religion, it was believed, would not prepare future generations to live cohesively in a multicultural province. It would not have hurt Tory's cause to have asked faith-based schools that receive funding to publicly address their approach to citizenship education. Not all faith-based schools would have done so.[9] For the faith communities that were interested in public funding and the politicians who sought to extend it to them, a discussion of citizenship education would have improved the unfortunately superficial public debate.

I suggested above that whether or not schools recognize and acknowledge it, there are ample conflicts, tensions, and disagreements that arise in every faith-based school. These events are more likely to surface in the

CONCLUSION

initial stages of founding a school, as Memon's and Pomson and Schnoor's chapters demonstrate, because parents, teachers, administrators, and community leaders have diverse aspirations and expectations and no institutional history exists that could offer a guiding vision. The perspectives of the many parties that establish a school must slowly be melded into a single vision. Additionally, a school operating in its early years will likely see the diverse aspirations and expectations of its constituents resurface.

Long-established schools, like Canada's Catholic schools, have a history and an entrenched culture of schooling. Even if parents had reservations about the school's policies and practices, they might not expect any opportunities to raise their concerns. Yet Catholic schools, like other schools, would benefit from engaging their students in meaningful deliberation about Catholic faith, as McDonough argues. Meaningful deliberation is important in schools because it is key to good citizenship. Democratic societies always feature conflicts among groups and individuals, and we are all inevitably forced to confront uncertainties about which we will need to make difficult decisions. Citizens who deliberate alone and with others in a manner that respects all other Canadians, those similar to themselves or different, are well equipped for citizenship in multicultural Canada.[10]

One of the problems with arguing, as I am, for the importance of promoting deliberation in schools and through schools is that deliberation, or dialogue, critical reflection or any of the related nexus of concepts that educational philosophers have promoted, is unquantifiable.[11] If political decisions about the status of faith-based schools are to be made efficiently and without great subjectivity, is it not much easier to ask that schools provide evidence that their curriculum satisfactorily resembles the provincial curriculum and that their teachers can provide documentation of their certification?

Without doubt, deliberation is a more difficult aspect of a school to quantify, but I believe that the contributors to this book have raised a helpful way to think about how it might be broached. At one level, schools may articulate responses to the question "how does your school approach citizenship education?" Beiles has provided an example of how a school official might offer such a response. More important, perhaps, than the response provided, is the discussion about the response that might take place in the school in the process of writing that response. As I argued at the beginning of this chapter, articulating an ideal of an educated student who is both a good member of the faith and a good citizen is itself a valuable exercise for a religious community. It provides an opportunity for thinking through

246

DIVERSITY AND DELIBERATION IN FAITH-BASED SCHOOLS | MINTZ

what kind of citizens the next generation should be. To borrow from Amy Gutmann, it is an opportunity to use schools to undergo conscious social reproduction, rather than replication.[12] And the type of deliberation that would support a community's conscious social reproduction is not limited to the classroom. Pomson and Schnoor's study indicates that adult members of the community can be called upon to participate in deliberation if a school puts in place mechanisms to address concerns raised about a school's policies and practices. Faith-based schools that might embrace the role of deliberation for renewing and rejuvenating the community's understanding of itself and its place in Canada could create a standing committee composed of parents, administrators, teachers, community members, and, for a high school, perhaps students as well. For meaningful deliberation to occur, the results of the committee's discussions would need to be addressed, even if their decisions were not binding. The type of committee to which I am referring here goes beyond the typical Parents' Association Committee. It is rather explicitly created to address the school's policies and practices, especially those that relate to the faith and those that animate the purpose and mission of the school.

Whether or not a province would require a statement about how a school's curriculum addresses citizenship education or a committee in the school that would have meaningful power to address concerns about policy and practice, these forums for deliberation would have value. There are faith-based schools in Canada that value obedience over critical dialogue, and many that are happy to stand apart from provincial oversight.[13] However, a school that embraces the idea that it serves the common good by cultivating Canadian citizens could use the opportunities for deliberation that I suggested to revisit its fundamental purpose for its students, for the faith community, and for Canadian society. It also serves as an opportunity for school leaders to share with other Canadians that a concern for citizenship is present in their school, an opportunity that might combat the widely held belief that faith-based schools necessarily compromise social cohesion.

The role of faith-based schools in Canada will continue to create controversy because the true nature of Canadian identity will never be settled. Recently *The Globe and Mail* ran an editorial with the provocative title "Strike multiculturalism from the national vocabulary."[14] The title is provocative because, as Paul Bramadat has put it, "the tradition of multiculturalism is, along with hockey and universal health care, a Canadian 'mom and apple pie' issue."[15] Yet the editorial in *The Globe and Mail* is more than merely a cynical attempt to increase readership by challenging a con-

247

CONCLUSION

cept dear to Canadians. The editorial reflects the fact that Canadians have a long tradition of thinking about—and often fretting about—Canadian identity. The ongoing conversations about multiculturalism indicate that Canadian identity continues to evolve, and I believe that this continued evolution should be viewed positively. I suggest that faith-based schools may contribute to the evolving Canadian identity by articulating how they understand themselves to be cultivating citizens. They may do so, I have argued, by establishing formal committees to facilitate deliberation about the school's policies and practices and by articulating a vision of how the school addresses citizenship education. Canadian faith-based schools that embrace the diversity within them and around them by creating meaningful opportunities for deliberation go some length toward ensuring that the institutions themselves embody and reflect democratic principles and engender democratic dispositions.

Notes

1 See the Multi-Faith Coalition for Equal Funding of Faith-Based Schools website, http://www.multifaithcoalition.com

2 *Adler v. Ontario*, [1996] 3 S.C.R.

3 Lois Sweet, *God in the Classroom: The Controversial Issue of Religion in the Classroom* (Toronto: McClelland & Stewart, 1997), 108.

4 Cited in Jasmin Zine, *Canadian Islamic Schools: Unravelling the Politics of Faith, Gender, Knowledge, and Identity* (Toronto: University of Toronto Press, 2008), 43.

5 Zine, *Canadian Islamic Schools*, 43–44.

6 Pomson and Schnoor's work has been particularly valuable in demonstrating the role that a faith-based school may play in affecting parents' lives and religious identity (as opposed to those of the school's children, the more common focus of research on faith-based schools). See their *Back to School: Jewish Day School in the Lives of Adult Jews* (Detroit: Wayne State University Press, 2008).

7 Such legitimizing of dissent is also prominent in other accounts of Jewish schools. Walter Feinberg describes a Conservative Jewish school in the American Midwest in which the seventh graders discuss the relationship between Jewish laws and customs and social and historical circumstance (specifically through the example of a religious candle-lighting ceremony). The teacher in the class conveys the importance of debate and dissent by noting that "Jews have always disagreed," and Feinberg remarks that such a comment "legitimizes disagreements and debate" (*For Goodness Sake: Religious Schools and Education for Democratic Citizenry* [New York: Routledge, 2006], 26). Daniel Pekarsky's study of a Jewish school in Manhattan depicts a learning environment in

which critical examination of both secular and Jewish beliefs and material pervades the curriculum (*Vision at Work: The Theory and Practice of Beit Rabban* [New York: JTS Press, 2006], xiv, xxi, 13, 17, 31, 60–61). On Jewish sources generally being well suited for this kind of educational experience, see Menachem Lorberbaum, "Learning from Mistakes: Resources of Tolerance in the Jewish Tradition," *Journal of Philosophy of Education* 29, no. 2 (1995): 273–84.

8   See Andrea Perrella et al., "The 2007 Provincial Election and Electoral System Referendum in Ontario," *Canadian Political Science Review* 2, no. 1 (2008): 80. See also Robin Sears, "How Ontario Got a One-Issue Campaign," *Policy Options* 28, no. 10 (Nov. 2007): 17–24.

9   It is rarely noted that in Ontario during 2007, only about half of the faith-based schools that would have been eligible to receive funding under Tory's plan would have applied for it. See Michael Van Pelt, Ray Pennings, and Deani Van Pelt, "Faithful and Fruitless in Ontario: Status Quo in Education Policy," *Policy Options* 28, no. 10 (Nov. 2007): 25–26.

10 I am drawing here on the seminal work on the importance of deliberation in democratic education by Amy Gutmann, *Democratic Education*, rev. ed. (Princeton, NJ: Princeton University Press, 1999): 50–52.

11 For a robust treatment of dialogue, see Eamonn Callan, *Creating Citizens: Political Education and Liberal Democracy* (Oxford and New York: Clarendon Press, 1997), 196–220. On critical reflection see Feinberg, *For Goodness Sake*. In addition, the kind of reflection and discussion that faith-based schools may or may not facilitate is central to much of the literature on strong versus moderate schools that Qaiser Ahmad discusses in chapter nine.

12 Gutmann's conscious social reproduction requires that citizens consciously consider the type of education required to enable future generations to contribute intelligently to the political sphere. Gutmann is a strong proponent of common schools, but she does believe that a liberal state should make accommodations for faith-based schools that are held responsible for providing students with a common democratic morality (i.e., one that involves deliberation, among other things). *Democratic Education*, 117–18.

13 The Accelerated Christian Education schools discussed in the Introduction would fall into the category of those that do not support critical thinking, and there are schools throughout Canada that decline public support even in provinces in which they are eligible for it.

14 The editorial argues that Canada's multiculturalism policy of 1971 has devolved into a mere celebration of differences. A stronger concept that emphasizes the rights and responsibilities of citizens is therefore in order. *Globe and Mail*, "Strike Multiculturalism from the National Vocabulary," 8 Oct. 2010.

CONCLUSION

15 Paul Bramadat, "Beyond Christian Canada: Religion and Ethnicity in a Multi-cultural Society," in *Religion and Ethnicity in Canada*, ed. Paul Bramadat and David Seljak (Toronto: Pearson Education, 2004), 10.

Works Cited

Adler *v.* Ontario, [1996] 3 S.C.R.

Bramadat, Paul. "Beyond Christian Canada: Religion and Ethnicity in a Multicultural Society." In *Religion and Ethnicity in Canada*, edited by Paul Bramadat and David Seljak, 1–29. Toronto: Pearson Education, 2004.

Callan, Eamonn. *Creating Citizens: Political Education and Liberal Democracy*, Oxford Political Theory. Oxford and New York: Clarendon Press, 1997.

Feinberg, Walter. *For Goodness Sake: Religious Schools and Education for Democratic Citizenry*. Social Theory, Education, and Cultural Change Series. New York: Routledge, 2006.

Globe and Mail. "Strike Multiculturalism from the National Vocabulary." Editorial. 8 Oct. 2010. http://www.theglobeandmail.com/news/national/time-to-lead/part-6-editorial-strike-multiculturalism-from-the-national-vocabulary/article1314363/

Gutmann, Amy. *Democratic Education*, rev. ed., with a new preface and epilogue. Princeton, NJ: Princeton University Press, 1999.

Lorberbaum, Menachem. "Learning from Mistakes: Resources of Tolerance in the Jewish Tradition." *Journal of Philosophy of Education* 29, no. 2 (1995): 273–84.

Pekarsky, Daniel. *Vision at Work: The Theory and Practice of Beit Rabban*. New York: JTS Press, 2006.

Perrella, Andrea, Steven Brown, Barry Kay, and David Docherty. "The 2007 Provincial Election and Electoral System Referendum in Ontario." *Canadian Political Science Review* 2, no. 1 (2008): 78–87.

Pomson, Alex, and Randal F. Schnoor. *Back to School: Jewish Day School in the Lives of Adult Jews*. Detroit: Wayne State University Press, 2008.

Sears, Robin. "How Ontario Got a One-Issue Campaign." *Policy Options* 28, no. 10 (Nov. 2007): 17–24.

Sweet, Lois. *God in the Classroom: The Controversial Issue of Religion in the Classroom*. Toronto: McClelland & Stewart, 1997.

Van Pelt, Michael, Ray Pennings, and Deani Van Pelt. "Faithful and Fruitless in Ontario: Status Quo in Education Policy." *Policy Options* 28, no. 10 (Nov. 2007): 25–26.

Zine, Jasmin. *Canadian Islamic Schools: Unravelling the Politics of Faith, Gender, Knowledge, and Identity*. Toronto: University of Toronto Press, 2008.

GLOSSARY

Aramaic Part of a family of languages widely spoken in the ancient world. Western Aramaic was a common vernacular in Palestine and Babylonia (see below) during the rise of Rabbinic civilization. The Talmud is one of the first Jewish literary works composed in this language, and consists of an Aramaic commentary on earlier Hebrew texts. The historical Jesus spoke Aramaic.

Babylonia An ancient region of Mesopotamia to which Jews were exiled in the sixth century BCE.

Bar and bat mitzvah celebrations Ritual ceremonies in which boys and girls make the transition to adulthood. A boy celebrates his bar mitzvah at thirteen and a girl celebrates her bat mitzvah at either twelve or thirteen. When a child emerges from the ceremony, he or she becomes responsible for adhering to the Jewish *mitzvot* (see *mitzvah* below). The ceremony is typically celebrated by family, friends, and community members.

Bobov This is a Chasidic dynasty originally from Bobowa in southern Poland. The current headquarters are in Brooklyn, and a strong branch exists in Toronto, which sponsors an elementary school for boys.

Catechism (Catholic) The Catechism is a comprehensive expression of the Catholic Church's teachings on faith and morals, although it is not a compendium of all magisterial teachings.

GLOSSARY

Chabad The term Chabad is an acronym for the Hebrew words *Chochma, Binah,* and *Da'at*—wisdom, understanding, and knowledge, the motto of the movement. This Chasidic court is also known as Lubavitch after the Russian city, Lyubavichi, where it developed until the early twentieth century. Its centre is in Brooklyn, and its various branches in Toronto operate several schools.

Chanukah Eight-day Jewish winter holiday celebrating the rededication of the Second Temple in Jerusalem.

Chasidic/Chasidism see *Hasidism*

Conservative Judaism Conservative Judaism is respectful of Jewish law as interpreted by the tradition and the movement's rabbis. However, it affirms the historical development of Jewish law and therefore is open to changes that are seen as necessitated by societal change.

Deobandi An orientation among Sunni Muslim communities that began in Deoband, India, in the late nineteenth century. It is most notable for establishing *madrassa* schools globally (see below) that aspire to train students in the religious sciences. The perspectives and interpretations of the Islamic tradition that are emphasized by Deobandi communities (and their offshoots) influence the content and approach to Islamic schooling.

Encyclical A document written by the Pope that gives teaching or guidance about a contemporary issue.

Hadith Hadith are the sayings and traditions of Prophet Muhammad himself and form part of the record of the Prophet's *Sunnah* (see below). The Hadith record the words and deeds, explanations, and interpretations of the Prophet concerning all aspects of life. They are found in various collections compiled by Muslim scholars in the early centuries of the Muslim civilization.

Halacha Jewish law. In the traditional understanding, this system is rooted in the 613 commandments (*mitzvot*) of the Torah (Bible), as elaborated by the rabbis over many centuries. The system includes core institutions that govern relations between human beings, and ceremonial obligations that define the believer's relationship with God. The *halacha* includes standards that enjoy wide acceptance, and customary observances that define smaller groups of adherents.

Hasidism (or Chasidism) A branch of Orthodox Judaisim that originated in eighteenth-century Eastern Europe. Various sects make up this community, whose shared values include joyful celebration and the charismatic leadership of a *tzaddik* (dynastic head), who represents the community before God. See also *Lithuanian-Yeshiva tradition*.

Islamization Also known as "Islamization of Knowledge," this is a discourse on the need to synthesize ethics and an Islamic world view across fields of thought. It began through the writings of a handful of Muslim scholars that then led to the establishment of model Islamic universities in Malaysia, Pakistan, and elsewhere. Although not a direct influence, the discourse on the Islamization of Knowledge that is intended for higher education coincided with the earliest Islamic elementary schools in North America, and by virtue influenced the discourse on Islamic schooling.

Kippah (pl. kippot) A head-covering worn by Jews. In Orthodox Jewish communities, all boys and men wear kippot throughout the day. In some egalitarian Conservative and Reform congregations, both men and women may wear kippot throughout the day or during prayer services, ritual meals or religious study.

Kosher A label for food that is deemed permissible for Jews to consume.

Lithuanian-Yeshiva tradition There are three main current traditions of study in Orthodox male academies (*yeshivot*): Lithuanian, Chasidic (see above), and Sephardic (see below). Within these categories there is a complex range of differences and nuance, but these broad terms refer to the early origins of study methods specific to different groups in the Orthodox world. The tradition that emanated from Vilnius (Vilna or Wilno, depending on who occupied this city in present-day Lithuania) is practised in so-called *Litvish* or Lithuanian Yeshivot.

Lubavitch see *Chabad*

Madrassa Literally translated as a place of study, *madrassa* (pl. *madaris*) has come to refer to schools generally and in particular has become synonymous with Deobandi-styled schools in North America where children are sent to learn the religious sciences for the purpose of becoming religious scholars.

Magisterium The office of teaching authority within the Roman Catholic Church, held collectively by the bishops and the Pope. It is exercised in various ways, including the Pope in his encyclical teachings, by a Vatican congregation with the approval of the Pope, by the bishops through their national and provincial meetings, by ecumenical councils (such as the Second Vatican Council), and by individual bishops teaching in their diocese.

GLOSSARY

Menorah A seven-branch candelabrum, which became a symbol of Judaism. The candelabrum associated with the festival of Chanukah (see above), the *chanukiyah*, has nine branches.

Mitzvah (pl. mitzvot) A commandment recorded in the Torah. In the traditional count, there are 613 positive and negative commandments that form the basis of Jewish Law (*Halacha*). The term has also taken on a colloquial meaning of "good deed."

Orthodox Judaism Orthodox Judaism can be divided into two large groups, sometimes referred to as Modern and Ultra-Orthodox. Both groups lead a fully observant lifestyle marked by strict adherence to *Halacha* (Jewish law; see above), as interpreted by Orthodox rabbis. For example, men cover their heads, as do most married women, and the Sabbath and the dietary laws are strictly adhered to. The groups differ in their relationship with the secular world and degrees of permissible contact. Modern Orthodox believers are generally more comfortable in their acceptance of modernity (television, for example) and their more open relationship with the general population and culture.

Qur'an The Qur'an is the holy book of Islam; it literally means "reading." Muslims believe that the Qur'an is the final expression of God's revelations, after the Torah and the Bible.

Rabbinic law This term refers to the laws codified during the Talmudic period (see *Talmud*) and afterward. These laws are frequently based in the Hebrew Bible, but they constitute an elaborate expansion and modification of older standards. This literature is marked by the Rabbinic interpretation of authoritative biblical texts, which are made to reflect changing standards of practice and belief. Judaism of the post-biblical period is based on Rabbinic Law.

Rabbinic literature This term refers to the full scope of writing during the Rabbinic period, including legal codes, legendary narrative, sermons, ethical teachings, mystical speculation, biblical interpretation, and records of discussion in the academies of learning.

Reform Judaism Reform Judaism is an outgrowth of early attempts at religious reform in nineteenth-century Germany. Originally, it rejected the binding nature of Jewish law, but recently it has become more traditional in its approach, and support for day schools is one illustration of that tendency.

Rosh Hashanah A holiday marking and celebrating the Jewish new year.

Salafi An orientation among Sunni Muslims that places particular emphasis on following the earliest generations of Muslim communities (*salaf*)

GLOSSARY

or pious predecessors. The perspectives and interpretations of faith tradition that are held by Salafis are considered relatively conservative and, therefore, influence the choices in curriculum and school policy in particular directions.

Satmar An anti-Zionist Chasidic group with split headquarters in Brooklyn and Kiryas Joel, New York. Its name derives from its origins in the Transylvanian city of Satu Mare.

Sephardic The communities of Jews that trace their origin to the exiled populations of Spain (*Sepharad*). See also *Lithuanian-Yeshiva tradition*

Shabbat The Jewish Sabbath, which begins at sundown on Friday and ends Saturday night after sundown.

Shariah Etymologically means "the way" ("the path leading to the source"). Shariah outlines a global conception of creation, existence, death, and the way of life it entails stemming from a normative reading and understanding of scriptural sources. It directs Muslim observance and practice.

Shi'a (pl. Shi'ites) This term, meaning "party" or "partisans," designates those Muslims who believe that the rightful successor to the Prophet Muhammad should have been Ali ibn Abi Talib, rather than the first caliph Abu Bakr as-Sadiq. The Shi'ites believe that the leader of the Muslim community had to be chosen by God and the Prophet Muhammad, not by the community, and therefore do not recognize the first three caliphs or the later Sunni caliphates. Shi'ites consider their leaders, referred to as *Imam*, as the only legitimate rulers of the Islamic community. Compare *Sunni* below.

Shumuliyat al Islam Translates to "the comprehensive character of the Islamic teaching."

Simchat Torah A Jewish festival at which the Torah is celebrated. Traditionally, throughout the year, the Torah is read portion by portion each week (divided evenly so that the cycle will be completed in a single year). Simchat Torah marks the end of the reading cycle and the beginning of the new reading.

Succot (or Sukkot, sing. Sukkah) A *sukkah* is a booth that Jews build in remembrance of the temporary dwellings that Jews lived in as they fled Egypt. The holiday of Sukkot celebrates the final harvest in Israel, and during it many Jews eat meals and sleep in a sukkah.

Sufi An orientation among Muslim communities, spanning across sectarian differences, that emphasizes inner purification (*tasawwuf*), often through ascetic lifestyles and devotional acts of invoking God's names

GLOSSARY

and attributes (*dhikr*). The perspectives and interpretations of the Islamic tradition by Sufi-oriented communities influences curricular content, instructional approaches, and aims of Islamic education in particular ways.

Sunnah Habit, practice, customary procedure, action, norm, or usage sanctioned by tradition, specifically referring to the Prophet Muhammad's sayings, practices, and habits. The *Hadith* of the Prophet (see above) constitute a written record of his Sunnah.

Sunni The term Sunni comes from *ahl al-Sunnah wa'l Jamā'ah*, followers of the *Sunnah* of the Prophet (see above), and designates those Muslims who recognize the first four successors of Prophet Muhammad as the "Rightly-Guided" caliphs. Sunnis attribute no special religious or political function to the descendants of the Prophet's son-in-law Ali ibn Abi Talib and Fatima, the daughter of the Prophet Muhammad. Sunnis hold that any pious, just, and qualified Muslim may be elected caliph, whose function should be to protect the divine law, act as judge, and rule over the community, preserving public order and the borders of the Islamic world. Compare *Shi'a* above.

Ta'dib Rooted in the word *adab* (comportment or appropriate behaviour), the word *ta'dib* refers to the process of imparting *adab* and is commonly considered another word for education or the process of educating.

Ta'lim Commonly translated to mean "instruct or study," and is often used to refer to formal instruction or schooling.

Talmud This term refers to a corpus of Rabbinic literature (see above) of the centuries leading up to and including the fifth century CE and consists of the *Mishna,* which is the first codification of Rabbinic law, and the *Gemara,* a wide-ranging commentary on the *Mishna.*

Talmud Torah A school that offers Jewish education.

Tarbiyah Commonly translated to mean "nurture, grow or increase" and in contemporary Arabic language used to mean education or the process of education.

Tazkiyah Commonly translated by some as self-development and by others as purifying the soul, both of which refer to an educative process; hence the term is also commonly used as an educational concept in the Arabic language.

Tikkun olam A Hebrew phrase originating in the Jewish mystical tradition that means "repairing the world."

Torah The five books of Moses, or the Pentateuch, consisting of B'reishit (Genesis), Sh'mot (Exodus), Vayikra (Leviticus), Bamidbar (Numbers), and D'varim (Deutoronomy).

256

GLOSSARY

Yeshivah (pl. yeshivot) Traditionally, a yeshivah was an academy or school for Orthodox Jewish boys and men, but some yeshivot are now open to girls and women as well.

Yom Kippur Also known as the Day of Atonement, Yom Kippur features prayer and a fast that begins at sundown and continues until after sundown the following evening.

Zionist ideology Ever since the evolution of political Zionism in the nineteenth century, different Jewish groups and religious denominations have identified with or rejected Zionism in a variety of differing modes. In the contemporary period, most mainstream Jewish groups support Zionism, i.e., the idea of a Jewish state in the land of Israel, but there remain nuances of identification depending on politics and religious affiliation.

THE CONTRIBUTORS

Qaiser Ahmad is a secondary-school Curriculum Leader of Guidance for the Toronto District School Board, and an education consultant for RAZI Group. He holds an Honours Bachelor of Science degree from the University of Toronto, a Post-Graduate Certificate in Education from the Institute of Education, University of London (UK), and a Master of Education in Curriculum, Teaching, and Learning from the Ontario Institute for Studies in Education, University of Toronto. Qaiser taught for six years at a private Islamic school in Toronto, considered one of the most well-established Islamic schools in Canada. In addition to teaching there, he was involved in curriculum development and program planning. For over a decade, Qaiser has been conducting workshops and presentations on Muslims and Islam to a wide variety of audiences, most notably educators and school administrators, in the Greater Toronto Area.

Asma Ahmed was an elementary-school teacher at the London Islamic School (Ontario) for five years. She graduated from a Scholars' Elective Program at the University of Western Ontario in London with Honours in health science and social justice and peace. She then completed her Bachelor of Education and recently earned her master's degree in educational policy with a leadership focus at the University of Western Ontario. Her thesis explored the purposes of Islamic schools, with specific reference to young Muslims finding their way in the modern West and building a robust Cana-

259

THE CONTRIBUTORS

dian and Muslim identity. Asma is currently enrolled in a Ph.D. program in educational policy at the University of Western Ontario.

Greg Beiles has been working in the field of Jewish education for the past 15 years. He began his career as a teacher, and for the past decade has been involved in school administration, teacher training, and curriculum development. Currently, Greg is director of the Lola Stein Institute for Leadership in Education, a think tank devoted to innovation and best practices in Jewish and integrative education. Greg also serves as the Curriculum and Training Consultant at The Toronto Heschel School. He holds an M.A. in the philosophy of education from the Ontario Institute for Studies an Education, and is a Ph.D. candidate at the Centre for the Study of Religion at the University of Toronto. His research interests focus on the relationship between Jewish epistemology and the purpose and practice of Jewish education.

J. Kent Donlevy is a barrister and solicitor and the former interim associate dean of the Graduate Division of Educational Research in the Faculty of Education at the University of Calgary. His doctoral dissertation and master's thesis focused on Catholic education. He has published several books, including *The Ten Dimensions of Inclusion: Non-Catholic Students in Catholic Schools*, as well as many peer-reviewed papers on Catholic education in several jurisdictions: Australia, United Kingdom, United States, and Canada. Moreover, he has been a public speaker on Catholic education issues in Canada and the United States as well as an expert witness on Catholic constitutional matters in the Alberta Court of Queen's Bench. He has been a Catholic school principal, taught grades 6–12, and recently conducted research in Catholic high schools in both Alberta and Saskatchewan. His research focuses upon the nexus of section 2(a) of the *Canadian Charter of Rights and Freedoms* (freedom of conscience) and Catholic schools.

Fr. Mario O. D'Souza CSB is Dean of Theology at the University of St. Michael's College, and a member of the Congregation of St. Basil. He holds the Basilian Fathers Chair in Religion and Education at the Faculty of Theology. He has earned degrees from University College, Dublin; the University of Calgary; the University of Toronto; the University of St. Michael's College, Toronto; and Boston College. His doctorate from the University of Toronto was on Jacques Maritain's philosophy of education. He teaches and researches in the following areas: the philosophy of Jacques Maritain,

THE CONTRIBUTORS

philosophy of education, Catholic educational theory, religion and education, the Catholic university, person and personalism, religion, pluralism, citizenship, and Lonergan studies. He is an associate member of the School of Graduate Studies of the University of Toronto and is cross-appointed to the Department of Leadership, Higher and Adult Education at the Ontario Institute for Studies in Education. Fr. D'Souza has also taught in the Faculty of Education at the University of Windsor and was the academic dean at St. Joseph's College, University of Alberta. He is past-president of Assumption University, Windsor, where he also held the Stephen Jarislowsky Chair in Religion and Conflict. He has served as a member of the General Council of the Basilian Fathers. He is a full member of the International Seminar for Religious Education and Values, and a member of the editorial board of the *Religious Education Journal of Australia*. He is a member of the Board of Directors of St. Michael's College School, Toronto, and a member of the Board of Directors of the Association of Theological Schools.

Seymour Epstein has been active in every aspect of Jewish education, formal and informal. He worked at United Synagogue Day School in Toronto and helped to found an experimental high school there in 1971. From 1973 to 1978 he was an assistant professor at McGill University, where he directed the Jewish Teacher Training Program of Montreal. He was actively involved in Camp Ramah and directed the Canadian Ramah for three summers. In 1981 Dr. Epstein moved to Morocco to become the educational consultant for the American Jewish Joint Distribution Committee in Casablanca. During his eighteen years of JDC work, he was active in Morocco, Western Europe, and the former Soviet Union. He served the JDC as Director of Jewish Education and was responsible for community development in Siberia, Russia. For the ten years from 1999 to 2009 he was the director of Toronto's Board of Jewish Education at UJA Federation. In 2009 his first book, *From Couscous to Kasha: Reporting from the Field of Jewish Community Work*, was published by Urim Publications.

Graham McDonough is an assistant professor in the Faculty of Education at the University of Victoria, where he is also an associate fellow at the Centre for Studies in Religion and Society. He teaches courses in the history and philosophy of education, social studies curriculum, and teaching methods; his research focus is on Catholic education. A graduate of the University of Saskatchewan's College of Education (B.Mus.) and St. Thomas More College (B.A.); and OISE/University of Toronto's Philosophy of Education

THE CONTRIBUTORS

Program (M.A. and Ph.D.), he is formerly a teacher with Saskatoon Catholic Schools and has published articles in *Catholic Education: A Journal of Inquiry and Practice, International Studies in Catholic Education, Religious Education, Journal of Religious Education*, and the *Journal of Moral Education*. His doctoral dissertation, "The Moral and Pedagogical Importance of Dissent to Catholic Education," received the 2009 Kuhmerker Dissertation Award from the Association for Moral Education. His book, *Beyond Obedience and Abandonment: Toward a Theory of Dissent in Catholic Education*, is published by McGill-Queen's University Press.

Nadeem Memon is the director of the Islamic Teacher Education Program (ITEP), a collaboration between RAZI Group and the Ontario Institute for Studies in Education, University of Toronto (OISE/UT). Over the past five years of envisaging, designing, and developing ITEP, Nadeem has been actively researching, writing, and presenting about the ways in which faith and spiritually based pedagogies provide alternative visions of education worthy of consideration in faculties of education. He earned a Ph.D. from OISE/UT in 2009 with a dissertation on the vision of Islamic education in North America. Within his broader interests in the field, Nadeem also facilitates teacher and faculty development workshops both in North America and abroad on the foundations of education and educating for civic engagement. Nadeem is currently also a sessional instructor at Wilfrid Laurier University's Faculty of Education and OISE/UT, teaching courses on equity in education.

Avi Mintz is an assistant professor in the University of Tulsa's School of Education. He earned B.A. and M.A. degrees in philosophy at the University of Toronto and a Ph.D. in philosophy and education at Teachers College, Columbia University. His doctoral dissertation, "The Labor of Learning: A Study of the Role of Pain in Education," received the 2009 American Association for Teaching and Curriculum Outstanding Dissertation in Curriculum Award, and his doctoral studies were supported by a Spencer Foundation Dissertation Fellowship and a Social Sciences and Humanities Research Council of Canada Doctoral Fellowship. He has published on the alleged threat of faith-based schools to social cohesion in the *Journal of Religious Education*. He is also interested in the history of educational philosophy, and has published articles on Plato and Rousseau in *Studies in Philosophy and Education, Educational Theory*, and *Journal of Philosophy of Education*.

THE CONTRIBUTORS

Alex Pomson is a senior researcher at the Melton Centre for Jewish Education at the Hebrew University. He trained in history at the University of Cambridge and received his Ph.D. in religious education from the University of London in 1994. He was founding head of Jewish studies at the King Solomon High School in London, England. From 1996 to 2004, he served as associate professor of Jewish Teacher Education at York University, Toronto, where he coordinated York's Jewish Teacher Education Programme. He is past chair of the Network for Research in Jewish Education. He is co-author, with Randal Schnoor, of *Back to School: Jewish Day School as a Source of Meaning in the Lives of Adult Jews*. He is co-editor of *Jewish Schools, Jewish Communities: a Reconsideration* and of the recently published *International Handbook of Jewish Education*. He is presently engaged in a longitudinal study funded by the Canadian government to study the transitions from Jewish elementary school to high school, and of a parallel seven-year study, funded by the Pears Foundation, of the journey through high school of Jewish families in the UK.

Randal F. Schnoor teaches at the Koschitzky Centre for Jewish Studies at York University in Toronto. He received his Ph.D. in sociology at McGill University in 2003. He is co-author, with Alex Pomson, of *Back to School: Jewish Day School as a Source of Meaning in the Lives of Adult Jews* and of the chapter titled "Bringing School Home" in *Jewish Day Schools, Jewish Communities: A Reconsideration*. He has also recently published two pieces on Jewish supplementary schools in *Learning and Community: Jewish Supplementary Schools in the Twenty-first Century*. He is the editor of a special volume of the journal *Contemporary Jewry* (2011) on "Canadian Jewry." His research on Jewish identity, including gay-Jewish identity, has been published in academic journals such as *Sociology of Religion, Canadian Ethnic Studies*, and *Canadian Jewish Studies*. Since 2005 he has served as president of the Association for Canadian Jewish Studies.

INDEX

9/11, 1, 8, 12, 90

Aboriginal people, 2
abortion, 196, 205
Accelerated Christian Education (ACE), 9,
    249. *See also* Evangelical Protestant
Act to Establish Public Schools, 3
adab, 77, 83, 256
Adler *v.* Ontario, 238, 248, 250
administrators, 16, 74, 167, 238, 246–47; in
    Catholic schools, 244; and dissent,
    14–15; Evangelical Protestant, 7; in
    Islamic schools, 225, 227; in Jewish
    schools, 240–41
Ahmad, Qaiser, 16, 242–43, 249
Ahmed, Asma, 14, 242, 244
akhlaq, 85
al-Attas, Naquib, 75–78, 83–84, 93n16
Alberta, 5, 25, 27, 46; Human Rights
    Commission (*see* Human Rights
    Commission)
amal, 76–77
aqida, 85, 154
Aquinas, Saint Thomas, 132–33
Arabic, 80, 84–85, 154; studies, 153–54, 161,
    162n6

Aramaic, 34–35, 111, 251
Augustine, Saint, 193
autonomy, 115–16, 135–36n2, 189, 205n3,
    227; and Catholic education, 49, 64;
    of disciplines, 53; and Islamic schools,
    16, 215–16, 227; and Jewish schools,
    118; moral, 103, 118

Babylonia (Babylonian), 35, 110–12, 251
bar and *bat mitzvah* celebrations, 114, 251
behaviourism, 198
Beiles, Greg, 12–13, 241, 244–45, 246
*Beyond Schooling: Building Communities
    That Matter*, 91
Bibby, Reginald, 195
Bible: Christian, 3, 10, 131; Hebrew, 33–36
birth control. *See* contraception
bishop, 121, 193, 196; relationship to
    Catholic school, 121, 126, 132; and
    separate school establishment, 3.
    See also Canadian Conference of
    Catholic Bishops
Bobov, 32, 251
Brighouse, Harry, 205n3
British Columbia, 5, 27
British North America Act, 4, 27

265

INDEX

British schools, 81
Bryk, Anthony, 189
Buddhist, 6, 239

Canadian Catholic School Trustees
 Association, 47
Canadian Conference of Catholic
 Bishops, 191, 194
Canadian law, 121–25, 132–34
Casti connubii, 193–94
catechesis, 56, 58
Catechism of the Catholic Church, 56, 72,
 124, 129, 130, 251
Catholic: anthropology, 11, 13, 49, 55,
 62, 64, 127–28, 131, 133; Church, 8,
 58, 192, 204, 243; clergy, 190, 201,
 209n55; community, 8, 15, 124, 126,
 129, 132, 201; educators, 46–47, 49, 50,
 53–55, 58, 59, 61, 63, 196, 198, 209n50;
 family, 45, 125, 130, 196; minority, 3,
 4, 46, 124; orthodoxy, 61, 190–91, 192,
 201, 209n50; parents, 15, 57, 190–1,
 202–3, 214, 244, 246; students, 10, 15,
 47–49, 50–64, 121, 134–35, 189–91, 192,
 195–204, 207n19, 208n43, 209n49,
 243–44, 246; teaching, 193, 209n50,
 209n54. *See also* Catholicism
Catholic education, 13, 190, 191, 200,
 202–3, 243; aims of, 11, 45–46, 50,
 51, 64, 121, 126–27, 134; defences
 of, 46; distinctiveness of, 45, 60,
 63; ontological concern of, 49;
 philosophy of, 8, 11; public funding of,
 1–6, 27, 46–48, 189; and theology, 11,
 46, 53. *See also* personhood
Catholic Insight, 122, 124
Catholicism, 4, 7, 11, 81, 122, 125, 190, 196,
 200, 203–4, 243; internal critique of
 (see dissent). *See also* Catholic
Catholic school: Catholicity of, 47, 50,
 51, 60, 196; and common good,
 62–63, 189–90; controversy within,
 15; paradox within, 134; public
 funding for, 5–6, 27, 46, 48; identity,
 190; methodological choice of, 8–9;
 and non-Catholic/non-Christian
 students, 46–47, 59, 62, 204;

relationship with State, 3, 12–13, 58;
 scholarship on, 7
Catholic University of America, 194
Chabad, 32
Chanukah, 42, 180, 252, 254
character education, 87, 157–58
Charter of Rights and Freedoms, 103, 121,
 125, 132, 135, 140, 141
Chasidic/Chasidism. *See* Hasidism
chevruta, 37, 116
Christian, 2–59, 61, 79, 128, 240, 234,
 249n13; anthropology, 50, 127–28,
 131, 139n40; belief, 56–57, 59, 126;
 education, 56; immigrants, 48;
 schools, 8–9, 214, 238; understanding
 of existence, 51, 54; virtues, 127
Christianity, common, 3–4
Chymyshyn, Deborah, 122, 123
civic education. *See* education, civic. *See
 also* citizenship
citizenship, 14, 17, 152–53, 160–61, 165n1,
 205n3, 226, 242; education for, 2, 9,
 12, 16, 46, 50, 101, 105, 214–16; loyal,
 38–39, 147; responsible, 109, 197
colonial classroom, 81, 87, 94n24
common good, 50, 60–62, 124–25,
 135–36n2, 189–91, 203–4, 215, 243,
 247; conceptions of, 13–14, 116, 126,
 128–31, 134–35, 189–91, 209n50;
 equality among, 223; as foundation of
 Catholic school, 11, 45–46, 62–63, 121,
 189; good, 197; loyal, 38–39, 153; Pope
 John Paul II and, 206n13; relationship
 with state, 48. *See also* multicultural
 citizenship
common schools, 3, 4, 159, 205n3, 237, 240,
 249n12
Confederation, 4–6. *See also* British North
 America Act
Congrégation de Notre Dame, 2
Congregation for Catholic Education, 127
Connolloy, William E., 102, 105, 107,
 109–10, 112, 116
conscience, 128, 151, 158, 164, 191, 199, 203;
 and contraception, 193–95; freedom
 of, 126, 133, 135, 244
Conservative Judaism. *See* Judaism

INDEX

conservatism, 86
Constitution, Canadian, 3, 147, 214
contraception, 15, 190–95, 205n8, 208n34, 237, 244
controversy, 1, 5, 125, 180, 203, 243, 247; intra-Church, 15, 191–93, 196–97; secular-civil, 196–97
convent schools, 81–82
Corcoran, James (Jim), 122, 124
corporal punishment, 9
Council of Islamic Schools of North America (CISNA), 87
Coyne, Andrew, 1
critical inquiry, 48
critical responsiveness, 102, 110
critical thinking, 199, 202, 216, 244; discouraged, 9, 163, 249n13; skills, 214. See also critical inquiry; critical responsiveness
culture, 13, 17, 125, 134, 151, 229n23, 239, 242; and Catholic education, 11, 47–48, 50, 56–61; Catholic school, 127, 246; cultural heritage, 32, 156, 218; cultural identity, 89, 152, 217; Islamic, 82, 165n1, 221, 239; Islamic school, 89, 150–51, 158, 160, 216–19; Jewish, 10, 29, 38, 40–41, 116, 176, 254; Jewish school, 13, 103, 105–6, 109–10, 113–14, 118, 178; nurturing of, 2; Yiddish, 10
Curran, Charles, 194
curriculum, 147, 245–47; in Catholic schools, 47–49, 51–56, 59–60, 126, 129, 189–90, 198–202; civics, 103–7, 109; integration, 33, 35–36, 56, 63–64, 83–84, 91, 103, 106, 109, 216; in Islamic schools, 11, 14, 74–75, 79, 82–91, 91n1, 150, 153–54, 159, 161–64, 216–17, 223, 239; in Jewish schools, 10–11, 13, 26, 29, 31–33, 35–38, 40–41, 102–3, 105, 109, 171, 176, 178, 240–41, 249n7; organization of, 55, 89, 202, 243; provincial, 5; transmission orientation, 192, 198–99; transaction orientation, 192, 199–200; transformation orientation, 192, 200–201, 209

Declaration on Religious Liberty, 189
deliberation, 16–17, 50, 57, 59, 84, 91, 240–41, 244–48, 249n10, 249n12, 250
democracy, 48, 61, 101–7, 121, 125, 131–31, 136n3, 146, 152, 243, 244
denominational schools, 3–5, 31, 171, 182. *See also* faith schools
Deobandi. *See* Muslim
Dewey, John, 52
dissent, 6, 10, 14, 15, 17, 19n18
diversity, 4, 16, 48, 57–58, 60–61, 63–64, 135, 206n17; within Catholicism, 48, 57, 58, 126, 204; of curriculum, 51–54, 64; and Islamic education, 11–12; and Jewish schools, 11, 15, 26, 28–31, 33, 37, 38, 41, 118, 173, 176, 180–81, 183
divorce, 48
doctrine, 9, 15, 31, 39, 46, 56, 59, 194, 216
domestic violence, 146, 220
Donlevy, J. Kent, 11, 13, 243–44
Downtown Jewish Day School, 14–15, 173–77, 180–83, 240–41, 242
Doyle, Brendan, 5
D'Souza, Mario, 11, 243–44
Dworkin, Ronald, 132, 136n2

ecclesia discens, 198
ecclesia docens, 198
Edmonton, 5, 26, 28, 89, 124; Pride Center. *See* Pride Center of Edmonton
education: arts-based, 10; civic, 9, 12, 243; and democracy, 61, 249, 249n12; health, 224, 225; moral, 3; policy, 3; special, 30, 37; state-sponsored, 4–5, 29, 46; and women, 79, 220–23
encyclical, 15, 62, 190, 193–95, 252, 253
Epstein, Seymour, 9–11, 241
Eucharist, 48
Evangelical Protestant, 7, 9
evangelization, 56, 58, 126–27
evolution, 82, 218–19, 237, 245
experiential learning or pedagogy, 53, 103, 105

fairness, 13, 55, 61, 121–26, 128, 130–31, 134–35, 135n1, 158, 243

INDEX

faith and culture, synthesis of, 11, 57, 58, 60, 127

faith schools, 190, 205n3

Feinberg, Walter, 101–2, 105, 107, 109, 113, 115–16, 120, 189–90, 199, 200, 248n7, 249n11

female ordination, 48, 196, 205n8

feminist theology, 200

fiqh, 85, 87, 149, 154

First Nations persons, 47, 104, 225. *See also* Aboriginal persons

First World Conference on Muslim education, 74, 75, 87, 92n5

Foy, Vincent (Monsignor), 194–95

freedom, 11, 48–51, 53, 55–58, 61–63, 126, 133, 135, 136n2, 244, 260; of religion. *See* religious freedom

Freire, Paulo, 209n50

French: language instruction, 154, 178; settlers, 2

fundamentalist, 7, 9, 31

Gemara, 35, 256

gender, 38, 40, 79, 83, 155–56, 164–65, 215, 219–220, 223, 225, 244

Gospel, 47, 54, 127

Greeley, Andrew, 195

Greenfield, Norm, 125

Groome, Thomas, 49, 138

Gutmann, Amy, 247, 249n10, 249n12

hadith, 154, 252, 256

halacha, 30, 35, 252, 254

halal, 149

Halstead, Mark, 189, 218, 221, 223–24

Hall, Marc. *See* Hall v. Powers

Hall v. Powers, 122–23, 128, 129, 131–34, 243–44

Hanukkah. S*ee* Chanukah

Häring, Bernard, 193

haram, 149

Hasidism, 31–33, 39, 251, 252, 253, 255

hayaa, 157

Hebrew, 10, 30–31, 33–35, 38, 40–41, 42n9, 178–79, 181, 251, 252, 254, 256

Henry, Frederick (Bishop), 122, 125

Heschel School. *See* Toronto Heschel School

heterodoxy, 15, 182

hijab, 153, 221–22, 230n33

Hindu, 6, 147, 214, 238, 240

Holland, Peter, 189

homosexual, 124; acts, 130; relations, 122; relationships, 130, 243; unions, 129–30

homosexuality, 48, 82, 125, 128, 225–26, 244; as "disorder," 129, 138n26

Holy Spirit, 127

Humanae vitae, 15, 190, 193–204, 206n14, 208n34, 209n50

human rights, 6, 13, 121–25, 128–29, 131, 133–35, 226

Human Rights Commission, 135; Canadian, 123–24; Alberta, 125

Human Rights Committee. *See* United Nations

Human Rights Tribunal, 13; British Columbia, 123; Ontario, 124, 141

ibadaat, 217

identity, 4, 13, 46, 62, 49, 103, 109, 118, 128, 215, 241–42, 247; Canadian, 4, 248; Catholic, 190, 196, 204; Jewish, 30, 38, 103, 112–16, 172, 180; Muslim, 83, 86, 89, 146–47, 149, 152–53, 155–60, 165n1, 216–18, 223; national, 4; religious, 14, 16, 62–63, 149, 215–16, 241, 248n6

ilm, 77

immigrants, 4, 47–48, 75, 239; Muslim, 78–79, 81, 83, 85–86, 89, 90, 92n3, 146, 148–50, 155; Yiddish-speaking, 30

immigration, 27, 39, 48, 74

individualism, 53, 54, 58, 59, 128

indoctrination, 147, 189, 198

informal logic, 200

integration, 16, 27, 40, 84, 146–47, 149–52, 154–55, 157, 159–61, 163, 219, 242, 244; curricular, 36, 64, 83, 88–89, 109; of faith and culture, 127; sense of, 14; social, 14, 83, 221

insular, 16, 50, 190, 219

interdenominational, 8–10, 12, 13, 101

in utero and in vitro fertilization, 196

268

INDEX

IQRA Education Foundation, 85, 86, 89, 154

Iroquois. *See* Aboriginal persons

Islam, 85, 86, 145, 148–49, 155, 158–59, 163–64, 214–16, 218, 219, 225, 227, 254, 255; conception of education in, 74–984, 91, 157; ethical code of, 86; foundations of, 79, 152, 157, 161, 217; homosexuality and, 226; misrepresentation of, 82, 242; Nation of, 92; relationship with Western society, 165n1; and sex education, 223–24; teaching, 84–85, 87, 91, 153, 215–16; and women, 221–23. *See also* Muslim

Islamic epistemology, 89

Islamic pedagogy, 74, 76, 77–78, 87

Islamic school, 8, 79, 87, 88, 91n1, 92n2, 94n24, 149–50, 153, 162–64, 165n1, 219, 239–40, 242, 243, 252, 253; concerns among Muslims about, 80–82 (*see* curriculum, Islamic schools); Edmonton, 5, 89; establishment of, 11, 12, 73–74, 78–80, 82–83; gendering of, 79; graduate students and, 75, 78, 81; and homosexuality, 225–26; and physical contact, 224–25; purpose of, 11, 73–74, 77–78, 82–83, 85–86, 90–91, 146–47, 157, 239; and sexuality, 223–26; and strong/moderate categories, 214–18, 219, 223, 224, 226–27

Islamic Society of North America, 12, 74, 78

Islamization, 75, 82, 92n5, 93n16, 253

Islamization of Knowledge. *See* Islamization

Islamophobia, 1, 17–18n3, 90, 148, 223

Israel, 26, 30, 32–36, 39, 40, 42n9, 88, 105, 111, 176, 179, 255, 257

Jesuits, 2

Jewish. *See* culture, Jewish; law, 30, 35, 39, 40, 114, 119n5, 248n7, 252, 254. *See also* halacha; metaphysic, 115–18

Jewish schools, 8–11, 241–42, 248n7; complementary,

26–27; congregational, 27; interdenominational, 8, 10, 12, 101–2; pluralistic, 172–73, 175–76; supplementary, 26, 171, 173

John XXIII, Pope, 193

Johnson, Carol, 125

Judaism, 109–10, 112–13, 115–18, 174–75, 182, 241; *Charedi,* 10, 28–37, 39–41, 241–42; Conservative, 31–33, 39, 172, 173, 248n7, 252; cultural, 38; Modern Orthodox, 10, 28, 30–36, 38, 254; Reform, 10, 27, 29, 31–33, 35, 39, 172, 254

Just Community School Project, 106, 118

Kaufman, Philip, 194

King, Martin Luther, 133

kippah (pl. kippot), 115, 253

Knights of Columbus, 123

Kohlberg, Lawrence, 106, 118

Kosher, 115, 177, 253

laity, 191, 198, 204, 209n55

law, Canadian. *See* Canadian Law

Lee, Valerie, 189

liberal arts, 55, 59

liberal democracy, 12, 101–3, 109

Liberal Party. *See* Ontario Liberal Party

Lithuanian-Yeshiva tradition, 32, 39, 253

London (Ontario) Islamic School, 14, 145

Lonergan, Bernard, 53, 59

Lower Canada, 3. *See also* Quebec

Lubavitch. *See* Chabad

Luther, Martin, 134

madrassa (pl. madaris), 18n3, 80–81, 91n1, 147, 252–53

magisterium, 48, 58, 126, 130–31, 190–94, 197–204, 209n55, 253

Manitoba, 5, 25, 27; Schools Question, 5

Maritain, Jacques, 49

McDonough, Graham, 15, 48, 244, 246

McGuinty, Dalton, 1–2, 8, 18n3, 162

McLachlin, Beverley, 132

McLaughlin, Terence, 54, 126

Mecca, 74, 92n5

INDEX

Memon, Nadeem, 11–12, 239, 245–46
menorah, 114, 254
Middle East, 79, 94n24, 148
Miller, J. Michael (Archbishop), 131
Miller, John, 192, 200, 207n19, 208n44
Ministry of Education, 40, 153
Mintz, Avi, 16–17
Mishna, 35, 107, 256
mitzvah (pl. mitzvot), 25, 108–9, 251, 252, 254
mosque, 73, 79, 80, 148, 153
Mulligan, James T., 47
multicultural, 158, 219–20, 226, 245–46; citizenship, 9, 12, 17, 216; education, 9–10, 245. *See also* multiculturalism
multiculturalism, 46, 102, 125, 216, 227, 245, 247–48. *See also* multicultural
Multi-Faith Coalition for Equal Funding of Faith-Based Schools, 238
Muslim: Canadian immigrants 74–75, 78–79, 81, 85–86, 90, 148–49, 239; Deobandi, 8, 252, 253; parents, 80–83, 85, 89–90; Salafi, 8, 254–55; Shi'a, 227, 255; Sufi, 8, 255–56; Sunni, 8, 213, 225, 227, 252, 254–56; women, 147, 220–23; youth, 14, 145–46, 148–50, 152, 155–58, 163. *See also* Islam
Muslim Canadian Congress, 239
Muslim Education Foundation, 89–90
Muslim Students' Association, 12, 74, 78–80

natural law, 129, 132–33, 194–95, 206n14
New Brunswick, 5
New France, 2, 18, 20
Newfoundland and Labrador, 4–5
niqab, 222
Northwest Territories, 5
Nova Scotia, 5
Nunavut, 5

On Responsible Parenthood, 193
Ontario, 1–6, 25, 27, 33, 46, 73, 84, 134, 145, 153–55; Equity and Inclusive Education Strategy, 134; Human Rights Tribunal (*see* Human Rights

Tribunal); Liberal Party, 1, 146–47; Progressive Conservative Party, 1, 147; provincial election (2007), 1–2, 6, 239, 245. *See also* McGuinty, Dalton; Tory, John; Upper Canada
Ontario Catholic School Graduate Expectations, 47
Ontario English Catholic Teachers' Association, 122
Ontario Multi-Faith Coalition for Equity in Education, 238
oral sex, 196
ordination of women. *See* female ordination
Orthodox Judaism. *See* Judaism
Other (concept of), 13, 105, 118, 121, 123–24, 126, 128–31, 134–35

Pastoral Constitution on the Church in the Modern World, 62, 193
Paul VI, Pope, 15, 190, 193–95
Pentateuch. *See* Torah
personhood, 45, 47, 49–51, 55–57, 60
Pius XI, Pope, 193
philosophy: Catholic educational, 8, 46, 53, 56, 244; Catholic vs. secular, 125–27; Islamic educational, 75, 91, 105, 118, 121, 123–24, 126, 128–31, 134–35; of personhood, 49
pluralism, 13, 60–62, 101–20, 175–76, 182, 190, 222; democratic, 60, 101–2, 107; interdenominational, 101; religious, 2, 15, 180
plurality, 11, 61–62, 104, 179
Pomson, Alex, 14–15, 89, 240, 245–47, 248n6
post-integration, 14, 146, 147, 149–54, 159–61, 163, 242
postmodern: approach to Catholic education, 200; "community of difference," 15, 182–83; culture, 47, 53
prayer: in Catholic schools, 54; in Islamic schools, 83, 86; in Jewish schools, 10, 33–34, 38, 154, 176
premarital sex, 48, 82, 86, 195–96, 208n34, 224

270

INDEX

Pride Center of Edmonton, 124
Prince Edward Island, 5
progressive education, 9, 181, 241
Progressive Conservative Party. *See*
Ontario Progressive Conservative
Party
Prophet Muhammad, 85, 217, 252, 255–56
prophetic tradition (Islam), 86
Protestant, 3–5, 7, 9, 27
provincial funding for schools, 1–6, 27, 33,
45–48, 147, 237–39, 245
public funding, 18, 166, 168. *See also*
provincial funding for schools
public schools. *See* common schools

Quebec, 3–5, 25, 27, 40, 48, 195, 222. *See
also* Lower Canada
Qur'an, 77, 79–81, 85–87, 89, 153–54, 157,
161–62, 213, 216–17, 221–22, 225, 254

Rabbinic, 34, 107, 114, 241, 251; law, 35, 254,
256; literature, 37, 254, 256
Ramadan, Tariq, 14, 146–55, 157, 159,
160–65, 242
Reform Judaism. *See* Judaism
relativism, 52, 53, 59, 126
religious: diversity, 4, 15, 17, 46, 48, 52,
54, 60, 61, 63, 182; freedom, 11, 48;
identity, 14, 16, 17, 38, 62, 63, 149,
172, 175–76, 215–16, 241. *See also*
pluralism, religious; minorities, 8,
124, 242, 245, 248n6; secular divide,
36, 82
Report of the Commission on Private
Schools, 147, 162
Rosh Hashanah, 175, 177, 254
Runnymede Trust, 148
Rushdie Affair, 148

Sacraments, 50, 60, 204,
Salafi. *See* Muslim, Salafi
same-sex relationships, 123–25, 129–30.
See also homosexuality and
homosexual
Saskatchewan, 5, 46
Satmar, 32, 255

Scheffler, Israel, 209n53
Schnoor, Randal, 14–15, 240, 245–47,
248n6
Scripture, 56, 129, 131
Second Vatican Council, 50, 56–59, 189,
190, 193, 253
secular: curriculum in Islamic schools,
81–82, 84–85, 89, 91, 216; curriculum
in Jewish schools, 29–30, 33, 36–38,
41, 106, 114–15, 118; and sacred
tensions, 121–44, 217, 241–42
secularism, 48, 114, 160
seerah, 85, 87
segregation, 86, 243, 245
Seller, Wayne, 192, 200, 207n19, 208n44
Sen, Amartya, 62
Sephardic, 32, 35, 40, 253, 255. *See also*
Lithuanian-Yeshiva tradition
sex education, 82, 223–24
sexuality, 52, 128, 195, 215, 223–26
Shabbat, 115, 255
shariah, 154, 255
Shi'a (pl. Shi'ites). *See* Muslim, Shi'a
shumuliyat al Islam, 152, 255
Sikh, 6, 147, 214, 238, 240
Simchat Torah, 177, 255
Smith, Tracey, 123–24
social cohesion, 1, 12, 147, 214–16, 226–27,
237, 247
social justice, 47, 63, 105–6, 204, 209n50.
See also tikkun olam
Society of Jesus. *See* Jesuits
solidarity, 63, 132, 194, 206n13
South Asia, 79, 81, 94n24
Succot (Sukkot), 177, 255
Sufi. *See* Muslim, Sufi
sunnah, 157, 161, 252, 256
Sunni. *See* Muslim, Sunni
Sweet, Lois, 219, 238–39
synagogue, 38–39, 172, 174–75, 177

ta'dib, 75–77, 84, 256
ta'lim, 75–76, 256
Taliban, 148
Talmud, 34–37, 107, 114, 118, 241, 251, 254,
256

INDEX

Talmud Torah (pl. Talmudei Torah), 26, 179, 256
tarbiyah, 75–77, 84, 158, 161–62, 256
Taylor, Charles, 128
tazkiyah, 75–76, 256
terrorism, 1, 146, 157
theology: Catholic, 8, 11, 15, 46, 51, 53, 56, 200; Rabbinic, 117; Shi'a, 227
tikkun olam, 105, 109, 256
tolerance, 16, 29, 158, 214
Tönnies, Ferdinand, 182–83
Torah, 34, 103, 107, 114, 252, 254–56
Toronto: Islamic schools of, 11, 16, 79–81, 213; Jewish schools of, 14–15, 262–69, 32, 37, 39, 40, 173–74
Toronto Heschel School, 12–13, 101–20, 241–42, 244
Tory, John, 1–2, 18n3, 147, 239, 245, 249n9
"Tragedy at Winnipeg," 194–95
Triune God, 198

ulema, 83
United Kingdom, 216
United Nations Human Rights Committee, 6

United States: Catholics' beliefs, 195–96; religious school funding, 29–30; Islamic schools, 78, 79, 85, 90, 92n3; Islamic organizations, 12; Jewish schools, 27, 171, 174
Upper Canada, 3. *See also* Ontario
Ursulines, 2

Vancouver, Archdiocese of, 123
Vatican II. *See* Second Vatican Council

Wells, Rob, 124
Wertheimer, Jack, 174
Wills, Garry, 194
Winnipeg Statement, 194–95
Wojtyla, Karol (Cardinal). *See* John Paul II, Pope

yeshivah (pl. yeshivot), 26, 31–32, 173, 253, 257
Yiddish, 10, 30, 34–35
Yom Kippur, 175, 177–78, 257
Yukon, 5

Zine, Jasmin, 156, 239
Zionism, 32–33, 36, 38–39, 179, 255, 257